DAWN

Alfred Draper s[...]
Lieutenant, R[...]
suffered the sink[...] beneath him,
one on D-Day and again in the Atlantic, before
going on to serve in India and the Far East.
After the war he worked on a weekly
newspaper, on the *Daily Herald* and from
there to the *Daily Express* for sixteen years,
during which time he covered many major
stories and trials at home and abroad. After a
year with the *Daily Mail* and another
scriptwriting for the BBC, he left journalism in
1972 to become a full-time writer. The author
of five previous non-fiction books and seven
fiction, as well as numerous magazine and
newspaper articles, he lives in Hertfordshire.

DAWNS LIKE THUNDER

The Retreat from Burma 1942

Alfred Draper

ARROW BOOKS

Arrow Books Limited
62-65 Chandos Place, London WC2N 4NW

An imprint of Century Hutchinson Limited

London Melbourne Sydney Auckland
Johannesburg and agencies throughout
the world

First published by Leo Cooper 1987
Arrow edition 1988

Printed and bound in Great Britain by
Anchor Brendon Limited, Tiptree, Essex

ISBN 0 09 955840 8

*This book is dedicated to those who survived
and to those who did not.*

ILLUSTRATIONS

ACKNOWLEDGEMENTS

"Tell it as *we* saw it," was a request I frequently heard during my research for this book. I have endeavoured to honour that plea.

This book, therefore, is not a detailed history but simply an attempt to recount what many soldiers, civilians and officials involved in the defeat of Burma felt at the time.

I have, of course, consulted the relevant official histories and numerous biographies and autobiographies in order to provide the necessary backcloth to their experiences. Understandably they often do not see eye to eye with the professional historians. Where possible I have tried to explain why.

I am particularly indebted to my friend Leland Stowe, that prince of reporters, who readily placed at my disposal his meticulously kept diaries of the campaign, and never failed to reply to my innumerable requests. I encountered the same generosity from his Burma 'stable mate', the late O. D. Gallagher, who let me quote from his despatches and writings, and Jim Nicoll, formerly Foreign Editor of the *Daily Express*, who made available the necessary newspaper cuttings.

I owe a special debt of gratitude to Major Bruce Kinloch, M.C., for the infinite trouble he took in recounting his experiences and placing at my disposal so many contemporary accounts.

I am indebted to so many people that it is impossible to detail just how much I owe them. The brevity of my acknowledgement is no indication of their great contribution.

My sincere thanks to:

Mrs Gwenllyan Moon (Coward), Mrs Finetta Bagot, Mrs Joan Morton, Mrs Anne Purton, Mrs Norma Morrison, Miss Violet Kelly, R.R.C., Mrs Nora Healy, The Reverend Wilfred Crittle and S. Farrant Russell, F.R.C.S., for their accounts of the trek through the Hukawng

Valley, and the latter for loaning me Private Warner's diary, and the account of his wife Muriel's escape.

Many soldiers from generals to privates readily gave up their time. The late Major-General David Tennant Cowan, C.B., C.B.E., D.S.O., and Bar, M.C., Major Bashir Ahmad Khan, Major Roy Hudson, Major-General D. C. J. Swann, C.B., C.B.E., the late Brigadier Sir John Smyth, V.C., M.C., for allowing me to quote from his memoirs. Lieutenant-Colonel Humphrey Purton for giving up much of his time and for introducing me to so many members of the Burma Forces Luncheon Club. Lieutenant-Colonel Henry Radice, M.B.E., for permitting access to so much invaluable material at the Regimental Headquarters and Museum of the Gloucestershire Regiment, Lieutenant-Colonel Terrence Dillon, Mr George Biggs, M.M., Mr N. Coppard, Brigadier John Randle, O.B.E., M.C., Mr Charles Coubrough, formerly 7/10th Baluch, Brigadier Tony Firth, O.B.E., M.C., (Duke of Wellington's Regiment), and Lieutenant-Colonel Tony Mains.

Captain Charles Fox (K.O.Y.L.I.), Mr Ken Chadwick, Lientenant-Colonel George Forty (Tank Museum, Wareham), Captain Mike Patterson, M.C., Col. the Rev. Neville Metcalfe, D.S.O., Major J. S. Knight, Headquarters the Queen's Own Hussars, Major D. S. Day, Hon. Sec. 4th P.W.O. Gurkha Rifles Officers' Association, Colonel F. W. Cook, M.B.E., M.C., Light Infantry Officer (Yorkshire), Major John Finnerty, B.E.M., Mr Ian Scott, Mr Alfred Dunn, M.B.E., the brothers John and George Robertson, and Mr Nigel Hogg.

A considerable time was spent in libraries and museums where I always encountered unstinting help and courtesy. Miss Patricia Methven, Archivist at the Liddell Hart Centre for Military Archives, University of London King's College, went to endless trouble helping me, especially with the collection of Lieutenant-General Sir Thomas Hutton, K.C.I.E., C.B., M.C., Mr Phillip Dymond and the staff at the India Office Library and records, Mr Tom Westmancoat at the British Newspaper Library, Mr R. R. Mellor, Public Records Office, Kew, Mr D. K. Smurthwaite, National Army Museum, and the Imperial War Museum.

Finally I would like to thank everyone for their generous hospitality which, alas, I have no hope of reciprocating, and to Barbara who lived through the campaign with me.

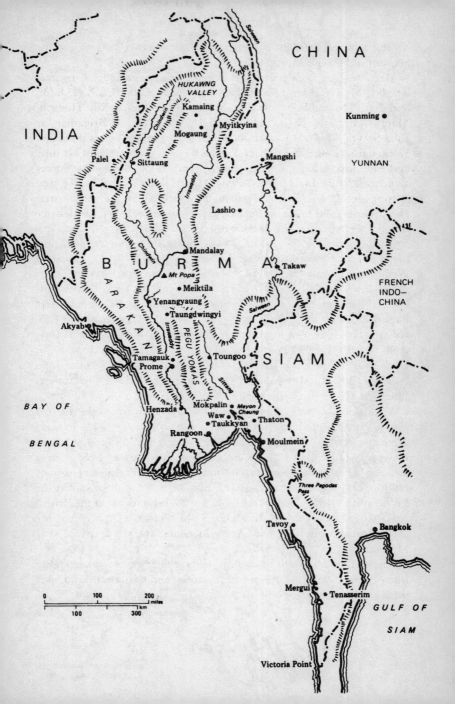

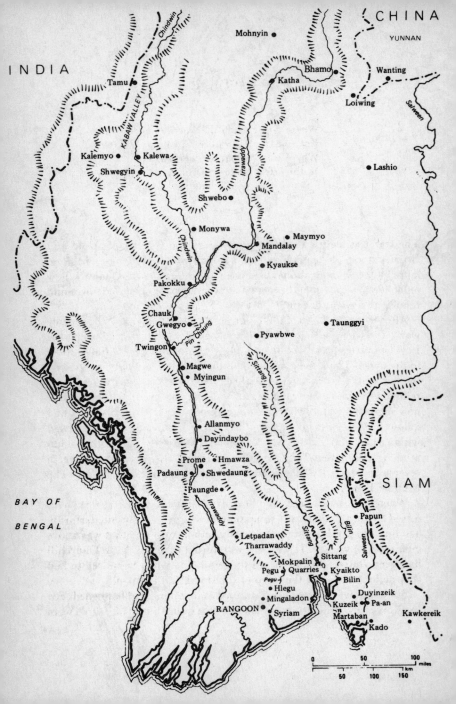

CHAPTER 1

Where was I when the war was on?
I can hear a faint voice murmur.
Where was I when the war was on?
In the safest place – in Burma.
                                        Soldiers' Song.

The war was a little more than two years and three months old and
Britain stood alone, fighting for survival and waiting for Hitler to
launch Operation Sealion – the invasion from across the Channel. Few
onlookers, even among her staunchest supporters, believed she could
repulse the might of Hitler's armies.

After the abrupt end of the soporific interlude known as "the phoney
war", Norway had fallen and as the tide of war engulfed Europe the
Low Countries had capitulated and a demoralized France had thrown
in the towel. The B.E.F., trapped on the beaches, had only escaped by
the skin of its teeth in what was called "the miracle of Dunkirk", and the
remnants of its near weaponless army, assisted by the Home Guard,
now mounted watch with antiquated equipment. More disasters had
followed: the ill-timed campaign in Greece had resulted in a scurried
withdrawal, culminating in the débâcle of Crete and another ignominious evacuation. The Middle East had also been the scene of
reversals, which led the troops doing the fighting to dub it "The
Muddle East".

When the Japanese attacked Pearl Harbor the event was greeted with
mixed feelings of shock and jubilation. It was a cowardly and dastardly
act, but it had at last brought America into the war and that was a sure
guarantee of victory. It was not an unusual reaction. Even Churchill
had been elated when he heard the news, and when he retired to bed
that night had "slept the sleep of the saved and thankful".

But in faraway Burma life continued as if nothing had happened. For
the Europeans the club continued to be the hub of social life; cards were

dropped with a meticulous regard to protocol; there was dancing, swimming, tennis, golf, bridge, polo, and one would never dream of not dressing for dinner. Race meetings continued to be attended by the Governor, Sir Reginald Dorman-Smith, at which the women wore beautiful dresses and wide-brimmed hats, yet still felt the need to carry a frilly parasol. Most of the men dressed as if it was Ascot Week.

It was not a completely ostrich-like attitude on the part of the ruling European community, neither was it due to a fatalistic belief that they were doomed and might just as well indulge in a bout of riotous living before the end came. It was brought about by a surfeit of optimism. Since the start of hostilities they had been repeatedly misled into believing that the war would never come to Burma.

In Rangoon's Silver Grill mercenary pilots of the American Volunteer Group danced to the latest hits, downed whisky as if they feared a sudden shortage, fired six-guns as if they were in a Wild West saloon and stood champagne for the "chi chi" girls who looked white but could never fool the European community that they were. In less expensive clubs sailors and soldiers drank and danced with the local prostitutes and their Chinese, Burmese and Anglo-Indian girlfriends.

As Christmas, 1941, approached, Burma prepared for an orgy of overeating and overdrinking, even though there was a vague awareness that the war was getting closer. Despite the heat, dinner would be traditional and certainly better than that available in shivering Britain; roast turkey, ham, Christmas pudding, and an infinite variety of drinks.

Joan Morton, wife of Major Victor Morton, Second-in-Command of the First Battalion of the Gloucestershire Regiment on garrison duty in Rangoon, was one of the few who had doubts that Burma would be spared the attention of the Japanese.

They took root with the sinking of the battleships *Prince of Wales* and *Repulse* which had been sent to Singapore by Churchill, who believed they would act as a deterrent to the Japanese.

Joan Morton said, "The news of the sinking was the biggest shock of all. Victor and I were quite stunned, and I think that was the moment when we fully grasped the seriousness of the situation. How extremely vulnerable we were and the very real possibility that our world might be about to fall apart."

Nothing, however, happened and a sense of complacency was restored. Those who still had misgivings were assured by the Governor that there was no immediate danger, and in any case Burma was ready to defend herself and was even preparing to take the offensive against the enemy.

They were further comforted by recalling the words of Alfred Duff Cooper, the Minister of Information, who, after a visit to Burma in November, during which he sympathized with the soldiers who would miss out on the fighting, had informed Whitehall, "I can find no support for the theory that war in Burma is imminent."

So, with their complacency officially approved by such a prominent public figure, the European community prepared for Christmas.

On Christmas Eve Rangoon was crowded with people intent on doing some last-minute shopping. Mrs Finetta Bagot, the wife of Lieutenant-Colonel Charles Bagot, MC, Commanding Officer of the Gloucesters, was on a shopping expedition with her young daughter Veronica. The Gloucesters had been abroad for eleven years and this was to be their third Christmas in Burma. But she knew that it would not be the jolly affair it had previously been, for Charles Bagot had not been beguiled by the propaganda and had long suspected that Burma would soon be in the front line, and on his insistence most of the wives and children had been sent up-country to Maymyo. So there would be no children's party with Colour Sergeant Victor Ballinger dressed up as Father Christmas. Apart from that, the festivities would carry on as normal.

Finetta Bagot was out shopping when the siren sounded. At first she thought it was a practice alert; then she heard the whistle of falling bombs followed by the crump of explosions. She grabbed Veronica's hand, hurried to nearby Sale Barracks and took shelter in a slit trench. The Japanese bombers were clearly visible, flying in tight formation as if on a practice run. Fires were springing up everywhere and the panic among the native population was pitiful to see. An officer of the Gloucesters ran over to the slit trench to see if they were all right, and as he glanced skywards three parachutes ballooned open and slowly began to descend. Thinking they were Japanese paratroops, he ran to his car, grabbed his revolver and braced himself to open fire as they got nearer. Then an anti-personnel bomb fell about ten yards away and the splinters ripped a jagged hole in his shoulder. Mrs Bagot scrambled out to render what first aid she could. "It wasn't much as I did not have anything with me," she confessed.

Her car was riddled with shrapnel, but she managed to drive it back to her quarters.

Sub-Lieutenant George Robertson, RNVR, had a grandstand view from the Burma Navy Headquarters less than a mile from the bombers' main target. "Several of us ran like hell for the open sand-bagged emplacement, cursing and swearing at having a practice alert at that particular time of day. Then I looked up and saw about a hundred aircraft flying in perfect formation. It thrilled me no end as I thought they were the R.A.F. reinforcements."

His delight was short-lived when the solitary ack-ack gun on Monkey Point opened fire and, within seconds, bombs were raining down on the riverside area, obscuring it in towering clouds of dust and smoke. The bombers flew straight on in tight formation and several fighters were seen darting among them. "I saw two bombers disintegrate in midair and then three parachutes slowly opened and began drifting earthwards. Later I was told that they were members of a bomber's crew who were armed with machine pistols and had fought to the death when they landed."

They were the same parachutes the Gloucester officer had seen, and the first kill to be made by the A.V.G. pilots. They claimed several others during the first raid, and the small R.A.F. unit, equipped with antiquated Brewster Buffaloes, also chalked up their first kill.

Rangoon was pathetically unprepared for the surprise raid; there were hardly any shelters worthy of the name and the warning system could have been devised by Heath Robinson. Apart from a well-worn and near obsolete R.D.F. set, it consisted of a chain of sentinels, perched on platforms, whose job it was to shin down at the sight of approaching aircraft and telephone a warning to Rangoon. They provided such a ludicrous spectacle that the natives at one post had mistaken the observer for a holy man and had placed food at the base of the tree. He had found this much more rewarding than scanning the sky.

It was the native population which suffered most, for they had not been warned of the necessity for taking cover during an air raid. So when the first bombers, escorted by tiers of fighters, appeared overhead, women in the markets left their stalls and stood in the streets in order to get a good view of the dog-fights taking place above. In crowded Strand Road the coolies stopped work and gazed skywards as the impressive armada flew over.

The main Japanese objective was to terrify the local population and this they did with hundreds of anti-personnel bombs. Within minutes the streets were strewn with the mangled and mutilated bodies of the dead, dying and wounded. When Robertson left his shelter to see what help he could give, he saw "bodies everywhere, and mangled bits of human flesh littering the ground". When the bombers departed some 3,000 had been killed and injured.

It was not wholly true that the city had no shelters; there were a few but they were made of clay bricks which offered little protection, or of cement which was so new it had not dried, and any explosion nearby would have resulted in those taking shelter being buried alive.

But the Japanese did not rely solely on anti-personnel bombs; they plastered the city with sticks of high-explosive bombs which demolished many of the stone-built buildings, and incendiaries which wrought total havoc in the native areas where the mainly wooden houses either disappeared completely or burst into flames that spread like fire in a field of stubble. Saboteurs added to the confusion with deliberate acts of arson and the panic that paralysed the city was an open invitation for the criminally minded to indulge in an orgy of looting.

There were deafening explosions as ammunition went up in great gouts of flame and smoke. Lorries were wrecked and huge quantities of goods destined to be transported up the Burma Road for use by the Chinese army were destroyed.

O. D. Gallagher, the *Daily Express* war correspondent, was on the front step of the Strand Hotel opposite Brooking Street Wharves when a stick of bombs straddled the docks. Gallagher, who had arrived in Rangoon after surving the sinking of the *Repulse*, suspected that he was in for a repetition of what he had witnessed in Singapore. There total apathy had reigned and few of the Europeans would face up to the realities of the Japanese threat. In the short time he had been in Rangoon, he had encountered a similar attitude and he had been astonished at the number of Europeans who had assured him that nothing would happen, adding, rather proudly, "Burma is a military backwater".

Most of the eye-witnesses grossly exaggerated the number of aircraft which attacked Rangoon. There were only fifty bombers, escorted by thirty-four fighters. But within half an hour they brought the country's most important city and major port to a chaotic halt. In the docks unloading stopped as coolies fled, bus and tram drivers left their vehicles, shops and business houses put up their shutters, hotel staff deserted, and the servants of the Europeans departed in droves.

As a mass exodus of refugees fled along the Prome Road, corpses lying in the street were already starting to become swollen and bloated in the afternoon heat, but there were no arrangements for the collection of the dead and so sacks were hastily thrown over them. The trains and convoys of lorries heading north were so crowded that they resembled branches on which swarms of bees had descended. There was stark terror on the faces of the wretched Indians and Burmese as they hurried away from the scene of devastation with the few pitiful belongings they had managed to salvage. But those with transport, no matter how primitive, were greatly outnumbered by those who were walking. There were women with bundles on their heads, babies on their backs, and screaming children clinging to the hems of their skirts and saris, all vaguely heading north towards India and possible safety. By nightfall many of the city's 500,000 people had left and packs of wild dogs and crows were already busy eating and pecking at the dead.

When they had finished pulverising the city, the aircraft attacked Mingaladon Airfield about fifteen miles north of Rangoon. They dived to within five hundred feet of the tarmac, raked the entire field with machine guns and cratered it with bombs. Hardly a building remained unscathed; the control tower was hit and badly damaged by a bomb which went through the roof carrying away the air-raid siren. Several men were killed, including the entire crew in a gun pit. As the attack intensified, some of the ground crew panicked and took off on lorries up the Prome Road, leaving petrol tankers exposed on the airstrip. Their departure was disgraceful but understandable; between them they had six rifles and three Bren guns to beat off the attackers. They returned next day to face a real blistering, but, as one unarmed airman pointed out, "What would you have done, sir, against machine guns without even a rifle?" Ironically, there were plenty of Lend-Lease anti-aircraft guns and other vital equipment desperately needed by the

6

British lying in the docks, but the Chinese would not part with any of it.

The Gloucesters at Mingaladon were also subjected to a concentrated attack when enemy fighters swooped down to roof height and straffed the barracks. The native staff fled as a stick of bombs fell on the parade square, while another demolished the married quarters, mercifully evacuated three days previously.

Although his prized barracks had been reduced to near rubble and Rangoon brought to a complete halt, Charles Bagot was determined that the Japanese would not deprive his men of their Christmas dinner, and he despatched a lorry to Rangoon, where someone obtained the keys of the warehouse and cold store, and soldiers loaded up with frozen turkeys, cigarettes, beer and the rest of the Christmas fare.

Joan Morton, working in the R.A.F. headquarters, first knew of the raid when the telephone rang to inform the staff that the city and airfield were under attack. She took cover and watched it from a slit trench. "No bombs fell on or near H.Q., but we could hear them falling on the city and we could see dog fights going on above us. It was all over in thirty minutes, and we returned to our desks where the telephones immediately began to ring furiously. The greatest anxiety was about the airfield, and for some time we could not get through to it as the Operation Office had been hit, but eventually a messenger arrived by road on a motor cycle to tell us that no one had been killed and no aircraft damaged."

The conflicting reports as to the extent of the damage and casualties reflected the inadequacy of the communications system.

Mrs Morton, with commendable coolness, was more concerned with the dinner she and her husband were giving for some young officers next day. "During my lunch hour I went to collect our turkey and found the shop deserted with the door unlocked and the fridge still working, so I was able to grab the turkey and take it away, without paying for it, of course."

If Rangoon's air-raid services were pathetically inadequate, so too were the medical facilities. As in the other essential services an appeal for volunteers had met with a lukewarm response.

Miss Violet Kelly, the Assistant Nursing Superintendent at Rangoon General Hospital recalled that "There was an appeal for nurses to join the Burma Military Nursing Service. One English woman who applied for a matron's post for which she was fully qualified with-drew her application when she learned that her personal equipment should include an enamel plate and mug. She considered it below her dignity."

Three or four large buildings in Rangoon had been set up as emergency hospitals, but only the Rangoon General was adequately equipped to deal with the non-stop flow of casualties that poured in after the first raid. Blast-proof walls had been erected round it, and most of the extensive and bomb-proof basement had been turned into an air-raid shelter where treatment could be carried out. During the first day 320 casualties were brought into the hospital, many of whom died of their injuries.

"We found our pre-arranged plans worked very well with this sudden influx, although only one V.A.D. turned up to help that day or later."

The ambulance service was a dismal failure, and many of the injured had to walk or even crawl to the hospitals. At the Rangoon General, where every available bed was filled, people were placed under them, or on the floors of the corridors and wards. The walls echoed to the moans and screams of the injured as they waited for the overworked doctors and nurses to reach them.

Fortunately the Rangoon General had built up a good blood bank, mainly donated by the Anglo-Indian and Anglo-Burmese staff. Again there had not been the anticipated response from the European community to a public appeal for donors.

And amid all the horror and human suffering, there were incidents which still brought tears to the eyes of the doctors, nurses and rescue workers who thought they were immune to further shock. One concerned the death of Harry Pope and his wife. He managed Watson's Garage, one of the largest in Rangoon. It was not just the death of two very popular people but the manner in which their 19-year-old daughter Norah learned about them.

"I was a volunteer with St John's Ambulance Brigade and working as assistant to Mrs Gertrude Murphy, the District Officer in charge of the canteen at headquarters in Rangoon Town Hall. My mother was an ambulance driver, but not on duty at the time of the raid. At some stage during the raid I was called from the canteen and told that my mother wanted me. I went out into the main hall and found her dead on a stretcher at my feet. Her wounds were horrific and I suppose I was in a state of shock for I went back into the canteen and carried on with the endless washing up."

More ships continued to arrive in the docks, adding to the congestion caused by those already loaded to the Plimsoll Line with Lend-Lease equipment. As most of the dock labour force had fled, there were resigned moans from some officials that the valuable cargoes would all be lost. But among the pessimists there were a handful of optimists who remained at their posts encouraging the few remaining coolies to continue unloading the vital stuff of war. Among them was Captain Bobby McClean Brown, a veteran naval officer, who, by example, got a team of Indians and Burmese to unload some of the ships moored alongside. "All you've got to do is stay with them," he said. "Those people at the top won't do anything about it. They don't know what to do in a tight spot, and they don't know how to handle the natives. All you've got to do is *stay* with them. Give them cigarettes, and *stay* with them, and they'll stick."

Far too many people, however, refused to allow the bombs and carnage to interrupt their way of life or affect hallowed customs. Incredibly, the banks closed the next day and remained closed until 27 December for the holiday. They reopened on the 28th, but only for a short spell as it was a Saturday, and then they were only open to receive payments. As 30 December was a Sunday they were closed again, and their doors remained shut on 31 December and 1 January because it was New Year's Day.

The prolonged closure was deeply resented by many people who were concerned with getting all their personal belongings packed and put aboard ships bound for Calcutta. Despite the devastation and human suffering, they crated their silver, cut glass, linen and expensive carpets and other valuables. They would have liked to leave with ample funds too.

Lady Dorman-Smith heard but did not see the devastation caused by the bombers; she and her family had gone to the deep shelter in the grounds of Government House when the first bombs fell. The shelter was to prove an albatross which Sir Reginald had to carry throughout the short-lived campaign. It had cost 30,000 rupees to build and, as the death toll mounted, so too did the criticisms that he had looked after his own first.

That night Lady Dorman-Smith religiously filled in her diary with her bold, upright, hard-to-read writing. She deeply lamented the loss of life, and had a special word of condolence for the Popes.

Ironically, only a short time before, Lady Dorman-Smith had recorded her impressions of a day at the Rangoon races where "Early Bird ran well". It seemed unbelievable that in such a short time, "all the shops have closed and there are no papers on the market".

That afternoon Sir Reginald toured the devastated city and cabled to the Viceroy in India, "Damage is not great but A.P. bombs were efficient," and, he added, "Apart from some feeling of helplessness from lack of labour civilian services are functioning well. There is a stoppage of retail trade which we are trying to remedy."

It was a message of remarkable complacency; Rangoon was already in its death throes. It was this urbanity which was to result in the Governor being branded the villain of the piece and the person mainly responsible for the shambles and eventual breakdown of civilized life in Rangoon. He was branded "Dormant Myth", "Dormouse Smith", and "Snoremouse Smith". Some of the criticisms were justified, but many of them were entirely unfounded; he had only arrived in Rangoon in May and there was little he could have done to remedy the results of years of decay and stagnation that characterized the life of the European community which virtually ran the country. Soon after his arrival he had asked for reinforcements for the army and air force. He also wanted more shelters, better medical facilities, blast and splinter-proof fire stations, more ambulances and a more efficient fire-fighting service. Little of what he asked for materialized.

He was a proud, somewhat aloof man, who adhered strongly to the view that representatives of His Majesty the King did not, in fact could not, answer their critics. He was, to his own detriment, first and foremost a politician, and in no way the inspired leader Burma so desperately needed.

Added to all that was the general feeling that he had been foisted on Burma by Winston Churchill who did not want him in his Cabinet as he was too closely associated with Neville Chamberlain and his policy of appeasement. It was character assassination without much justification. The neglect of Burma was due more to the penny-pinching policies of Westminster and the military experts before the war than anything His Excellency did. Nevertheless, he was a far from ideal choice; he had no experience of the Far East, while his political career had hardly been distinguished. But his background was impeccably patrician. He had been educated at Harrow and the Royal Military Academy, Sandhurst, had served with the 15th Sikhs, and came from that class which genuinely and sincerely believed they had a right and duty to govern. At the remarkably young age of 32 he became a Justice of the Peace and a County Alderman. Four years later he was a Member of Parliament and President of the powerful National Farmers Union. At 38 he was knighted and soon afterwards became a Privy Councillor, it was by any standard a meteroric rise, made all the more remarkable by the fact that there were no visible signs of an outstanding talent.

When the war in Europe started he was Minister of Agriculture and Fisheries, entrusted with the task of getting men on the land and increasing food production. He promised there would be a million more people on the land and more acres under the plough, but somehow he managed to lessen both of them.

When he arrived in Rangoon those who did meet him were impressed by his charm and readiness to listen. To the 'old hands' he was a bit of an upstart who had arrived to teach old dogs new tricks, but even his most outspoken critics were prepared to swallow their pride for an invitation to drinks in his garden., For, whatever his limitations, he represented the apex of the social pyramid.

The Japanese returned again on Christmas Day in much bigger strength; this time there *were* a hundred bombers escorted by a large group of fighters. The native casualties were lower, but still tragically high. Dorman-Smith reported that "they had learned a lesson". How, he did not explain. They had certainly not taken to the shelters. If the death roll was lower it was only because so many had fled, an action which he personally deplored.

The mass exodus certainly had catastrophic results. At the Dufferin Hospital the entire Burmese nursing staff left, leaving 280 wounded to their fate. The Myoma Boys High School, which had been turned into an emergency hospital, also packed up through the desertion of menial staff and nurses. Many of the new casualties and those admitted to hospitals the day before died through inadequate treatment and the delays in collecting the injured because of the shortage of ambulances.

At the Rangoon General Hospital, just before the beginning of the second raid, the Nursing Superintendent, Miss Mabel Maxfield, was handed twenty-five envelopes. "Before opening them she thought they were Christmas cards, but they contained the resignations of some of the indigenous nursing staff who wanted to return to their homes away from Rangoon," said Violet Kelly.

The airfield at Mingaladon and the barracks of the Gloucesters were again attacked, just as the cooks were preparing Christmas dinner.

C.Q.M.S. George Biggs recalled, "Preparations for the festive day were more or less complete, the turkeys were in the ovens half-cooked when the sirens went around 10 am. D Company were near the church and we had trenches dug between the church and our barrack block. We had hardly time to get there when over the church came Japanese fighters blasting away with all guns firing. I saw a Jap fighter coming for us, and as my rifle was fully loaded I stood up and fired five to seven rounds at it, but was disappointed I did not bring it down. I believe I was the first one in the Battalion to have a shot at the Japs."

With extraordinary equanimity George Biggs recalls, "With everything in confusion the question was – were we going to have our Christmas dinner? Well, by running to and fro to our cookhouse, we managed to have all ready for the men's dinner and the meal was taken with no further incident."

General Sir Archibald Wavell, Commander-in-Chief India, who had been given the added responsibility of Commander-in-Chief South-West Pacific, flew into Mingaladon under a cloak of secrecy in the middle of the raid and had the humiliating experience of having to dive headlong into a slit trench. One bomb landed less than thirteen paces away which provided a good laugh for the airmen and soldiers, and proved a great boost to morale. He was driven to Government House where he disclosed that he had sent for Lieutenant-General Thomas Hutton, a soldier of "real organizational ability" to take over from Lieutenant-General D. K. McLeod. He did not stay long in Rangoon as he wanted to be back in Delhi in time for the Viceroy's Cup.

Lieutenant-Colonel Charles Bagot, who had won a Military Cross in Flanders, was a tough, professional soldier dedicated to the welfare of his men who would have walked over a cliff edge if he had given the order. But even his most ardent admirers had to concede that he possessed a fiery temper for which the back of his neck acted as a barometer. In Rangoon during the first two raids it was invariably crimson, for he could not stand incompetence and what he had witnessed was the inevitable consequence of the apathy he had been forced to observe in silence ever since the Battalion arrived in 1938.

Now he was appalled at the way in which the great port was being allowed to disintegrate and decided that the Gloucesters would do all they could to halt the rot. The men were questioned about their past, something which many had enlisted to bury, but Bagot was not interested in opening cupboards to expose old bones; he simply wanted to know their peacetime occupation.

Former butchers became slaughterers, bakers made bread, men with no special training were detailed to unload ships, dig trenches, repair the damaged airfield, help out at the hospitals, work in river launches, stoke the engines of ambulance trains, work as porters on the platforms, clear the city of mounting refuse and remove some of the corpses. Others armed with rifles patrolled the streets with orders to shoot on sight anyone seen looting.

It was largely due to the Gloucesters, and those civilians who stayed at their posts until some measure of morale was restored, that Rangoon was kept ticking over. Naturally there were many civilians who had not raised a finger to help who readily claimed the credit. Charles Bagot, never a man to mince his words, commented laconically, "Certainly in Rangoon, as elsewhere in the campaign, reputations were fought for, and earned, to the last Gloster."

Winston Churchill sent a message of congratulations to the dock workers and public services and sweepers for standing by their posts. Not unnaturally, it provoked some ribald comments from the troops.

Leland Stowe, America's most celebrated correspondent, had been busy gathering material for his story to the *Chicago Daily News* which would be syndicated throughout the United States. What he had seen had thoroughly depressed him; he feared he was witnessing the collapse of the entire country. It was just after 8 pm when he decided to try and get something to eat in the Strand which was still littered with broken glass and debris. "Two Englishmen, attired immaculately in dress shirts and black ties, walked in with a woman who was togged out in a sweeping evening gown. They were bound for a chota peg in the bar, according to a ritual which was undoubtedly of many years' standing. They did not seem remotely aware that Rangoon's fires were still smouldering, or that parts of the city were a shambles, or that its hospitals were overcrowded with some two thousand wounded. It seemed that these three hadn't seen a thing all day — perhaps not for years and years. They were sleepwalkers among the bombs."

Joan Morton and her husband managed eventually to sit down with their guests and enjoy the turkey she had purloined from the abandoned cold store. "Mercifully we did not know this would be our last Christmas together," she said.

Finetta Bagot and her daughter had watched the raid from under a tree by the roadside where her husband had driven them when the alert sounded. When it was over he collected them and took them back to the barracks. There he announced that the few remaining wives and children would be leaving next day to join other families in Maymyo. On Boxing Day he drove them to Rangoon station where he was able to find an engine in a siding, but there was no driver and so his men stoked up the boiler, pushed it into the station and coupled it up to some carriages.

At the close of that historic Christmas Day a depressed Lady Dorman-Smith confided in her diary, "Can't believe it is Xmas. Masses of servants have departed including thirty-seven Government House malis . . . The position of no sweepers is going to be very awkward." The sight of the refugees pouring out of the city had distressed her considerably, and her heart went out to the air-raid victims. "The patients are not getting their food as there are no cooks. . . . It was a most tragic sight at the General."

She was also gravely concerned that General Wavell's presence in Rangoon had become common knowledge. "How does it get out? Going to stick up warning notices, 'Walls have ears' etc."

The Governor had toured the city and at the end of the day had cabled his report to the Viceroy: "Our Christmas pie from Japan duly arrived in the shape of (estimated) eighty bombers and about twenty fighters. Present figures show that we accounted for fourteen fighters and seven bombers with four probables. Our losses were two Buffaloes shot down and two missing. A further two were shot up on the ground while being serviced, one more being damaged." Two of the American Tomahawks had also been written off. Once again he reiterated his urgent appeal for more aircraft as the Buffalo losses meant the small R.A.F. unit had almost been wiped out in the two raids.

He added, "The great exodus from Rangoon continues", and went on to say that the desertions had presented urgent problems at the hospitals and there was a desperate shortage of doctors, nurses and orderlies.

In the city those who had remained behind were all asking the same question: Why doesn't the Governor declare martial law?

Only a gallant band of men had prevented Rangoon from being totally destroyed – the pilots of the R.A.F. with their antiquated, unreliable Brewster Buffaloes, and the highly-paid mercenaries of the A.V.G. with their vastly superior P.40 fighters. Throughout the two raids they had scrambled time and again to battle against overwhelming odds. It was an achievement to have even become airborne in time, as the warning system was woefully inadequate and messengers on cycles had to pedal like fury from the orderly room at R.A.F. headquarters to warn them of approaching aircraft.

The A.V.G. had only fourteen Tomahawks and the R.A.F. ten Buffaloes, but together they had taken on two vastly superior enemy forces and inflicted heavy losses.

If the Japanese had persisted they could have won the battle for air superiority there and then, for the A.V.G. were so short of ammunition that a request was made for 70,000 rounds to be flown down from Lashio. Apart from suffering heavy losses, the R.A.F. was perilously low on fuel. Fortunately there was someone capable of meeting the crisis. Captain Harry Stott, R.A.M.C, a burly, outspoken Yorkshireman who refused to be intimidated by officialdom or bureaucracy, heard of the plight of the pilots and set off to find 80-octane petrol. "I went to five petrol dumps in Mingaladon before I found one drum. Four dumps were clean dry of petrol and the bloody Japs had been at war with us for sixteen days."

Through sheer persistence and bullying, he managed to assemble twenty trucks and move 1,000 tons of high octane petrol from a ship in the docks. With the lorries loaded and lined up on the quay, Stott set off to seek authorization to move it to the airfield, but to his dismay a Burma Army colonel turned down his request for the necessary port permits. "Today is Saturday. We cannot interfere with the weekend amenities." And with that he went off to play a round of golf. Stott, who had survived Dunkirk, exploded: "Just bloody colonial rot," but his outburst got him nowhere; he still had to wait until Monday to move the much-needed fuel.

Rangoon was in dire need of more men like Captain Stott. While others were bemoaning the lack of transport, he accumulated a sizeable fleet. When asked how he obtained the vehicles he answered tartly, "I swiped them." The Chinese would not release any of the Lend-Lease vehicles choking the port, so he had helped himself, and when a Chinese officer had warned him that he was taking property belonging to his Government, he replied, "No, you're mistaken. They belong to the British Army now."

Another man who refused to throw up his hands in resignation was David Maurice, an Australian Buddhist employed by Imperial Chemical Industries. He knew the natives intimately and by labouring himself at the quayside had been able to get a gang of terrified coolies to remain at their posts. Among the goods they unloaded was a consignment of gelignite, which if it had exploded would have destroyed a large part of the docks. Typically, when he had offered his services earlier he had been turned down; there was an inbred mistrust of men who were too close to the native population. Previously he had warned about the dangers of a fifth column, and he strongly advocated enlisting the support of the Burmese before they fell prey to Japanese propaganda. Anti-Japanese propaganda, he was reminded, had been officially banned in Burma.

As December drew to an end Sir Reginald was able to inform the Viceroy that the position had improved as some of the labour which had deserted had reported back for work, but the situation in the hospitals was still critical and there was discontent in the underpaid and undermanned police force.

As the fettered war correspondents toured the ravaged and near-deserted streets, they had already written off Rangoon as a 'doomed city', but such a defeatist opinion was not allowed to find its way into their copy. It would have had a detrimental effect on morale.

CHAPTER 2

"Government Officials just did not talk to box wallahs"
Mrs Gwenllyan Coward

At 6.30 am on Monday 8 December, 1941, Sir Reginald Dorman-Smith had been shaken awake at Government House by his Military Secretary, Lieutenant-Colonel C. T. Miller, and told, "The Pacific balloon has gone up." News had just come through of the attack on Pearl Harbor. He wasted little time in driving to Rangoon radio station to tell the country that the Japanese had "out-Hitlered the Führer". "There is only one thing that decent people can and will do, that is fight and continue fighting, no matter what the cost, until these forces of all that is evil, corrupt and vile are eradicated from the face of the globe for all time."

He appealed to them to carry out their duties calmly and efficiently and to remain at their posts, adding comfortingly: "As far as human ingenuity can devise, we are ready. Our armed forces are at their action stations. Our civil defence forces are ready for action and as keen as mustard. Everything which can be done is being done both to contribute to your safety and to the defeat of the enemy."

It was a total travesty of the truth, and most Europeans, who bore a heavy share of the responsibility for the lack of preparation, knew it, but that did not prevent them from indulging soon afterwards in an orgy of denigration and accusations that His Excellency had deliberately misled the country. It *was* true that Dorman-Smith was guilty of deception and he knew it. But he could not go to the microphone and admit that Burma was totally unprepared. Neither was he blind to the appalling state of the civil defence and medical services. The rescue, demolition and debris-clearing services existed only on paper; they were untrained and had no equipment. The fire service was abysmally short of vehicles, while roof-spotters and fire-watchers were non-existent. No organization existed for the reception of bombed-out people and the canteen services were poor. Much depended on the telephone system, but there were too few telephones and an acute shortage of staff, which meant it was impossible to work in shifts.

London had responded to his appeals in a manner which had characterized the conduct of war to date: "too little too late".

Shortly after his arrival, Sir Reginald had cabled the British Government urgently requesting that an expert, with personal experience of bombing, should be sent out to help set up an efficient organization. As a result Mr de Graaff Hunter was sent to Rangoon as Defence Commissioner. When he arrived he found things far worse than he had anticipated. The situation, he confessed, "scared me stiff". He was told there were no shelters because it was impossible to provide them. It was as simple as that. With the time available he was confronted with an impossible task. He would, he said, need at least two years to set up an efficient organization, not the few months which he knew was the most he could hope for. But he did what he could and he achieved miracles in the time available; but for his efforts the disaster of Rangoon would have been even more catastrophic.

It took outsiders to put their finger on just what was wrong with Burma; it was the system – a system which *encouraged* apathy and allowed a creeping rot to set in undetected. There was an odour of decay which the Europeans seemed incapable of smelling, or, if they did, they kept quiet about it, having learned that social survival depended on conformity. It was not something that was unique to Burma; it existed in neighbouring Malaya and Singapore on which a successful defence of the Far East was based.

Lady Brooke-Popham, wife of Air Chief Marshal Sir Robert Brooke-Popham, Commander-in-Chief Far East, encountered it soon after arriving in Singapore. "I went as a newcomer after experiencing the London blitz. I was struck immediately by the deadly inertia of the white population. They were utterly dormant." And she was astounded at the reply she received when she asked a woman to help with A.R.P. work: "I'm awfully sorry Lady Popham, but I've already entered for the tennis tournament; civil defence will interfere with my tennis."

Few people in Britain had any real idea what life was like for the European in the East. They imagined that the whites were spurred on by a deep sense of vocation, with little or no regard for financial reward or official recognition. It was true in some cases but the majority were there because it promised rewards far greater than any they could hope to obtain at home. And nowhere did this apply more than in Burma.

In shape Burma is rather like a withered hand with a long index finger pointing southwards. The northern end is an extension of the mountain mass of Central Asia, the bleak and desolate domain of llamas and pandas which had been given the rather romantic title "Roof of the World". As the human hand divides into fingers so does Burma, split into ranges stretching southwards with the mighty rivers Chindwin, Irrawaddy and Salween running between. This comprises the bulk of the country. Tenasserim, the forefinger, stretches down the western shore of the Malay Peninsula towards Singapore.

Although hot and steamy, the Europeans found it a country of breathtaking beauty, a land of golden-domed pagodas and saffron-robed priests, with an abundance of game and wild life, plus superb fishing and shooting. On the more material side it boasted vast oil fields, silver, tin, copper and tungsten, vast forests of teak, precious stones, wolfram, rice and rubber.

To understand Burma one has to know the social structure of the country, which was cone-shaped and many-tiered. At the summit was the Governor. Sir Reginald lived with his family in Government House, an architectural monstrosity with large, lofty rooms and long, echoing corridors, where an army of uniformed servants, who moved as silently as if on well-oiled castors, waited upon their every need.

Just below His Excellency were the senior officials of the elite Indian Civil Service who worked with him in the Secretariat and were responsible for the day-to-day running of the country.

Then there were the Divisional Commissioners, Deputy Commissioners, District Officers, Forestry Officers, Senior Police and Railway Officers.

The next in priority were the "box wallahs", the European employees of such powerful companies as Steel Brothers, the Bombay-Burmah Trading Corporation, Foucars, Jardine Matheson, Burmah Oil, Ellerman and the large banks. Contrary to what the ICS might think, they considered themselves the real rulers. "Steel Brothers is Burma," summed up their attitude. Gwenllyan Coward, married to a senior railway man, considered it an empty boast, for soon after arriving in Burma she was told, "Government Officials just did not talk to box wallahs."

But whatever level you were on, appearance was everything. Arthur Dunn, who was a young locomotive foreman in Leeds before he answered an advertisement in *The Times* for a job with Burma Railways in 1922, was astonished at his London interview to be given a list of essentials to take with him; it included full morning dress. And at Maymyo he found he was expected to dress for breakfast in the club at 11 am and again for dinner, and that promotion was by way of "dead men's shoes".

The timbermen, rice growers, oil engineers and rubbermen were all loosely lumped together as "jungle wallahs", men who worked hard, played hard and drank too much when they visited one of the larger cities.

There was also a relatively small group of whites who did not really have an established niche in an otherwise perfectly layered society. They were the missionaries who spread the gospel in the more remote areas. They were an enigma to the Europeans in the larger towns who saw no point in living in an inhospitable climate if you did not benefit financially.

Next on the scale were the Eurasians, the Anglo-Indians and Anglo-Burmese who were described in a variety of ways, none flattering and all contemptuous – "café au lait", "chilly crackers", "two of coffee, one of milk". They suffered from a sense of inferiority which they tried to hide by becoming more pukka than the genuine sahib. But they filled a vital role in performing many duties essential to the efficient running of the country.

Yet they were never allowed to forget that they were inferior. George Robertson, son of Andrew Forsyth Robertson, a Scottish Forestry Manager for Steel Brothers, and a Shan lady from Bhamo, enlised in the small Burma Navy as soon as war looked imminent. "I recall the first day of my commission in the Burma R.N.V.R. I was instructed by the C.O. to go with a fellow officer in his car. He was an expatriate from one of the British firms in Rangoon and during the trip I tried to strike up a conversation, but he would have none of it. He neither spoke nor took any notice of me. It was infra-dig for him to converse with me, even though we were so-called brother officers."

Then there were the million-odd Indians, coolies, gardeners, house servants, ayahs, scyces and others who performed the tasks that no one else would tackle; they emptied the "thunder boxes", collected the refuse and were the main source of labour in the docks. But not all were poor and subservient. Among them were craftsmen, stone masons, carpenters, mechanics, along with shrewd businessmen who ran lucrative bazaars and shops, and traders who were extremely wealthy. And, of course, there were the money lenders, the most despised and yet most sought-after group.

There were also 300,000 Chinese who kept very much to themselves, maintaining their age-old customs and devoting their energies to what interested them most, accumulating wealth.

The indigenous population of Burma numbered some 15 million, consisting of the Shans in the east, the Chins in the west, the Kachins in the north and the Karens in the south. There were also numerous other tribes scattered over the country. They were an easy-going people with a marked antipathy to heavy manual work, content to grow their crops, smoke opium and chew betel nut.

For some time the more intelligent and educated Burmese had been taking a closer interest in the government of their own country and the British were constantly reminded that if they were to stay they had to encourage progression towards independence. Some measure of self-government had been achieved. The Premier, U-Saw, was Burmese and several others held high positions. But the reins of government were still held firmly by the British.

Many of the older Burma hands had not taken kindly to the idea of U-Saw holding such high office, but his subsequent fate forced them to concede that it had not been such a bad step after all; it proved how unreliable the Burmese were. Before war was declared in the Far East, he had travelled to London with the support of the Governor on a good will mission to try and persuade Churchill to grant full independence when the war was over. He was extremely bitter when his appeal was rejected; he was on his way home and had reached Hawaii when Pearl Harbor was attacked, and he was forced to fly to Lisbon where he offered his allegiance to Japan, which promised what Britain would not countenance. He was subsequently arrested by the British and interned for the duration.

The British in Burma were quick to point out that they were not motivated by self-interest in their opposition to the political aspirations of the Burmese. Any objections were purely in their own interests and they had a gruesome allegory, that was worn out with the telling, to justify their attitude.

In the Southern Shan States near Loikam, it went, lived the giraffe women whose necks were stretched to twice their normal length by the gradual addition of metal rings. One of the women developed a bad neck ulcer which required urgent surgery necessitating the removal of the rings. Unfortunately, while she was sitting up in bed, well on the road to recovery, she sneezed and broke her neck. And that, the story concluded, was what would happen if Burma was granted independence – for the British were the rings.

With no visible place in the order of things were the Japanese, obsequious, ingratiating, ever-smiling and always ready to serve. They were dentists, doctors and photographers, but their main occupation was spying and every town of any importance had a well-organized ring, which over the years had insiduously sown discontent among the Burmese: Asia should be for the Asiatics and Japan was going to put and end to their servitude.

They kept a careful log of troop movements, noted new military installations, checked the movement of shipping and reported with satisfaction the absence of any civil defence. With an audacity that was hard to believe the photographers who took pictures of bouncing babies also photographed anything of military value. And they passed it on to the Japanese Consul who enjoyed a remarkable popularity; his party held in the Consulate in 1940 was voted the social event of the year.

There was little room on the social pyramid for the British soldier, who detected a "prison hulk" mentality among the whites; they appreciated the need for garrison troops but preferred to have them out of sight. The clubs were closed to them, and few ever saw the inside of a white person's home. Most of their off-duty time was spent in the wet canteen where beer was cheap and plentiful, with the inevitable result that some soldiers soon became confirmed soaks.

The European community took it for granted that the young soldiers who were paid next to nothing unquestioningly accepted that it was *their* duty to defend their properties and commercial interests and uphold the prejudices in which they were included.

*

The task of the Gloucesters was to maintain internal security and they were quickly called upon to do this when severe rioting broke out in Rangoon. But for the more serious purpose of war they were woefully ill-equipped. "Guts and esprit de corps were the only weapons a cheese-paring government could not deny them," said Charles Bagot.

When Neville Chamberlain announced on the BBC that Britain was at war with Germany, Ann Purton had decided her place was beside her husband in Burma. She had recently married Humphrey Purton, a subaltern in the 4th Battalion, Burma Rifles, and on hearing the declaration of war promptly booked a passage to Rangoon.

She arrived on 17 October, 1939, and was immediately struck by the contrast between wartime England and Burma. She was greeted at the dockside by her husband and his Christian bearer Anthony who was splendidly attired in snow-white trousers, a knee-length coat with a cummerbund of gold and peacock blue (the regimental colours) and a white pugaree bearing the same colours.

In Mandalay, where he was stationed, she quickly learned that as a memsahib she was not expected to do anything for herself; there were plenty of servants to do everything. She was, however, expected to do child welfare in the lines once a week and make bandages with the other ladies of the station, attend knitting sessions and make comforts for the troops back home. Neither did her husband lead a spartan existence; his clothes were laid out every day, and he seldom put his shoes on or took them off; his personal bearer did that. The officers changed at least three times a day and always dressed for dinner.

It was understandable, said Mrs Coward, that the women "found it difficult to think of the war at home".

Gwenllyan Coward was simply living for the day when her husband would retire and, when she was not playing golf, tennis, riding, sailing or swimming, she contemplated a life of leisure back home. "We thoroughly enjoyed ourselves and felt remote from events at home, for the Government had assured us that, although Burma had no defence of her own, naval units and fighter aircraft and troops from Singapore would come to our aid in the extremely unlikely event of Burma being attacked."

On Sunday mornings, Mrs Coward recalled, there were paper chases on borrowed police ponies, or hunts with the better riders acting as the quarry.

"Life," she said, "was happy and very pleasant."

One reminder that there was a war not far from their doorstep was the day-and-night din of heavy lorries and jeeps careering up the Burma Road towards Lashio, bearing crated Lend-Lease equipment for the Chinese army which had been fighting the Japanese for some time.

"It displayed a sense of urgency so sadly lacking in those of us who had sweated it out for years in Burma," said Mrs Coward.

For Ian Scott, a Second Lieutenant of the Army in Burma Reserve of Officers, soldiering was "a lot of fun". His first posting was to Pyawbwe, headquarters of the Burma Frontier Force, about 300 miles north of Rangoon on the road to Mandalay. The Commanding Officer was Lieutenant-Colonel Hugh Childers.

"The Colonel always came dressed in a dinner jacket, and his wife Gladys in a long evening gown with gloves. In fact Hughie and Gladys dressed for dinner every night, even when on their own. I well remember him saying to me once when we were discussing this, 'I presume you take a bath and put on a clean shirt every evening before dinner?' 'Yes sir,' I replied. 'Then why not put on the correct clothes after your bath? You will find that dinner tastes so much better when you are properly dressed.'"

Dinner at the Colonel's residence was always a memorable occasion. Troopers of the Governor's bodyguard, which was stationed at Pyawbe, were on duty in full dress uniform and the meal was served by mess waiters in ceremonial dress. "It was all very splendid and very British," said Scott.

Lieutenant-Colonel Bagot, convinced that the Japanese *would* invade, was determined that the Gloucesters would be ready. He ignored red tape and put his officers and men through a period of intensive training, which included illegal exercises in the jungle. He told them, "You are going to be hungry, tired and thirsty before this war is over, and I'm personally going to see to it that you are ready for whatever lies ahead."

He knew however, that physical fitness alone would not defeat the Japanese; he needed more equipment of all kinds, but his requests were never met. When he asked for such basic requirements as sandbags, barbed wire and extra ammunition he was greeted with a chilly response and advised to use string in place of barbed wire.

The Gloucesters were not only undermanned, they were disgracefully ill-equipped. They had some new weapons, but little ammunition – a paltry ninety rounds for the Thompson sub-machine guns which would prove so effective in the jungle, while there were only twelve grenades for the entire battalion, and in the past three years only thirty-six men had been allowed to throw one. There were no mortar bombs and the forty mules needed to transport the mortars had no saddlery, while the Carrier Platoon had no carriers; what signal equipment they had was obsolete, consisting mainly of telephones, heliographs and lamps, none of which were suitable for the terrain, while the odd radio sets that were beginning to arrive were insufficient for the minimum requirements.

It was not until the day of Pearl Harbor that the battalion was mobilized, the number of grenades increased to ninety-six and 400 mortar bombs were allowed to be drawn. Even so the battalion was still twelve officers and 340 other ranks short.

The only other regular British infantry battalion in Burma was the 2nd King's Own Yorkshire Light infantry stationed in Maymyo. Its officers and men were fit, tough and second to none in spirit and courage, but they lacked even the most basic requirement of a fighting soldier – a tin helmet. Instead they were expected to make do with the regulation topee. There were no entrenching tools, only ninety-six shovels and forty-six pickaxes, which were extremely cumbersome and difficult to carry. There were no heavy knives for cutting through the jungle, only a few locally-made dahs which broke on the stout bamboo. A most essential item of equipment for jungle warfare was a compass, but only twenty of these had been issued. The battalion had no 2-inch mortar which, because of their mobility and accuracy, were invaluable against small, well-concealed forces. Four 3-inch mortars were received but no means existed for carrying them or the ammunition. Although many of the men prided themselves on their skill as marksmen there were no sniper rifles, while the machine-gun platoon had its .303 Vickers taken away and handed to a Burmese unit on aerodrome defence. There were no wireless sets, no mines, no materials for making booby traps. They should have had fifty-two lorries, but had been issued with seven. The ten Bren carriers were in India.

Something less than 2000 men constituted the British Army in Burma, and they were expected to repel an invader with little more than rifles, cold steel and courage. Yet they were given some encouragement. Military Intelligence, such as it was, assured them that the Japanese soldier was even worse off when it came to equipment; furthermore, he was a squat, myopic little man who could not shoot straight and was incapable of fighting in the dark. As a final comfort they were assured that a full-scale war was out of the question because of the terrain. Had not a colonel, on being sent to Rangoon to organize training, retorted, "Training? It is out of the question – there is nothing but jungle"?

While the politicians and military experts continued to issue the same soporific pronouncements, the Japanese were preparing to invade. Two divisions slipped across the Indo-China border into Siam where the Thais offered little resistance after being assured that their sovereignty would be honoured. On the Burma-Siam border the 55th and 33rd Japanese divisions waited for the order to attack.

CHAPTER 3

"I've heard of holding the baby, but this is twins"
                                                                    General Wavell

When war came to the Far East, the Commander-in-Chief was a man who had forfeited Churchill's confidence. General Sir Archibald Wavell had been kicked sideways and sent to India where the Prime Minister thought he would be out of sight and out of mind in a military cul de sac. In wartime reputations rise and fall like a barometer in unsettled weather, and Wavell's fortunes were at an extremely low ebb. Having enjoyed the respect and affection of everyone, his reputation was now very bruised, following the series of disastrous reversals in the Middle East, Greece and Crete.

The first hint of dissatisfaction in the soldier-scholar came in a letter from the Chief of the Imperial General Staff, General Sir John Dill, to General Sir Claude Auchinleck, who was tipped to replace him in the Middle East.

Dill wrote:

"For your eyes only: I would like to tell you that the P.M. has lost confidence in Wavell – if he ever had any. I maintain that in war you must either trust your general or sack him. That being so we *may* be faced with the withdrawal of Wavell from the Middle East – even before you get this letter. If that happens you may succeed him."

Dill understandably resented Churchill going over his head on such matters as the appointment of commanders and the tactical handling of their men. He was convinced that Japan *would* enter the war and wanted Auchinleck to remain in India and Wavell to have a long and well-deserved rest in the United Kingdom. Churchill, however, was adamant, and justified his decision with, "At home we had the feeling that Wavell was a tired man. It might well be said that we had ridden the willing horse to a standstill."

Wavell *was* tired and it was noticeable to those who were close to him; Anthony Eden thought he had aged ten years almost overnight. Wavell was aware of it too and had repeatedly asked for leave. Dill's opposition to the switch was more practical; he thought Auchinleck was better for India and he let Churchill know exactly what he thought. The move was also opposed by the Viceroy, Lord Linlithgow, and Leo Amery, Secretary of State for India, who feared "everybody would feel that India was being saddled with a cast-off, whether for reasons of failure or mere fatigue." Churchill, however, was convinced that "the public interest will best be served" by the change.

Wavell took his transfer with quiet resignation and his face registered as much emotion as his glass eye when he was told the news. Five days after handing over to Auchinleck he flew to Delhi where his "heart bled" at the lack of preparedness and the shortage of all types of equipment. The country was carrying on as if it was still peacetime, and many people had already retired to Simla. When Wavell took his own family there he was shocked at the air of complacency. He was convinced that Burma should come under his command instead of Singapore and the War Office should be responsible for the supply and allocation of materials. On his own initiative he went to Burma to see for himself how things stood and suffered another shock when he saw how ill-prepared the country was.

Four days after Pearl Harbor the War Office, with almost indecent haste, informed him that Burma was now under his command, and Wavell again listed all he required to defend it: modern fighter squadrons, two squadrons of Blenheim bombers, air-raid-warning equipment and anti-aircraft guns. Responsibility for the defence of Burma had been tossed like a shuttlecock between London, India and Singapore for some time and in the vital period between November, 1941, and February, 1942, there were to be no fewer than five separate headquarters.

At the time of the first raids on Rangoon Churchill was in America, and it was there he learned that the Americans wanted a Supreme Allied Command in South-East Asia and the man they wanted to lead it was Wavell; and so the short-lived and cumbersome ABDACOM was born. Wavell accepted it with the laconic comment, "I've heard of holding the baby, but this is twins."

Wavell's choice as C.G.S. to replace the retiring Major-General Donald McLeod was Lieutenant-General Thomas Hutton, a gunner and first class officer with an excellent First War record. "Grannie" Hutton, as he was unkindly dubbed behind his back, was not everyone's choice for the job; some said he lacked imagination and was not a "fighting soldier". It was a churlish remark to make about a man who had been wounded thrice, four times mentioned in despatches, awarded the Military Cross and Bar, the Legion of Honour and the French and Italian War Crosses. To say he did not *look* the warrior was nearer the truth. But he was a brilliant organizer, and a man of strong character and firmly held views. And he had the courage to stand by his convictions, even when they were unpalatable to his civil and military superiors. His outspokenness, however, was not appreciated and it was not long before his ability to fulfil the task was being questioned.

As the situation in Rangoon worsened Wavell made a decision which was to have a profound effect on the war in Burma and result in a bitter controversy.

He appointed Major-General Jackie Smyth to command the 17th Indian Division which would provide the backbone for the defence of Burma. With hindsight, Smyth recognized it as an appointment he should have refused on medical grounds, but professional soldiers are ambitious and when he concealed the state of his health he had no reason to believe it would have such a calamitous outcome. But it was not merely a simple question of ambition over-riding all else; Smyth had placed himself in a position from which he could not extricate himself without admitting he had been guilty of a serious breach of army regulations.

Stocky, restless, full of self-confidence that some thought bordered on arrogance, and a harsh critic of anyone he did not feel was up to the job, he was one of the army's most celebrated officers. In the close-knit community of senior officers it was confidently predicted that he would attain the highest possible rank. As a junior officer with the 15th Ludhiana Sikhs he had won a Victoria Cross in France in 1915, been awarded an M.C. in the Afghan War, fought in seven Indian Frontier campaigns and been mentioned in despatches six times, the last for his outstanding work commanding a brigade at Dunkirk. A man with a long and honourable family tradition of military service and an impeccable background of Repton and Sandhurst, he was also endowed with dashing good looks and was a sportsman of outstanding talent.

In 1941 he had spent two periods in hospital suffering from malaria and an anal fissure which required surgical treatment. On 2 October he was informed by Army Headquarters in Delhi that he was being offered the command of the 18th India Division which was due to form in Secunderabad. It carried with it promotion from brigadier to acting major-general and he accepted, thinking that it would be at least six months before the Divison would be fit for active service, by which time his physical condition would have improved. Nevertheless he consulted the senior medical officer in Quetta who took the view that he did not wish to upset the apple cart by making an adverse report; in any case he had not been notified of the appointment nor asked to carry out a medical examination. Smyth accepted, but events changed dramatically and on 4 December he received an urgent message that General Wavell wanted him to take command of the 17th Indian Division, and, five days after the first bombing of Rangoon, he was summoned to Flagstaff House, Delhi, and told his Division was to go to Burma. It was not the kind of news an officer commanding his first division wanted to hear, for he knew it was ill-equipped, had many raw recruits and had been trained for desert warfare. An added problem was that the 17th would, in fact, have to be reformed as two of its original brigades had been diverted to Singapore.

At the interview Smyth formed the opinion that Wavell was a tired man, and at the age of 59 ought not to be indulging in such hectic pursuits as pig-sticking. But what perturbed Smyth more was the General's low opinion of the Japanese as fighting soldiers. It was not a view that Smyth shared. He was also informed that Hutton had been sent to Rangoon as Burma Army Commander, an appointment which he personally considered a great mistake as "he was no commander of troops in battle", but his fears were allayed when he was told that Hutton would look after the administration while he would do the fighting.

The Japanese had already started their infiltration into Burma when Smyth arrived in Rangoon on 9 January by flying boat. An air-raid warning sounded as he stepped ashore, which brought even more chaos to what was already almost a ghost city. At his first meeting with General Hutton he was given a precise and accurate rundown of the situation; the Japanese had already advanced rapidly from the south and captured Victoria Point and its airfield in the southernmost tip of lower Burma. But Hutton shrewdly calculated that the real threat would not come from this direction; as Rangoon would be the main target, he believed the main thrust would come from the direction of Raheng via Kawkareik-Paan-Kyaikto and Sittang.

To meet this threat the 16th Indian Brigade, commanded by Brigadier John Keane Jones, had been sent to Kawkareik on the Siam border. It was one battalion short, for the 4/12 Frontier Force Rifles had been sent to stiffen the 2nd Brigade which consisted largely of Burma Rifles battalions which were covering 300 miles of jungle country and the vital airfields at Mergui and Tavoy.

The area which fell under Smyth's command was vast, considering the number and quality of the men at his disposal. It stretched from Papun in the north to Mergui in the south and eastwards to Reheng and the Three Pagoda Pass. For this daunting task he had just the 16th India Brigade and the 2nd Burma, although the 46th Brigade was due to arrive in Rangoon within a few days.

After touring his command Smyth went to Moulmein, where his headquarters had been established with a system of communications which was "completely Heath Robinson".

The complacency which still existed in Burma was unforgiveable, but there was some justification for the people in Britain not being unduly worried about the situation, for the outside world was being deliberately deprived of the real truth as the Burma Government had agreed to censor all defeatist reports. Reports which had appeared in the London newspapers on 18 December and datelined Rangoon mentioned the arrival of another big convoy of Indian troops with full equipment: "The well-chosen and well-trained troops made a splendid showing on arrival." Among the troops was the 16th Indian Infantry Brigade which consisted of poorly-trained and inadequately-equipped soldiers, most of whom were little more than raw recruits. None of the officers had any experience of the jungle except a few senior officers whose experience was confined to "Shikar". The British officers of the 13th Indian Infantry Brigade, which had arrived in Burma some weeks previously, had clearly become victims of the propaganda which ridiculed the prowess of the Japanese, for they took their chargers, full peacetime mess kits and dinner jackets to Mandalay.

In the same edition the Governor was reported as saying, "We are here to defend Burma, and, more than that, we are preparing to take the offensive against our enemies." From the outset the attitude of the Government towards the reporting of the war did not make for a happy relationship with the correspondents, neither did it establish a mutual trust.

In Burma correspondents found they were in a position of playing false to all their better instincts by painting a cosy picture which bore no relation to the truth. They wanted to look at the war objectively, not through rose-coloured spectacles prescribed by the Government. They could see no sense in covering up ineptitude and inefficiency, for in doing so nothing would be changed. Neither did they want to cable misleading information about the quality and quantity of the troops.

If the war correspondents were pessimistic, Major-General Smyth was buoyantly confident. "My job would be to do the fighting. That suited me. It was the job for which I had been trained all my military life. Fighting was my business and I was the only General in India who had already had experience of modern war fare against the Germans."

In a short time he was to discover that the experience gained in France was of little use in Burma where the enemy introduced a new kind of warfare.

Christmas found the 2nd King's Own Yorkshire Light Infantry stationed at Takaw on the Salween River, a swollen expanse of muddy water of no use except as a possible military barrier. Fast-flowing, with numerous waterfalls, it presented a picture of unbridled power as it roared through a deep gorge with almost vertical sides. There they dug in, poorly equipped and inadequately dressed. They had not seen the enemy although their casualties were high as it proved to be a malaria trap.

It was just one of many incidents which revealed how ignorant commanders were of the conditions in Burma and how abysmal military intelligence was. When the Japanese invaded it was far from where the KOYLI were entrenched and they were hastily ordered south.

On 20 January the Japanese attacked with tactics that completely confused and unnerved the defenders. They avoided the roads and moved through the jungle and undergrowth, launching surprise attacks in which they blew whistles, fired Verey pistols and tracer bullets, let off fire crackers and emitted spine-chilling screams.

At Kawkareik where the 16th Indian Brigade was positioned it developed into a riot that became a shambles. An angry Wavell thought the men had not stood their ground and his despatch expressed his disappointment: "It is quite clear that the enemy were allowed to gain cheap initial successes through bad handling through the local commanders, lack of training, and in some instances lack of fighting spirit on the part of the troops. It was an unfortunate beginning to the campaign and had serious results in raising the morale of the enemy and depressing that of our own troops." He still could not concede that the Japanese soldiers had outfought and out-manouvred the Indian and Burmese troops.

Kawkareik was without question a resounding defeat, but it might have been wiser for General Wavell to have paid more attention to the cause than the effect. The raw recruits had been thrown into action without proper equipment or training in the use of the most basic weapons. If there were moments of panic and instances of cowardice at Kawkareik, there was also incredible valour and self-sacrifice which went largely unnoticed.

It was true that some of the Burma Rifles did break and run, but when Smyth had visited them before the battle he found that four hundred were suffering from malaria. No criticism, however, could be made against D Coy of the 1/7th Gurkha Rifles who more than lived up to their splendid tradition. They fought with incredible tenacity against odds of five to one, making every shot count. It was then that the officers first knew that they faced an enemy of the highest calibre to whom death did not matter, but to whom capture or surrender was an undreamed-of disgrace. The Gurkhas held their fire until the enemy were almost touching the muzzles of their light machine guns, but there were always others to take the place of those who fell. For five hours the battle raged without pause, and it was only when the Gurkhas faced certain annihilation that they withdrew. The 1/9th Jats also acquitted themselves with commendable courage.

The skirmish, or pitched battle, depending on whose view one wished to take, set the pattern for what was to follow with horrifying swiftness. In the early hours of the next day things started to go wrong and after that nothing went right. Unnerved by the tactics of an enemy who in the dark remained largely unseen, the raw troops became trigger-happy, began to fire at imaginary targets and hurl grenade after grenade which exploded harmlessly in the jungle. In an attempt to reveal the enemy, Verey lights were fired into the air, achieving nothing, but merely adding to the confusion. Bound as they were to motorized transport, the jittery troops could find no effective answer to the jungle tactics and flanking movements which the enemy developed to a fine art.

Rumours spread among the troops, sapping their already sinking morale: they were faced by an enemy numbering several thousand; the brigade commander had been killed; the Japanese were about to launch a gas attack.

Brigadier J. K. Jones was far from dead and anxiously debating what his next step should be. His orders were not exactly clear. He was not to become so involved with a numerically superior force so as to make withdrawal impossible; at the same time he was not to surrender more ground than was necessary. Whatever he did would be wrong.

As the battle continued he realized that he had no option but to withdraw; the situation was out of hand and in a short time it developed into a scene of utter chaos. The 4th Burma Rifles fired on the Gurkhas, mistaking them for Japanese. The 1/9th Jats fired on both of them. Trucks were shot up or were cannoned into each other by terrified drivers. The Japanese tossed firecrackers under the hooves of the mules which panicked and fled into the jungle with their precious cargoes of ammunition. To add to the débâcle a rogue elephant appeared and inflicted more damage on the already depleted mechanized transport and terrified some mules carrying six of the brigade's seven wireless sets; they ran off and were never seen again. Much of the confusion was due to the sinking of a river ferry by an overloaded ammunition truck which meant the bulk of the transport and their loads had to be destroyed as the only available track was unsuitable for motorized vehicles. The wounded were sent to Moulmein by boat while the remainder of the brigade marched down river for two days until picked up by steamer and taken to Martaban.

Altogether it was a grim picture, lightened only by the occasional act of outstanding courage. Captain Eric Holdaway of the 1/7th Gurkhas, who had led his men in a gallant charge against a vastly superior force and had been given up for dead, arrived at Martaban with a handful of survivors after cutting their way through a circle of Japanese, marching across country with the aid of a compass and then floating down the Salween by barge. He was awarded the Military Cross. One Gurkha who had been badly shot in the stomach and almost beheaded by a Samurai sword demonstrated the legendary indestructability of the Gurkha by walking sixty miles to rejoin the battalion.

It was a disastrous start that did not augur well for the future. The brigade arrived at Martaban without mules, lorries and many of its weapons. It would need reorganizing before it was ready for action again.

Brigadier Jones was criticized for withdrawing too soon, for the road to Moulmein was now open and the Japanese 55th Division was poised to take it. Both Generals Hutton and Wavell held the view that the attack was not nearly so heavy as was reported, and were in no doubt that more seasoned troops would have held the position.

Smyth prepared to meet the enemy and as he surveyed the battleground he reflected ruefully that it was "a swine of a position to hold", and he told Hutton quite bluntly that he needed to be reinforced by at least two additional divisions. As a first step the 48th Gurkha Brigade training in Secunderabad for desert warfare should be sent without delay. Wavell was now pressing for two Chinese divisions to be sent in support, which re-opened old wounds between him and the Americans who had been angered at his earlier refusal to accept the offer of Chinese troops. Wavell's view at the time had been that it was preferable that a country in the Empire should be defended by Imperial troops rather than by foreign soldiers, as the Chinese might feel they were entitled to a say in Burma's future when the war was over. But President Roosevelt, who held the Chinese in high esteem, took the view that America was not in the war to support what he regarded as a backward colonial policy. Lend-Lease was sustaining the Chinese and he could not understand Wavell's reluctance to use them. Around this time Churchill realized that Singapore was gravely imperilled and his thoughts turned to holding Burma to ensure that the vital Burma Road remained open. An "ugly decision" might have to be taken to abandon Singapore and concentrate on Burma; he told the Chiefs of Staff, "As a strategic object, I regard keeping the Burma Road open as more important than the retention of Singapore," and he asked them to consider the problem and let him have their opinion as soon as possible;

he warned them that by hesitating to take a decision both Singapore and Burma could be lost.

Supported by Mr Roosevelt, he asked the Prime Minister of Australia, Mr John Curtin, to divert a Division of troops to Rangoon.

Whether by mistake or deliberately, a copy of the minute suggesting the possible abandonment of Singapore fell into the hand of the Australian representative in London who promptly fed the contents back to Mr Curtin. The effect on the Australian Cabinet was devastating and Mr Curtin cabled a furious protest to Churchill:

"After all the utterances we have been given the evacuation of Singapore would be regarded here as an inexcusable betrayal. Singapore is a central fortress in the system of the Empire and local defence. We understand it was to be made impregnable, and in any event it was to be capable of holding out for a prolonged period until the arrival of the main fleet."

Mr Curtin went on to say that if there was to be any diversion of reinforcements they should go to the Netherlands East Indies and not Burma; if this was not done the Dutch might make a separate peace. Understandably Mr Curtin was extremely worried about the growing threat to his own country and he had no intention of becoming involved in another Gallipoli.

Australia had provided unstinted help in men and materials since the start of the war, but Churchill's proposals brought British-Australian relations to near-breaking-point. The requested division did not sail for Rangoon.

General Smyth's earlier buoyancy was now being replaced by a growing sense of frustration. He did not see any point in holding Moulmein, a city which he considered of no military value, but General Hutton was insisting that it should be held and this Wavell fully endorsed.

Wavell was sending a constant stream of signals from Java, often via Delhi, so that when they arrived in Rangoon the situation had changed completely, while General Hutton was also issuing instructions to the commander on the spot which showed a regrettable ignorance of the true position.

As the situation in Burma began to deteriorate even further Wavell cabled General Hutton and emphasized that in his opinion he saw no reason why, with the troops available, Moulmein should not be held. The nature of the country and the resources available would surely limit the Japanese effort. The same signal contained the depressing news that he had no resources with which to assist.

The Commander-in-Chief announced that he intended to visit Rangoon, but the message did not reach Hutton who was at the front with General Smyth. When the two men did eventually meet at Government House Wavell expressed his displeasure at the failure to halt the enemy at Kawkareik and insisted it be done at Moulmein. Smyth's limited forces would, however, have to achieve it with a minimum of air cover for the enemy had gained possession of three vital airfields on the Tenasserim coast – Victoria Point, Mergui and Tavoy – from which they could provide fighter cover for their own bombers.

General Hutton was particularly dismayed at the fall of Tavoy for a battalion of the Burma Frontier Force had put up a very spirited resistance until they saw the R.A.F. ground crew handing in their rifles, which had been on loan to them from the armoury at Tenasserim, before leaving by lorry. Mergui had been evacuated when it became isolated, an action which prompted the Deputy Chief Commissioner, Mr F. H. Yardley, to say, with justifiable bitterness, "We will never be able to hold up our heads again in Mergui."

The hasty withdrawal resulted in the enemy capturing a considerable amount of stores and equipment, but, more important, 300,000 gallons of high octane fuel which the Japanese used for their own aircraft. The stores and petrol had been prepared for demolition, but it seemed that no one was prepared to give the order for the destruction of the fuel for fear that the noise of the explosion would have an even more demoralizing effect on the already jittery Burmese troops.

Throughout the campaign commanders were repeatedly to blame the lack of intelligence for many of the setbacks, but the attack through Tavoy should not have come as any surprise; some police agents who had been captured in Thailand and later released said they had heard some Japanese officers boasting at the beginning of January that an advance was planned through Tavoy. It was either ignored or the information was pigeon-holed.

CHAPTER 4

"We have had a great deal of bad news lately from the Far East,
and I think it is highly probable we shall have a great deal more.
Wrapped up in this bad news will be many tales of blunders
and shortcomings, both in foresight and action."

Winston Churchill, 27 January, 1941.

After the two big raids on Rangoon and the mass exodus of people, the
Japanese bombers began to concentrate more on military targets,
particularly the airfields. The Japanese saw no point in inflicting further
damage on port installations; they would need them when the time
came for them to land their own troops and equipment. And so, as the
danger from the skies diminished, people began to trickle back and
Rangoon returned to some degree of normality. A skeleton staff, mainly
of Anglo-Indians and Indians, continued to man the telegraph office,
although communications with the rest of the country remained very
much on a hit-and-miss basis. Regrettably in a short time the old
lethargy also began to creep back and the war effort once again became
strangled by red tape.

Major Tony Mains of the 9th Gurkha Rifles, who had specialized in
Intelligence work, experienced it at first hand late in January when he
was rushed to Rangoon to take up an appointment as GSO II in the
headquarters of the Burma Army. He had been appointed by GHQ
in India but the position still had to be formally created by the
Government of Burma, and it was then that he stumbled against the
unyielding bureaucracy that was gnawing away at the vitals of the city.
Although he was paid by India, and the Burmese Government should
presumably have been grateful to obtain his valuable services free, he
found himself enmeshed in an agonizingly drawn-out procedure which
involved the exchange of long, windy letters which were larded with
formal phrases which characterized the official jargon, before he
received one, "I have the honour to convey the sanction of the Governor
of Burma . . .", which meant his appointment had been confirmed.

As his work primarily concerned Field Security he immediately set about enlisting men, there being none for him to take over. He called for volunteers and explained to them that they would be paid by India, although they would be under the jurisdiction of the Rangoon authorities. Incredibly the Defence Department refused to sanction it without first receiving full details and approval from India. As the postal system to India was almost non-existent it resulted in a long delay at a time when speed was essential.

Soon afterwards Mains set up base at the main police headquarters known locally as the Mogul Guard. Not once did the Governor visit him, and, despite the urgency of the situation, he found it difficult to obtain the co-operation of many officials who had "delusions of grandeur". "So many were prisoners of the system, and the memsahibs were the worst." In exasperation he decided to do things his own way. Looking back, he reflected, "I could have been cashiered for what I did in Rangoon."

But not everyone was indifferent to what was going on. There were still those who deplored the inability of the Government to set the city on an efficient war footing and one of them was Mr E. W. R. Stone, the outspoken editor of the *Rangoon Gazette*. To the fury of the Governor and officials, a headline was blazoned across the front page which summed up exactly what so many who had not joined the exodus felt: "Our finest fighting efficiency will be when the bureaucrats have gone."

And even more contemptuously: "Faith in our fighting men: but save us from the non-belligerent dopes. . . . There is little doubt that there are ships in Rangoon, and coming to Rangoon, loaded with goods, both for civil and military use. The difficulty apparently is to get them unloaded, and as the Government fights shy of the excellent suggestion for labour battalions (although we cannot think why) we support the suggestion. Let us cut yards and yards of red tape, wound round the customs and port officials, and get down to essentials. The goods are here, and they have got to be unloaded, so let us get down to it and hang the cost. After all there is a war on."

Leland Stowe and O. D. Gallagher, who had teamed up, had so far refrained from writing about the chaos in the port for fear that it might boost Japanese morale, but when they read the *Gazette* they no longer had any qualms about sending the truth to Britain and America. They were aware that the Burmese Government had agreed as early as

27 December that defeatist reports would be censored, but as the truth had now appeared in print they felt free to sit down and type their own despatches. They considered it was their duty to expose the complacency in the hope that it would lead to rigorous action being taken in London and Washington.

The response was far chillier than they had anticipated. The Chief Civil Censor, Colonel Raymond, a retired soldier, simply refused to look at them. To Gallagher's consternation he found himself subjected to a vicious personal attack.

"Oh, you're Gallagher, are you? God, how I hate the name. What part of Ireland do you come from?"

Gallagher curbed his temper and politely explained that he was South African and had never set foot in Ireland.

"Oh," said the deflated colonel, "I thought you were one of those irresponsible Irishmen."

Leland Stowe tactfully steered him back to the purpose of their visit, but the censor was adamant. "Take them up to Government House and tell the Governor's private secretary I would not look at them."

The two fuming war correspondents picked up their stories and trudged off to Government House where Mr Bernard Ottwell Binns was even more unyielding "Are they about this stuff Stone wrote about this morning? Because if they are I simply refuse to show them to His Excellency. He's absolutely furious with Stone. If he doesn't stop it we will pre-censor his paper."

The two reporters had no alternative but to pick up their despatches and leave; without approval of the censor there was no way of getting their stories through.

Stowe, a Pulitzer Prize winner, had never written anything that would adversely effect the war effort, but there was a vast difference between that and covering up for an inefficient administration. When he tried to make this point, Colonel Raymond said blandly, "I always ask myself if my dear, devoted daughter in England would be alarmed by this."

It was not an isolated incident; often correspondents' stories lay on desks unread for days on end. Instead they were given official handouts which often bore little resemblance to the true situation.

In the eyes of veteran reporters the system of censorship was an appalling abuse of official power. Mr Binns was particularly hostile and said he objected strongly to any reports being sent to England, especially to the B.B.C., which made any mention of the disloyalty of the Burmese. Pretending it did not exist seemed to convince Government House that it did not. The stupidity of it was, said the reporters, that nearly everyone in Rangoon had witnessed blatant examples of fifth-column activities. Night after night traitors succeeded in establishing chains of bonfires on the high ground which acted as guiding beacons for the Japanese bombers seeking troop positions.

"Nothing was passed that they thought might cause offence to the Burmese, or encourage the Japanese to believe that their agents were having any success."

Sir Reginald simply could not understand the attitude of the newspapermen and he confided to the Viceroy that he found them "somewhat of a nuisance".

Sometimes Army Headquarters had "nothing to report" and this lack of news was reflected in the newspapers in Britain which day after day made scarcely any reference to events in Rangoon.

It was hardly unexpected therefore that an atmosphere of cynicism began to pervade the city. The local radio station spent much of its time playing records and there were bulletins invariably prefaced with, "Here is the news – do not listen to the rumours," but as the days passed a disillusioned public began muttering, "Here are the rumours – we haven't got any news."

The Government did its utmost to portray the war correspondents as peevish defeatists who went into childish tantrums whenever a "good story" was ruined, and to convince the population that everything was under control. But nothing could prevent the real truth from filtering through the clubs and bars that all was not well in the Far East, especially in Malaya. By the end of January it was common knowledge that the British had withdrawn across the Johore causeway and Singapore was under siege. On the same day the Japanese captured Moulmein and were about to cross the Salween, only 100 miles east of Rangoon.

Stowe found, as he moved around the city, that the main topic of conversation was evacuation; every conversation seemed to be prefaced with "When are you getting out?" or "When do we leave?" The newsmen, however, were not able to report what was being said in the clubs and hotel bars.

One English girl who had stayed out of a sense of duty volunteered her services as a typist or driver at General Headquarters. "I was given an Oldsmobile, but I only drove it once a day, or not at all. I just sat in the office all day, perhaps typing one letter. It was the same for the other girls. I had my own car which I offered but they did not want it. The half-dozen or more jeeps at H.Q. were used for nothing but officers to drive home for lunch and back."

The hapless Gloucesters, confined to security duties in Rangoon when they would have preferred to be in the front lines, were forced to requisition ponies, buses and cycles for added mobility, and to improve communications and patrolling Lieutenant-Colonel Bagot even enlisted the services of a privately owned aeroplane to carry out twice-daily patrols in order to keep abreast of the situation outside the city. Meanwhile his battalion continued to be 'milked' for work in the hospitals and other menial tasks which could easily have been undertaken by requisitioned labour. But whenever men became available Bagot turned a blind eye to regulations and employed them irrespective of their background. When seven White Russians who had been trained in the Shanghai Volunteer Force arrived on the scene after escaping through China, he had no hesitation in recruiting them. One of them was to become an honoured and proud name in the regimental archives before the campaign was over. Bagot also issued paybooks and numbers to camp followers, sweepers, storemen and gardeners who had not deserted after the first raids.

He saw to it that his men fulfilled all the duties, many of them unpleasant and unsoldierly, with efficiency and determination. Among their many onerous duties was to help maintain discipline at the overcrowded railway station where there was always a long queue of people waiting to get on one of the few trains heading north, and at the ferry points where similar crowds gathered to try and get aboard one of the Irrawaddy Flotilla steamers evacuating people up-river.

With great effort, Bagot kept his innermost thoughts to himself, which was just as well for they would only have added to the growing sense of disillusionment which was spreading throughout the city. In the rare quiet moments allowed to him he reflected on the civilian officials, "few and far between", who still tried to instil some organization into the running of the city. "But mainly the backbone of Rangoon was either inept, frankly frightened, or hysterical. It did not take more than a couple of air raids and the promise of more to cause the

Burmese Ministry to contemplate a premature move to their hot-weather estates in Maymyo." It pained him a great deal to have to order his men to hold back homeless families with nothing but a pitiful bundle of belongings from boarding trains in order that officials should have priority and be able to proceed to Maymyo "without undue inconvenience".

"Some of us felt we would have preferred to see the Burmese Ministers remain in their doomed city to look after their people, and leave the only means of transport to Indian refugees among whom were so many old men and women, stranded a long way from their own country and having little chance of reaching it."

As the days passed and the situation worsened on the military front an appalling inertia gripped the city. When Eve Curie, the daughter of the discoverer of radium, arrived to report the war she detected the "ghastly odour of defeat, of retreat, of fear, that I knew only too well". As a Frenchwoman she had seen it in her homeland. "Rangoon was already a dead city, as good as lost."

She tried to hail a taxi but there weren't any, and the public transport system seemed non-existent. She was, however, surprised at how little bomb damage had been inflicted on the residential and commercial areas of the city; most of the bombing had been concentrated on the native quarters. The shells of burnt-out cars littered the street. At night on the surrounding hilltops she saw the lines of fires which were mysteriously lit to guide the approaching bombers.

Her escort was an Indian captain and she was astonished to find that in a city that was in its death throes it was still considered quite out of the question for her to take him to dinner in one of the few restaurants still open, as they would not serve Indians.

In the Rangoon General Hospital Violet Kelly and her senior colleagues, with a handful of loyal nurses, continued to administer to the sick and wounded with little idea of what was going on outside. "The Inspector General Civil Hospitals was up-country looking for a suitable site for a hospital in the dry zone, as the idea seemed to be that the hospital would move north for the duration of the monsoon and then return to Rangoon when the rains were over. No mention was made of possible evacuation, and the assumption was that by the time we returned the Japanese would have been driven out of Burma."

In the absence of real news rumour began to take over and more and more nurses left, as an air of panic developed and the lack of faith in the authorities increased. "On top of that there was disturbing news and rumours of frightening happenings at Tavoy and Moulmein as well as the repeated stories of wholesale rape by the Japanese."

Many of the remaining white women took the rape warnings seriously and began to carry suicide pills. Joan Morton recalled being offered one, "which I could take if I fell into Jap hands, on the basis that it was preferable to 'a fate worse than death'. I refused it, as I could not seriously imagine the possibility of such a fate, and was sure I would not be brave enough to take it."

One of the more persistent rumours was that the Governor had left the city for the safety of Maymyo, and as Sir Reginald was seldom seen in public it gained credence. An incensed Lady Dorman-Smith confided in her diary, "On the strength of that he dashed off to the studio and spoke after the news and told the idiotic people that he is in charge here and intends to stay. It is really quite inconceivable the stuff they believe."

Those banks which had reopened refused to deal in foreign currency, not even dollars. Soon afterwards the Governor informed the Viceroy, "Owing to almost complete desertion of the staffs, banks here regret that they are quite unable to continue business in Rangoon." Even Government House, he added, was now on a cash basis with the local shops.

General Hutton, meanwhile, was finding it harder and harder to exercise the administrative skills for which he was renowned. Although outwardly giving the impression that all was going well, he felt shackled and impotent in the face of the unyielding attitude adopted by the authorities. The bitter lesson, he told Wavell later, was that the civil and military administrations should have been placed on a war footing before hostilities started. His headquarters was hampered from the start by the fact that the civil departments just would not recognize how quickly events moved in war, and the result was interminable committee meetings which took up valuable time and achieved little. The same reluctance existed in the railway service which could not be persuaded, until it was too late, that there had to be unified control. He had little comfort, however, for those who argued that the Burmese should have a bigger say in the running of the country, for he found that with the appointment of Burmese Ministers there had been a gradual deterioration in the public services. "Nepotism, bribery and inefficiency," he told Wavell, "were widespread and it is fair to say that many of the senior British Officials had in consequence lost heart and in some cases even interest."

With the city in such a disorganized state it was essential to have a good police force, Hutton wrote, but they were poorly paid and for the most part corrupt, which left Rangoon at the mercy of looters and arsonists.

"Long before the threat of enemy occupation it became normal for the police to depart on the first alarming rumour and to take an active part in looting which their officers appeared unable to suppress."

Some of the British officials, he conceded, were good, but, "There were, however, others whom long service in the East, the gradual deterioration of the public services under self-government, and the slow pace of administration in peace, had rendered incapable of the vigorous action and quick decisions necessitated by war conditions. Unfortunately, considerations of pay and pensions were thought to prohibit their replacement by younger men, even in the face of invasion, and the administration suffered accordingly."

The imposition of martial law could have remedied many of the shortcomings, but the Governor was adamantly opposed to such a step and so things got worse.

A week after Sir Reginald spoke on the radio his wife was helping their married daughter to pack her belongings, which included her silver and wedding presents. When the news leaked out it did nothing to raise morale.

CHAPTER 5

"The Burma Road was the greatest racket in the Far East"
Leland Stowe

The Burma Road which ran for nearly 1500 miles from Lashio to Chungking was China's lifeline in its long battle against Japan. Along it travelled the Lend-Lease materials provided by Washington which viewed its existence as an insurance policy; it was buying time for an unprepared America. There was also a twinge of conscience behind the gifts; America knew it had not helped the Chinese cause by sending iron, petrol and other strategic materials to Japan. The Americans were also aware that in the defence of their own democracy they were propping up a despotic regime overlorded by Chiang Kai-shek. But Chiang Kai-shek was vital to America's interests and any qualms there might have been were assuaged when the Generalissimo assured Roosevelt that he would never arrange a secret peace treaty with Japan.

The Road was an incredible feat of civil engineering that ranked alongside the Great Wall of China, for it had been built by thousands of coolies without the aid of any mechanical equipment. Mile by mile they had hewn through solid rock in the hills and mountains with primitive picks, shovels and rock-crushing hammers, carrying away the earth in baskets, to prop up the red soil and prevent landslides.

It has been completed at the cost of countless lives in September, 1938, and in the spring of 1941 the United States Congress had made its first Lend-Lease allocation of nearly $5,000,000,000 in aid to China.

When Leland Stowe arrived in Burma he had already heard disquieting stories about the abuse of Lend-Lease and the rackets which were being operated by the Chinese, many in high places, who had no concern for the welfare of their own country or the successful prosecution of the war. "It was a story which, to my surprise, had never been reported in anything faintly resembling its factual nakedness throughout more than three long years of chequered operation."

Stowe decided to investigate and what he saw shocked him. Before he started off he was advised to take a gun, for law and order ceased to exist beyond Lashio. Choking clouds of thick red dust were thrown up by the lorries as they careered madly along the road which seemed to consist of nothing but hairpin bends and precipitous drops. The only rule of the road was "To hell with everyone but yourself". The beds of the rivers hundreds of feet below were littered with wrecked and overturned vehicles, their wheels still spinning. Trucks were needlessly wrecked by running them without oil in the sumps or air in the tyres, and when they seized up or spun off the road they were simply abandoned. People who fell off were run over and left in the dust to die.

Six hours' drive from Lashio was the border and the start of the Yunnan, and the worst part of the journey. Governor Lung Yung, the virtual warlord of the Yunnan, amassed a fortune by imposing a tax on all trucks passing through. Sixty miles further on lay the town of Mangshi, but few of the Indian or Burmese drivers would go that far; too many had been robbed and beaten by the Chinese bandits who terrorized the area. The vehicles that roared along were the most modern that America's factories could turn out and nearly every vehicle was loaded with cardboard cartons of English cigarettes which sold for a handsome profit in Kunming and beyond; smuggling was considered a legitimate perk of the drivers.

Accidents were frequent and often fatal but no one ever bothered to stop and attend to the victims. Stowe, who was a passenger in a station wagon destined for the Chinese Air Force, recalled one incident, "As we burst suddenly over a slight rise in the highway a sickening sight struck my eyes. Exactly in the middle of the road lay the body of a man. The side of his head was bashed wide open. His face and shoulders were covered in blood. He was trying to crawl – to lift the upper part of his body on his hands. I saw all this as the car swerved and we sped past. I grabbed the knee of the driver and shouted, 'Stop! He's dying. We've got to help him. Stop!' Though he couldn't understand a word of English, of course he knew exactly what I meant. But the driver pressed down on the accelerator. I looked back. I thought I had seen pieces of brain bulging from the wound in the man's head. The driver did not stop because he knew that if he did he would be accused of knocking him down."

Not all the fatalities were due to traffic accidents. Drivers were frequently hauled from the cabins by Chinese soldiers and beaten to death for refusing to give someone a lift. Anyone who tried to intervene was likely to be shot.

Yet the brutality paled into insignificance when weighed against the effects the corruption and profiteering were having on the war effort. Stowe decided to expose it. "Unless the abuses were eradicated the Chinese armies would never stage a large-scale offensive against the Japanese." His investigation lasted on and off for three months and he was staggered by the scale of the black marketeering. He also discovered that much of the equipment ordered by the Chinese had little to do with the war effort; the Chinese were simply getting America to underwrite the industrialization of their country.

He drew up a list of some of their major requirements:

The construction of a rolling mill costing $1,000,000 which would not be producing for at least two years.

A huge iron and steel works costing $4,500,000; a steam power plant to supplement the steel works costing $1,500,000; a blast furnace costing $737,000; equipment for a coal mine estimated at $500,000; machinery for an iron ore mine worth $500,000; more than twelve hydro-electric plants, most of which would take eighteen months to three years to build and equip after they had been transported along the Burma Road. That was just a part of the massive shopping list.

Lend-Lease had become a bandwagon on which many Chinese capitalists were determined to jump aboard and the racketeering was so taken for granted that the owners of private industries made no attempt to hide their dishonesty. "Can you tell me how I can get the materials I need through Lend-Lease?" was a frequently heard request.

The Chinese were, of course, ordering and receiving a great deal of legitimate war materials, but much of it, such as 600 armoured cars and a large consignment of light tanks, were useless in the terrain in which they were fighting. In addition to which they did not have the trained men necessary to man them.

In Rangoon Stowe saw large stocks of raw materials which had been lying rusting and rotting in the docks for more than a year because it was more profitable to use the Burma Road for smuggled goods which could be sold on the black market.

In Kunming he saw a new Buick car intended for the army sold to a wealthy Chinese for $6,000. Stolen petrol sold for $1.50 a gallon. When he asked why seventy or eighty percent of the tonnage along the Road was petrol he received the remarkably bland reply, "Well, petrol is a splendid commercial commodity."

In Chunking a bottle of gin brought £2.10, whisky £10, an aspirin tablet £1.10s, a typewriter £200, and a camera £1000, while a suitcase of drugs would change hands for a small fortune.

The drivers who swaggered around with pistols on their hips had pockets bulging with money made from contraband. It was all so blatant they stood beside their vehicles at the roadside bellowing at the top of their voices what they had for sale.

"Along the road there were scores of government-owned Dodge trucks standing idle, rusting in the rain, because no spare parts were available for them. But in privately-owned accessory shops in Kunming anyone could purchase parts for Dodge trucks or cars. They had simply been lifted off the stranded vehicles down the road. The trucks should have been carrying war materials into China."

Even the attack on Pearl Harbor did nothing to curb the racketeering, or instil a sense of urgency into the Chinese.

"In Rangoon the docks and warehouses were bulging with some 85,000 tons of American Lend-Lease supplies – a simply tremendous haul for the Japs if they broke through from nearby Thailand soon," said Stowe.

Waiting to be uncrated and assembled were 2,000 trucks and cars and more were arriving every day. It would take six to eight months to transport the 85,000 tons to China, but it was extremely unlikely, he thought, that the Japanese would wait so long before invading Burma.

Ironically the British troops who would have to meet the attack were desperately short of many of the things lying neglected in the port. In response to their request for 300 lorries, the British were offered near-wrecks at three times their market value. The blankets they were offered were rotting and the gas masks useless.

When a ship docked with 300 Lend-Lease Bren guns the British asked for some. "The Chinese refused and cleared them out of Rangoon the next day," said Stowe.

It was not only the British who were treated so churlishly; the Chinese had no qualms about biting the hand that fed them. Stowe discovered that a consignment of spare radio sets for the P40 Tomahawks flown by the two A.V.G. squadrons in Kunming had been shipped along the Burma Road in crates marked China Defence Supplies which guaranteed they would not be opened for inspection at Lashio. But a British officer thought they smelled rather strange for radio sets and ordered the crates to be opened. They contained perfume and women's toilet articles. There was no sign of the radios which had been sold at a handsome profit.

"The road had made a good many Chinese millionaires in its tawdry history, and was still making Chinese millionaires as the Japs prepared to strike at Rangoon – and its 85,000 tons of Lend-Lease supplies – from Thailand," said Stowe.

Stowe wrestled with his conscience, undecided as to how much of the truth should be told. "If the scope of the Burma Road racket was reported, I knew it would come as a tremendous shock to an American public which had come to look upon all Chinese as Sir Galahads."

After much heart-searching he decided that only the whole truth would suffice; he owed it to the Chinese soldiers who were dying, to the British who were about to, and to his own integrity as a newspaperman.

Stowe retired to his room in Rangoon and hammered away at his typewriter until he had completed seven feature articles on the Burma Road for the *Chicago Daily News* and the fifty other newspapers to which his reports were syndicated.

The British civil censor read the first three instalments with obvious dismay and reluctantly passed them, although making it abundantly clear that he accepted no responsibility for their contents.

Soon after the first three articles had been filed, Rangoon received its first two bombings which delayed transmission of the remainder of the series.

Because of the confusion in the telegraph service the series was not published in chronological order, but it did not affect their impact and Stowe received a cable from his office; "Burma roadsters causing sensation," and he was asked about the remaining articles. Stowe, who suspected that they had been deliberately held up in India, filed the whole lot again.

Soon afterwards he received another cable from Chicago:

"On urgent suggestion higher-ups publication remainder of China series suspended pending upclearing present crucial situation stop. Heavily uplayed fourth fifth and third which provoked bitter criticism threats reprisals stop personally appreciate your courageous coverage."

Unknown to him the Chinese Embassy in America had taken violent exception to the stories and pressure had been brought to bear on the newspaper by the American authorities. In addition a signal marked Secret was sent from London to the office of the Chief Censor in Rangoon, which said the criticisms were "justified but undesirable".

"Could you approach him [Stowe] and inform him that his articles are creating friction with the Chinese which is clearly undesirable at present juncture, and suggest he might stop sending reports of such nature."

Rangoon was still reeling from the effects of the bombing when Stowe received an urgent message asking him to call upon the Governor.

"He received me in a most gracious manner and made me at ease with a Scotch and soda, whisked expertly to my side by a perfect Indian servant. Eventually without undue haste, His Excellency revealed what was on his mind.

"'It appears, Stowe, that your articles about the Burma Road have provoked a rather violent controversy,' Sir Reginald began.

"'Yes, Your Excellency, I'm afraid they have.'

"Sir Reginald cleared his throat and took another sip of Scotch. 'I've just received a message about them from my Secretary of State in London. It says something like this, in effect: Stowe's reports are undoubtedly justified, but can't you persuade him to discontinue a pursuance of the subject? It would make co-operation with the Chinese much easier . . . I imagine you understand how things are?'"

Stowe replied that he understood perfectly well; in any case the message he had received from his own office made it clear that he would be wasting his time pursuing the matter.

"Well, I've been up against the same sort of thing," confessed Sir Reginald. "I know you are right about this, but . . ."

Stowe said, "I'm glad to have the opportunity of knowing what you think about it."

Nearly eighteen months were to pass before Stowe learned that his disclosures had reaped a just reward. A senior officer on General Magruder's staff told him, "Your stories were the one thing that got immediate action out of the Chinese. Do you know that more Lend-Lease tonnage was transported over the road during the next two months than at any time in its history?"

CHAPTER 6

"It can be said that the campaign was lost on the Salween for nowhere else in Burma did so good a defensive line exist"
History of the King's Own Yorkshire Light Infantry

As a young subaltern in the First War, Jackie Smyth had seen countless men perish in France for the retention or possession of a few hundred yards of shell-cratered mud of no strategic value whatsoever. He saw Moulmein in much the same context.

There were local people who could recall it when it had been no more than a fishing village which did not even merit a mention in an atlas. Now it was a busy port and, although its loss would be a commercial blow, it had little military worth. General Hutton, however, did not share his view. Smyth was also concerned with the difficulties of defending the position; in his eyes Moulmein was a far from suitable place in which to make a stand, especially when the forces at his disposal were so limited and disorganized.

Situated on the mouth of the Salween, it had a river frontage, facing westwards, of some six thousand yards and another frontage facing north about two thousand yards long. Running north and south like a spine was a steep ridge, while to the east flowed the Ataran River. Apart from paddy fields and patches of jungle to the south it was almost encircled by water, which meant that any withdrawal would have to be by boat.

Having toured the area, General Smyth was more in favour of establishing a secure base in the Bilin-Kyaikto-Sittang area from which to deliver a counterattack, while Moulmein would be held by a skirmishing force of not more than one battalion. But Hutton was adamant that Moulmein should be held for as long as possible by a much stronger force and he promised to send the 2nd KOYLI as reinforcements as soon as possible. Although preparation should be made for withdrawal, the prime consideration was to regain contact with the enemy which had been lost as a result of the withdrawal from

Kawkareik. This was a view General Wavell fully endorsed. Smyth was far from happy at the way in which his own proposals were constantly overruled, contrary to what he had been told before setting off for Burma. The General Staff had said that Hutton would deal with the administration side while he would do the fighting. Now he was being denied the right to choose his own positions. Hutton, of course, had never heard of any such directive and, when he heard later of Smyth's claim, could not believe they had ever said anything at all like it: "It is almost incredible and is of no credit to Smyth."

When Moulmein was attacked by a force of enemy bombers escorted by fighters, Smyth ordered the evacuation of all European and Indian women and children and two days later moved his own headquarters to Kyaikto on the Sittang estuary and prepared for the attack on Moulmein. He knew he could not count on any air cover as the enemy now occupied the airfields at Tavoy, Victoria Point and Mergui. Although he had no reliable information about the enemy strength he estimated that it was not less than one division. To meet it he had to cover an enormous perimeter with a widely dispersed 17th Division.

Moulmein, which was being defended by the 2nd Burma Brigade under Brigadier A. J. H. Bourke, consisted mainly of untried Burma Rifle battalions, the 4/12th Frontier Force Regiment, the 12th Indian Mountain Battery and one troop of the 3rd Indian Anti-Aircraft Battery. The 16th Brigade was withdrawing towards Martaban after the mauling at Kawkareik, while the partly-trained 46th Brigade, commanded by Brigadier Roger Ekin, which had recently arrived from India and was still without its transport, was in the Bilin area.

Smyth was doubtful of the fighting qualities of the Burma Rifles and would have preferred to use them as guerrillas instead of having them alongside troops they might unsettle. Again Hutton disagreed; he thought it would affect their morale even more if they knew they were not rated very highly. The 8th Burma Rifles were excluded from Smyth's misgivings as they were locally enlisted Sikhs and Punjabi Mussulmans who could be relied upon in a tight corner, as could the Gurkhas at his disposal.

As Brigadier Bourke had his hands full with administrative units and the civil population, Brigadier Ekin was placed in charge of the fighting units, a decision which Bourke readily accepted.

Apart from knowing he was chronically short of men, Smyth was now suffering a recurrence of the fistular trouble and was in constant pain as he prepared for the inevitable attack.

It came early on 30 January when the Japanese attacked the perimeter from the south and east. On receiving a report that one thousand troops had entered Kado across the river to the north of Moulmein and were busy building rafts, Smyth requested the R.A.F. to carry out a bombing attack but he was told there were no aircraft available; all the Blenheims were attacking Bangkok.

When Ekin arrived in Moulmein he learned that, although the 8th Burma Rifles had repulsed several attacks, the enemy had managed to cross the Ataran, occupy two villages and overrun the forward posts of the 3rd Burma Rifles. They had withdrawn to Myenigon but had disintegrated in the face of further attacks.

The 4/12th Frontier Force was now clearly engaging a powerful enemy force along the entire length of the ridge and the supporting 12th Mountain Battery was firing over open sights at the Japanese swarming into the port. Although they successfully fought off several attacks the enemy seemed to have inexhaustible replacements.

As darkness fell Ekin was faced with a fresh danger; the enemy were crossing the river by boat while the 8th Burma Rifles were rapidly becoming exhausted. He promptly shortened his perimeter and withdrew the 18th towards the southern end of the ridge and the river to form a tighter box.

Smyth, who had been following events with mounting concern, reported to Hutton that the situation was so serious that the garrison should either be reinforced by two battalions or withdrawn. As there was insufficient time to provide reinforcements he was in favour of withdrawing. It was an opinion Ekin endorsed, for the simple choice now facing him was whether to sacrifice more lives to no useful purpose or save as many as he could.

Hutton reluctantly agreed, but insisted that the line of the Salween including Martaban must be held.

Later that night the situation in Moulmein deteriorated even further when the Japanese made a landing at the northern end of the perimeter and brisk fighting broke out in the position held by the 7th Burma Rifles. Ekin was now doubtful whether the town could be held during daylight and he ordered a fleet of fifteen river boats to sail over from Martaban. As the civilian crews were reluctant to sail them under the fire from guns sited on the ridge, the boats were manned by Sappers.

The enemy attacked from all fronts, but too late to prevent the forward troops disengaging and Ekin gave the order for evacuation to start at 0730 on the morning of 31 January. By 2 am the 7th Burma Rifles had been driven back still further and had lost some Bofors. Badly shaken by the bombing and surprise attacks at night, they anticipated the evacuation and headed as fast as they could for the boats, where they had to be held back to allow some 500 wounded to embark first.

Their action was in stark contrast to the resolute resistance put up by the 4/12th Frontier Force Regiment and the 8th Burma Rifles who disputed every yard as they withdrew to the river. The commander of the 12th Mountain Battery, on being told that one section of guns was missing, called for volunteers to reclaim them, and the gunners in the unaccustomed role of infantry fought through the enemy lines and brought them back.

By 10 am most of the troops had embarked, with the exception of the 4/12th FFR which was holding the bridgehead protecting the two southernmost jetties. The Japanese reached the Mission Street jetty, the southernmost of the five on the waterfront, as the rearguard and Brigade headquarters left on the last boat. They made it just in time, for as the boat was pulling away a party of Japanese, led by an officer brandishing a sword, tried to board it, but the gap between the ferry and the jetty was too wide and they ended up in the water.

The small fleet of boats was mortared and shelled all the way to Martaban which was also being attacked by bombers. Fortunately only one boat was sunk. It was a colossal blunder by the bombers. If, instead of attacking Martaban, they had concentrated on the jetties at Moulmein the evacuation would have been disastrous.

Although the withdrawal had been brilliantly executed it had nevertheless been an overwhelming defeat in which 600 men had been lost, along with a considerable amount of equipment which included a valuable stock of petrol.

General Hutton was far from pleased as he did not consider a withdrawal on that scale was justified, although he conceded that with one exception the troops had fought well. The Japanese too spoke highly of the resistance of the enemy, especially in the hand-to-hand fighting.

Jackie Smyth watched the weary soldiers arrive at Martaban and considered it was no more defensible than Moulmein, but his orders were explicit; there was to be no further withdrawal without permission from Army Headquarters.

The loss of Moulmein was serious but not disastrous, for ahead of the advancing Japanese lay the wide Salween River, a natural obstacle even for an enemy who had introduced a completely new form of warfare. And in Rangoon everyone was assured that that was where the enemy would be halted, for the river, the broadest in Burma, was two miles wide in places, deep and fast-flowing, and lacking in ferrying stages.

At one of his briefings General Hutton, who had earlier been so angry about the loss of Moulmein, now seemed to have adopted the attitude that it was not such a bad thing after all and he told listening reporters that it had not been the kind of place in which to lock up a large number of troops. The Salween provided a much better line. "We are in a far stronger position to cry halt to the Japanese than we were a few weeks ago."

Jackie Smyth, who had been ordered to hold the line on the Salween, was not so optimistic, for he was confronted with an enormous task. The crucial sector on the west bank stretched from Martaban, almost directly opposite Moulmein, northwards for some sixty miles. In addition he was expected to hold Papun which was a further 100 miles to the north. The lines of communication which were also his responsibility ran back by rail and road through Thaton via the important town of Bilin to Kyaikto and on to the Sittang River. In order to cover such a vast area his troops were so stretched that some battalions were as much as forty miles apart.

Smyth inspected the whole line from Martaban to Sittang and noted with some dismay that the road ended at Kyaikto and from there to the Sittang Bridge, now being boarded by Sappers in order to take motorized transport, was little more than a rough track that was either ankle deep in dust or a porridgy morass of thick mud. This was where he must stand and fight.

On 6 February General Wavell flew in from his Java headquarters and went with General Hutton on an inspection tour of Smyth's divisional area. It was not the most cordial of meetings, for Wavell, clearly still fuming over the loss of Moulmein, lived up to his reputation for taciturnity; he did not ask Smyth about his men, his plans or his dispositions; in fact he did not say much at all during the long inspection. But the little he did say was of vital importance to the defence of Burma; having studied the terrain and decided it was suitable, he sought to confirm his opinion by asking Smyth if there was any scope for tanks. Smyth responded eagerly, saying they would make a valuable contribution to his forces. Whereupon Wavell announced that he would cable the Chiefs of Staff and ask for the 7th Armoured Brigade, consisting of two regiments of light cruiser tanks, one Royal Horse Artillery Battery and one Anti-tank battery, on its way from the Middle East to Malaya, to be diverted to Burma. At a rough estimate they would reach Rangoon about 21 February and could arrive at the Sittang three or four days later.

A visibly relieved Smyth asked General Wavell to address the troops, but was disappointed when he did so, for the General reverted to the old theme of the poor fighting qualities of the Japanese, which was the last thing the men wanted to hear, for they knew otherwise.

Despite the immensity of his task, Jackie Smyth had reason to be optimistic. On Sunday, 8 February he was heartened to hear of the arrival of the 48th Gurkha Brigade which consisted of the 1/3rd Queen Alexandra's Own Gurkha Rifles, the 1/4th Prince of Wales' Own Gurkha Rifles and the 2/5th Royal Gurkha Rifles, Frontier Force. It was commanded by Brigadier Noel Hugh-Jones, whom he knew well and held in high regard. He had specially asked for the Brigade to be sent as reinforcements.

The three battalion commanders – Lieutenant-Colonels George Ballinger, Joe Lentaigne and Ronnie Cameron – were all superb fighting soldiers who had seen action in the First War and on the North-West Frontier.

True, they had arrived in Rangoon with untrained mules and without pack saddles or leading ropes, but the reputation of the diminutive mercenaries from Nepal was enough to put a spring in the step of any divisional commander; when it came to the kind of fighting that was taking place there were no better men than the Gurkhas. Soon after disembarking at Rangoon they moved into reserve bivouacs near the Divisional Headquarters at Kyaikto.

Martaban was an important rail and ferry terminus on the west bank of the Salween and the responsibility for holding it rested on Lieutenant-

Colonel 'Red Steve' Stevenson, commanding officer of the 3/7th Gurkha Rifles. His task was formidable but the troops at his disposal seemed more than adequate. In addition to his own Gurkhas he had the 1/9th Jats, the 7/10th Baluchis, the 5th Mountain Battery and the comforting presence of A Company of the 2nd King's Own Yorkshire Light Infantry, a group of tough and wiry professionals. But the KOYLIs had been moved about so often without officially belonging to any brigade that they began to refer to themselves as "nobody's child". It was, on paper, the ideal balance, for experience had shown that Indian troops invariably performed better when supported by white troops. As one KOYLI put it, "Give me a Gurkha on my right side and an Indian on my left and nothing will stop us."

On 8 February the 16th Brigade, which had been responsible for the Salween line, was relieved by Brigadier Ekin's 46th Brigade, although some of the 16th remained in the forward area under his command owing to a shortage of troops.

The Japanese meanwhile began their softening-up of Martaban with heavy shelling and bombing and soon afterwards enemy troops landed west of the town and set up a road block some eight miles outside it. As a result the vital telephone link with Thaton was cut. An attempt to clear the block resulted in the loss of two armoured cars, but the 3/7th cleared it with a valiant bayonet charge. The enemy's task was made easier by Burmans who lit fires to guide the bombers on to military and civil targets, and by showing the advance troops secret jungle paths.

Just how well-organized the Fifth Column was was revealed when the bodies of some Japanese were found dressed in native costume and carrying maps and details of the British Army's strength and dispositions. It was in stark contrast to the almost total lack of British military intelligence which was largely due to a failure to utilize the services of Europeans who could speak Burmese.

Ekin, with Smyth's approval, decided to withdraw the Martaban garrison, and the Jats, Baluchis and the Mountain Battery were pulled out. As Ekin was unable to make contact by wireless, he sent orders to Lieutenant-Colonel Stevenson through a liaison officer accompanied by a small party of Gurkhas to withdraw. But the party was ambushed and wiped out and the orders were never received.

As more and more Japanese were reported to be landing and approaching the town along the flat coastal belt, Stevenson decided that

Martaban could not be held and he started to withdraw. As the Japanese swarmed in the Gurkhas and KOYLI put up a desperate fight, often at close quarters with kukris and bayonets matched against enemy swords. The Yorkshiremen were the first British troops to go into action in Burma, and they lived up to all the cherished traditions of their famous regiment. But they were outnumbered by at least three to one and the outcome was inevitable. Apart from the natural anxieties of going into action for the first time the KOYLI were burdened down with other problems that preyed on their minds. Some had left wives and children behind in Maymyo, while others had Anglo-Indian and Burmese girl friends. As they had moved into the war area they had witnessed the disintegration of the civil administration and the terrible plight of the refugees, and it was natural, therefore, that they should be worried about the fate of their loved ones. Furthermore they were fighting another enemy even more invincible than the Japanese. The effects of the spell in the malarial gorges at Takaw began to be felt.

Colonel Stevenson mustered his small force and, after destroying his motor transport, moved out as night fell, and after a march of fifty miles reached Thaton.

Some of the Yorkshiremen, when interviewed by reporters, spoke out forcefully about their poor and wrong equipment, the lack of artillery support and no air cover, the hostile natives and malaria. But they were still defiant and full of fight. And there was no doubt in the minds of the rugged northerners that the failure to hold the line of the Salween was a grave defeat, for it provided the finest defensive line of the country. They were also scathing of the way the troops had been deployed; they had proved that man to man the British and Indian troops were more than a match for the enemy, but they would not defeat him unless they adopted similar tactics.

CHAPTER 7

"The story of the young 7th Baluchis is one of the immortal tales
of the old Indian Army. The eyelids prick and the pen stumbles
to record it in words"

Compton Mackenzie

Pins with coloured heads are often the remote symbols on battle maps
depicting the position of real people. They are moved like pieces on a
chess board and too often they only assume human proportions when
things go wrong. Then the hand that moves the pins apportions the
blame on the men they represent – a military analogy to the poor
workman blaming his tools.

This was a view that was shared by many front-line soldiers in
Burma, and the repeated criticisms of the fighting qualities of the troops
aroused a lasting and deep resentment among officers and men. There
were isolated cases where some units panicked and broke, but they were
mainly Burmese units; in the main the British, Indian and Gurkha
troops fought with a fanatical bravery that had not been matched in any
other theatre of war.

Stowe and Gallagher, who together covered the campaign until they
were forced to leave for India, were as resentful of the critics as the
soldiers, and they did their utmost to let the outside world know how
magnificently they were facing up to an almost impossible task.

As Gallagher put it: "The courage of the small British army in Burma
is something that *must* be remembered. Though there were blunders,
though their tale during those months is one of continual retreats, they
were the men of a scratch army who stood up to an infinitely more
dangerous enemy, an enemy superior in everything except courage, and
made him pay in blood for every advance he made."

Nowhere was this truer than at Kuzeik.

Hardly anyone in Britain had ever heard of the place, and the few in
Burma who had recalled vaguely that it was a small village somewhere

61

near the Salween River. It was there that the 7/10th Baluchis were almost annihilated in a battle in which they carved an imperishable niche in military history.

On 8 February when Brigadier Roger Ekin's 46th brigade was scattered and trying desperately to reorganize, and the troops at Martaban were heavily engaged by a vastly superior enemy force, the Baluchis were perilously exposed at Kuzeik village. They had arrived there three days previously and their Commanding Officer, Lieutenant-Colonel Jerry Dyer, had set them to work on the task most detested by infantrymen – digging in. Anticipating heavy air attack he told them it was that or be killed, and they went to work with a zest that surprised even the phlegmatic Dyer.

Within a short time they appreciated that their commanding officer had not exaggerated the dangers. Early in the morning of 11 February twenty-seven enemy bombers attacked the battalion's position for ten hours, but due entirely to the deep and well-dug trenches there was not a single casualty. The bombing, as everyone was aware, was only the prelude to a fierce onslaught by Japanese troops.

It was not an ideal spot for the Baluchis to stand and fight off a major assault; they were entrenched in a saucer-shaped area of paddy fields about six hundred yards wide, with the river to the east and the road to Duyinzeik skirting the southern side. The rim of the saucer was fringed by deep, dense jungle which limited the field of fire. Approaching snake-like through the jungle were a thousand highly skilled Japanese who had been blooded in China. They also had the added advantage that they were being led along uncharted paths by traitor Burmese guides.

To the waiting soldiers they really were an unknown enemy. Intelligence had issued pictures of a Siamese soldier, saying that the Japanese *might* look like that. The Siamese were, of course, Allies and the clumsy attempt at identification merely added to the confusion.

The Baluchis were mainly young men with only a few months service who looked towards their officers and the relatively few regular soldiers for support and example in what was to be their first encounter with the enemy.

Colonel Dyer's position was made more precarious because he had to send out regular patrols along a large stretch of the river bank which widened his position. By now the Japanese were crossing the Salween in considerable numbers and near Pagat two patrols were attacked and overrun while the progress of a third was being signalled to the enemy by Burmese tapping on the bamboo canes. An attempt to surround the patrol was defeated by light machine-gun and rifle fire and the patrol managed to return to its position in Kuzeik.

Twenty-year-old Lieutenant Charles Coubrough, the signals officer, who was without a job as the enemy had cut the wire to Brigade headquarters, preventing all contact, had been impressed at the way the young soldiers had withstood the dive-bombing, as he clambered out of his trench to attend to the casualties which he felt were inevitable from the number of anti-personnel bombs which had been dropped. "I found none in the immediate vicinity, but met a number of leaderless men from one of the Rifle Companies unsettled by the bombing coming up the hill. They told me the Japs were attacking. I took over command, steadied the men and placed them in defensive positions. Although there was a lot of noise I did not personally believe that there was a Jap attack. But it was possible that they had infiltrated a number of men through the jungle and that the bombing was a prelude to an attack."

His Urdu was not perfect but he could make himself understood. No one was to fire without his order. It was just as well as out of the jungle into the field of fire there appeared not the Japs but the C.O. and the Subedar-Major.

Dyer knew that the main attack would not be too long in coming but felt confident that he could hold his positions long enough for the 5th Dogras, who had been promised in support, arrived. But as patrols brought in news of further enemy movement, he sent a patrol to the Dogras asking them to waste no time in arriving. He also gave orders for Brigade headquarters to be informed of the enemy's movements, and to stress the urgent need for reinforcements. The situation was desperate, as five platoons still out on patrol were cut off and his strength had been sapped by the earlier casualties.

12 February was three-quarters of an hour old when a lance-naik commanding a section of C Company saw a large body of troops approaching from the west, and he experienced a feeling of deep relief, thinking they were the long-awaited Dogras; he realized his error when they opened fire. His section immediately retaliated with their light machine guns and rifles, and the Japanese were forced to deploy. Fifteen minutes later the enemy attacked in force from the west and south-west.

The inexperienced Baluchis were subjected to a terrifying ordeal.

The enemy advanced shoulder to shoulder in compact formations, firing rifles and automatic weapons, screaming unintelligible, stomach-churning screams, and led by officers brandishing swords. They fired red and green tracer, let off noisy fire-crackers and hurled countless grenades.

The Baluchis were unnerved by tactics they had never been told to expect and they momentarily recoiled, but they quickly steadied and gave the Japanese a taste of their own medicine. As they worked the bolts of their rifles as quickly as their fingers could move, and changed magazines on the machine guns with a speed never accomplished during training, they responded with Mianwali and Dogra warcries. But no matter how hard they fought back, or how many enemy they killed, nothing seemed to be capable of stemming the human avalanche.

As the battle raged everyone, including the mess servants, signallers and medical orderlies, was brought into the fight and as ammunition became scarce the order was given to make every shot count. This they did, inflicting such heavy casualties that the enemy was forced to adopt different tactics. They advanced in small groups under cover of intense machine-gun fire, then when within a few yards of the Baluchis fell flat and loosed a barrage of grenades.

The battle soon developed into desperate hand-to-hand encounters. Outnumbered by at least five to one and with their casualties steadily mounting, the young Indians showed that they were prepared to die as resolutely as the enemy.

There was still no sign of the Dogras and doubts were beginning to surface in Dyer's mind that perhaps the signal had never reached them; but there was no way of finding out as the telephone wires had been cut and there was not one serviceable wireless set. And when there was a temporary lull in the fighting it was only to enable the Japanese bombers to swoop low and dive-bomb.

Like so many young officers, Second-Lieutenant John Randle had gone into action armed with nothing more effective than an army issue pistol. "The Japs formed up shoulder to shoulder and on the right there was a warrant officer with a sword who was coming straight at me. My first shot went over his head, the second hit the ground. The third killed him, but he still managed to throw a grenade."

Naik Amir Khan was awarded a posthumous Indian Order of Merit for shooting dead twenty Japanese with his Tommy-gun and clubbing three more to death when his ammunition ran out. Havildair-Major Ali Haider Khan strangled a Japanese with his bare hands.

Captain Siri Kanth Korla was awarded an immediate D.S.O. for his bravery. He led several bayonet charges, shouting war cries which led the enemy into thinking that he was leading a much larger force of men than he had. And when the enemy captured most of the reserve ammunition of A Company, swarmed into the position of B Company, overcame the remaining survivors and cut off C Company which was perilously short of ammunition, he and Jemadar Anant Ram and seven Sepoys hacked their way to A Company and collected two boxes of ammunition which they distributed among the hard-pressed soldiers.

Siri Kanth Korla, credited with killing ten Japanese with his revolver and several more with his 'Dah' slashing knife, bore a charmed life throughout the hours of non-stop fighting, and this was certainly borne out when he was captured along with his Lieutenant. Instead of shooting or bayoneting them, which had been the fate of most of those captured, for the Japanese did not believe in taking prisoners, they were bound hand and feet. Seeing the two men trussed like chickens the Japanese were unwise enough to leave their arms only a few yards away. Although it took Korla and his Lieutenant several hours of wriggling and squirming to reach the unguarded weapons they managed to free themselves and grab the arms. Korla shot dead one of the guards and killed the other with his knife. The two officers spent the remainder of the night hiding only fifteen yards away from where the furious Japanese were searching for them. Korla struggled through the dense jungle and finally managed to report back to Thaton.

Denied the promised support of the Dogras, Colonel Dyer realized that even the unbelievable courage displayed by his men was incapable of halting the Japanese. His battalion had been divided and had suffered enormous casualties and, although isolated groups were still fighting doggedly, he knew the end could not be far off. He turned to Charles Coubrough and indicated that they should advance. To those close by it seemed almost a death wish for immediately he was hit by three bullets. Before the battle started he had enjoined his men to fight to the last round and he had set a magnificent example. Coubrough carried him out of the line of fire, although he was aware that his colonel's wounds were mortal, and with the aid of a soldier carried him to the river. He then hid him in some bushes and did what he could for his wounds. He knew that the only hope was if the Dogras counter-attacked, but as time passed that possibility became more and more remote. Coubrough stayed with Dyer until he knew there was nothing more he could do. Like so many others in the battle he was confronted with an almost impossible choice – he could stay with a friend for whom he could do nothing, or escape to fight again. He heard the Japanese thrusting into the undergrowth searching for hiding soldiers and at one point a Japanese officer appeared within inches of him. Coubrough raised his pistol but the officer moved off. He whispered goodbye to Dyer and began making his way back to headquarters. He holed up for some time, intending to set off under cover of darkness. For two days he crawled through the jungle before he was betrayed by some Burmese who pinpointed his whereabouts and he was suddenly confronted by a Japanese officer brandishing a sword. Coubrough raised his pistol and pulled the trigger, but it misfired and he was overpowered and dragged off to spend the remainder of the war in one of the infamous prisoner-of-war camps. He was one of the few who were taken prisoner; most of the Baluchis were killed.

A similar fate befell the Quartermaster, Captain Bruce Toothill. Soon after the death of Jerry Dyer, he had set off with a small party to try and relieve a group of men who were surrounded.

He and his seven men were making their way through the jungle when they were encircled by howling Japanese who were standing less than ten yards away with their bayonets thrust forward. Toothill charged through a gap and, as he had no wish to be shot in the back, he hid behind a tree and emptied his revolver at them. The Subedar Major tried to throw a grenade, but he was too close to the enemy and was bayoneted to death. Toothill was immediately surrounded and found himself gazing down the barrels of a dozen rifles. He loaded his revolver with a none too steady hand and "wondered what it was like to be on the Other Side".

"The fight lasted a few minutes. Had they been Germans and better shots it wouldn't have lasted more than seconds. The first bullet got me through the leg just above the ankle, the second a couple of minutes later scraped my shoulder; the third knocked the smile off my face in no uncertain fashion, removing fourteen teeth and breaking my jaw prior to leaving via my left cheek. I am afraid I packed it in at that stage as I felt I had tried to kiss an express train."

The badly wounded captain tried to indicate by sign language that he would like to be finished off as he had no wish to be left to the vultures. The invitation was declined and instead an attempt was made to interrogate him, but he was unable to speak, and to his immense surprise he was placed on a makeshift stretcher. He was allowed to put a field dressing on his leg and one of the Japanese gave him a bandage to put on his shattered jaw.

When the sun rose there was a brief and welcome lull in the fighting. Battalion headquarters and part of A Company were still a fighting force, but D Company had almost ceased to exist.

A Japanese officer stood on a slight ridge, which shortly before had been B Company's position, and called upon the battle-weary remnants to surrender. He was answered by a burst of machine-gun fire and the battle resumed. A heavy barrage of mortar and artillery fire opened up with devastating effect and the remnants of Battalion headquarters and A Company attempted a counterattack across the paddy fields in an effort to reach C Company. Although casualties were heavy the objective was achieved, but there were few men left in C Company to greet them.

The Japanese promptly attacked with heavy automatic fire and in a short time organized resistance came to an end. The mountain battery which up till then had been able to provide valuable support was lost.

Day after day small groups began to trickle back to the British lines. Siri Kanth Korla was just one of many who trudged as many as twenty-five miles. The Baluchis as a fighting unit had almost ceased to exist. Three companies had very nearly been annihilated; only five officers, three VCOs and sixty-five other ranks succeeded in rejoining the 46th Brigade at Thaton.

The surviving officers almost unanimously agreed that the battle had been grossly mismanaged and that they and the men under them had been sacrificed. What, they asked, had happened to the Dogras? But they were given no satisfactory answer.

John Randle, who commanded B Company, was able to fight his way out with a small party. Weak with fever, it took him and his men two days to reach their own lines. At one stage Randle was forced to lie up near the side of a track while an entire battalion of unused Japanese soldiers passed, heading northwards on a line parallel to the Salween. He reported this on his return, for it was obvious that the enemy were intending to swing in a big right-hand sweep towards the Sittang Bridge.

CHAPTER 8

"I've had rather a blow this morning which I will tell you about
at once"

Major-General Smyth to General Hutton

When the news reached Rangoon that the Japanese were crossing the
Salween in strength it was received with astonished disbelief and the
already demoralized population vented their feelings in a bitter attack
on the army. "What's the matter with it? If they can't stop them at the
Salween where can they stop them?"

It was while the enemy were crossing the Salween that Sir Reginald
Dorman-Smith chose to broadcast to the people of Rangoon. It was an
unfortunate moment to assure the public that the city would become
another Tobruk and would never be allowed to fall. The rallying call fell
on deaf ears and rumours abounded that he had only made the broadcast
on the insistence of the military. It was increasingly clear, even to those
who did not possess a modicum of military knowledge, that the enemy had
set his sights on Rangoon, and if the series of withdrawals were anything to
go by there was no way of stopping him, certainly not with words.

The only ray of hope for Smyth, who was at the receiving end of most of the
criticism, was the presence of the 48th Gurkha Brigade and the promise of
more reinforcements in the form of four British Infantry battalions: the
2nd Battalion, Duke of Wellington's Regiment, which had been kicking
its heels in Delhi; the 1st Cameronians, and the 1st West Yorkshire
Regiment, who were in Secunderabad and Barrackpore, and the 1st Royal
Inniskilling Fusiliers who would be flown in from Meerut.

The 48th Gurkha Brigade, the despatch of which had so delighted
Smyth, had been mobilized with a sense of urgency that was in marked

contrast to the apathy which had existed for so long in military circles in India and the Far East. Sadly, the speed was not matched with comparable efficiency or realism, so that when the Brigade finally reached Rangoon the three Battalion Commanders were acutely conscious that their soldiers were short of everything except indominatable courage and unquenchable pride.

The 1/3rd Queen Alexandra's Own Gurkha Rifles had been on Frontier service for two years when it was moved to Secunderabad to become part of the 48th. The Battalion armament consisted of .303 rifles supported by a platoon of Vickers medium machine guns; there were no 2-inch or 3-inch mortars, although the men were expert in the use of grenades.

It was anticipated that the Battalion would have until April to be welded into a modern fighting outfit, but orders were received that they were to mobilize by Christmas Day. A period of frantic activity followed and new arms and equipment poured in, including the much-needed mortars and Bren guns which were an entirely new weapon to the soldiers.

Captain Robin Bishop, the Adjutant, who was killed later in Burma, recalled, "We fired our 3-inch mortars only once before we left, but we didn't fire our Bren guns, Tommy guns or our 2-inch mortars at all. No compasses were tested, and we hadn't seen our wireless sets."

Before leaving Secunderabad the officers had been asked to hand in their .45 pistols as they were to be issued with .38 pistols. But as the ship prepared to leave Madras on Christmas Day the replacements had still not arrived. "Hawsers were hauled inboard, sirens were blown and assorted WVS ladies waved goodbye," said Captain Bishop. "The Quartermaster was still trying to do something about the .38 pistols as the ship crept from the quay. Then a lorry came speeding towards us. The gap between the ship and the quay was widening as a box was thrown aboard. The Quartermaster opened it and fell back with a screech. They were .45 pistols."

When the Brigade arrived in Rangoon an air-raid warning had sounded and the port was devoid of all labour. Having unloaded all their own equipment and transport the Brigade was ordered to set up camp near Taukkyan north of Rangoon.

General Smyth's intention was to hold the newly arrived brigade in reserve and they were moved near his headquarters at Kyaikto where they started concentrated training.

Captain Bruce Kinloch, at 22 a veteran of many clashes with hostile Pathans on the Frontier, was in hospital suffering from quinsy when the order to mobilize was received, and he was put in charge of the mules and horses which would follow the Battalion by train four days after it left.

The horses and mules travelled by train to the docks in Calcutta where the Movement Control Staff were renowned for their inability to achieve either movement or control. After frantic searches a ship, the S. S. *Manon*, was located, but was completely inadequate for the job of transporting 600 horses and mules, along with a large number of men, line gear and extra baggage. Kinloch was told that only two officers and one man for every six animals would be able to board, but he was not to worry, another vessel would be provided that would follow on with the remainder of the men and equipment.

When the last animal was aboard a lorry roared up and a breathless corporal ran up the gangway to confront Kinloch with a last-minute consignment.

"'Here you are, sir,' he said, 'two Lewis guns and 20,000 rounds of ammunition for anti-aircraft protection.' We sailed at midnight, but next day when we prepared to mount the Lewis guns for battle a Naik who had been directed to deal with them said, 'Sahib we can't fire these guns.' Why not, I asked, and he replied, 'They came straight from Ordnance and they have no bolts.' So we sailed with a full armament of 30-odd rifles and three revolvers, plus two useless Lewis guns to protect us from sea and air attacks."

What should have been a short voyage to Rangoon dragged on for six days and nights as the ancient *Manon*'s maximum speed was about four knots, and it repeatedly broke down. When the ship finally staggered up the Rangoon River nothing had been done to recruit dock labour and a unit of Madrassi troops were enlisted to help unload the animals.

Because of the shortage of staff and the refugee problem the main railway station could not be used to transport the mules and Kinloch had to go to a station some distance from the town to take over two trains which had been made available.

"Suddenly a dust cloud appeared on the horizon and I was greeted with a most interesting spectacle – a large edition of the Grand National. Seventy-odd mules and horses were running flat out across the country led by five chestnut geldings. They went through gardens, rubber plantations, taking fences and ditches in their stride. It was an eye-opener. Some of the donkeys were shifting fast enough to make a steeplechaser at home sit up and look at their odds. After the first big bunch had come up the home straight, the odd also-rans started coming in, followed a long time afterwards by the Madrassis carrying their boots in their hands. Only one in fifty was leading an animal."

A quick head count disclosed that a large number of the animals were missing and a massive round-up was launched. The animals became widely dispersed and the round-up lasted all night; it was not until 4 a.m. that the trains pulled out of the station. When Kyaikto was eventually reached a staff officer announced that the animals had to be unloaded, only to be overruled by a more senior officer who said that the animals were to be taken seven miles in the opposite direction to where the Brigade was stationed.

Soon afterwards Kinloch encountered streams of vehicles and men who had lost contact with their units following a series of withdrawals from the Salween area. "It was here that I saw some of the armoured cars that were being used. Relics of the last war or before, with solid rubber tyres and armour that was pierced by Jap rifle and light machine-gun fire. Many men were killed in them before they were destroyed, and someone deserved to be shot for sending men into action in them."

On 8 February, the day before the fall of Martaban, Major-General Jackie Smyth had written a confidential letter to General Hutton which was the first intimation the Army Commander had that his senior commander was in no condition to be living in the harsh conditions of the front line, let alone conduct a full scale battle campaign.

"My dear General,
    I've had rather a blow this morning which I will tell you about at once. In September I had a rather bad operation for an anal fissure and piles which wasn't too well done. I went back to work too soon and had a go of acute nervous dyspepsia (most unpleasant thing) for

which the doctors advised at least a month's leave. However, I was at once posted to Command 18 Division and thought I would recover at Secunderabad. As you know I had to take over 17 Division in a hurry and then came on here (with a week in Delhi in between). The wound only stopped bleeding 10 days ago and is still discharging. I didn't feel too grand yesterday and your DDMS insisted that ADMS should have a look at me.

He finds nothing *organically* wrong with me that a few months' comparative rest wouldn't put right. I should hate to go sick – it's a thing I've never done in the whole of my service. I feel if I could have a month off – as Bill Slim and Messervy had done lately – and swop jobs with someone in a more sedentary job in India for a few months I should be absolutely OK for a command in the field again (if required).

Actually I've only had a week's leave since Dunkirk and have been in command of war formations all the time.

I'm terribly fed up about this but thought you ought to know.

Meanwhile I shall carry on here perfectly happily as long as you like. So sorry.

Yours ever,
Jackie Smyth

It was an astonishing request which could not have been made at a worse time; if granted it would have a most demoralizing effect on the fighting men to be told that their commander was going on leave in the middle of a battle.

The next day Jackie Smyth's depression was lifted somewhat by the arrival of Brigadier David "Punch" Cowan who had been sent to Burma as a reserve Brigade Commander in response to a personal request from Smyth. Cowan was a tough, aggressive soldier, though his nickname owed more to the seaside puppet than his pugnacious qualities. Although they were old friends, Cowan had no knowledge of Smyth's illness and was surprised when, as soon as he arrived at headquarters, Smyth took him for a private walk. Cowan found him in a "very nervous and jittery state; not at all the Smyth I knew," and he was amazed when Smyth said, "I am a sick man, I want you to take over". The newly arrived Brigadier told him quite bluntly that it was out of the question as it would have a very adverse effect on the men. It was, he said, no time to go on leave.

The following day Smyth had a conference with his Brigade commanders and as a result of their deliberations he telephoned Rangoon to say that he was sending Cowan to Army Headquarters with an important request.

Cowan's brief was to impress upon General Hutton the need to concentrate on the Bilin River and then, without delay, withdraw behind the Sittang River. Another purpose of the visit was to get the Army Commander to approve his appointment as Brigadier General Staff to Smyth.

Cowan returned with a firm refusal from Hutton: under no circumstances could he agree to a withdrawal behind the Bilin. It was General Wavell's policy, and one which he endorsed, that the army should fight as far forward as possible. This made little sense to Smyth who had a low opinion of Hutton as a fighting soldier, and scant respect for Wavell, who was trying to conduct the campaign by shuttling back and forth from Java and had no real appreciation of how events actually stood in Burma.

There was, however, something to be said for each man's attitude. Hutton and Wavell staunchly believed that Burma without Rangoon and its lifeline to China meant nothing and therefore must be held at all costs, and only by fighting forward would the 7th Armoured Brigade, due to arrive soon, be given the time to be in position to halt the advance of the enemy. Jackie Smyth took the view that his Division would be "eaten up in penny packets" if he adhered to Hutton's strategy.

It was an irreconcilable conflict of opinions. Hutton believed the coming battle should be fought on the east side of the Sittang, while Smyth favoured the west bank.

The day before he wrote to Hutton, Jackie Smyth had been visited by Major-General Treffry Thompson, the Deputy Director Medical Services to Burma Army, at his headquarters, who insisted, despite Smyth's protests, that he should have an immediate medical board. A date was fixed and, according to Smyth, the President of the Board went sick and his own ADMS, Colonel Mackenzie, was appointed in his place. "I had a word with him beforehand and begged him to let me carry on anyway until the crucial battle for Sittang was resolved.

Colonel Mackenzie gave him some arsenic and strychnine injections to keep him going and when the Board was duly held he was pronounced fit, although it was recommended that he took two months' rest at the first available opportunity. No one disputed Jackie Smyth's courage or dedication to duty, but by continuing he certainly jeopardized the entire campaign. He had covered up his illness in India with some justification, for he was of the opinion that he had plenty of time to recover, but to do so now at such a crucial time seemed incomprehensible to many close to him.

Understandably General Hutton was bitter, for soon after the disaster at Sittang his own military career was ended and, as he said later, "His state of health must have been known to a number of senior officers in India, including General Hartley, the Army Commander-in-Chief, and possibly to some of my own staff, though nobody felt it was his duty to tell me. It seems extraordinary that he was ever allowed to go to Burma by GHQ India. I have since heard, unofficially, that once or twice during the campaign he was virtually in a state of collapse."

Ironically Smyth took the view that the disastrous course of events in Burma was due to a large extent to the ill health of General Wavell and General Hutton. Both were involved in serious aeroplane accidents which, he was convinced, impaired their judgement to make sensible decisions.

On the night of 10 February, as General Wavell was leaving the now doomed Singapore, he had a very heavy fall as he was about to board his flying boat and tumbled six feet off the pierhead onto some rocks and barbed wire breaking two bones in his back. He refused to go on the sick list and after a short spell in hospital in Java he discharged himself and continued to direct the campaign in Burma. Smyth, forgetful that he was being kept going by a series of injections, believed that the "stream of ill-judged and ill-informed directives which he fired at Hutton during the next fortnight and the unwise decisions he made could only have been the vagaries of a very sick man".

Smyth adopted a similar attitude towards General Hutton, whose aircraft had run out of petrol and crashed into dense jungle during a visit to the Chinese in Lashio. Although badly bruised, Hutton had beaten out the flames with his greatcoat and rescued the pilot, who unfortunately did not survive.

Around this time Hutton was perturbed to hear that Smyth had withdrawn from the Duyinzeik-Thaton position, for there seemed no reason for it, and he wrote disapproving of the action which he considered premature. He informed Wavell, "I shall endeavour to stop this withdrawal but Thaton has already been evacuated."

He then travelled to the headquarters of the 17th Division and reiterated his orders that the Bilin was to be held as long as possible, and there was to be no withdrawal without his permission. At the same time he broke the news that Singapore had fallen and 100,000 troops captured.

To Jackie Smyth his superior's insistence was due to two things: his adherence to Wavell's orders and the effects of the crash. "General Hutton made light of this incident but it had naturally shaken him badly and he was obviously in pain. He looked ghastly and was really in no fit state to face the ordeals of the next few days."

He *was* undoubtedly under tremendous pressure from Wavell not to permit any further withdrawals but he was not browbeaten; he believed that Wavell was right and Smyth was wrong.

Soon afterwards Churchill realized what had long been patently obvious to most people, that it was ridiculous to try and conduct the campaign in Burma from somewhere as remote as Java, and he informed General Wavell that ABDACOM was to be disbanded and he would again become Commander-in-Chief India. But by then nothing short of a miracle could have saved Burma. On 15 February almost the entire 17th Division was concentrated on the Bilin, and one Japanese division was pressing in front while another was attempting a flanking movement.

The next day the Japanese reached the Bilin and dug in. Smyth's fears had been confirmed – it was not a good place to stand and fight. The river turned out to be no more than 100 yards wide, littered with sandbanks, and in most places little more than knee-deep.

CHAPTER 9

"Our troops are not fighting with proper spirit"
                              Lord Linlithgow, Viceroy

It was ironic that it was the administrator who favoured the more aggressive role and the fighting soldier who favoured further withdrawals. But with two generals holding such diametrically opposed views about the conduct of the campaign, disaster was almost inevitable.

Smyth, who believed that Hutton adhered too slavishly to the Commander-in-Chief's orders, found it difficult to accept that he had a mind of his own; no matter how hard he pressed his case Hutton remained adamant and he interpreted this as a sign of weakness. It was not the ideal relationship on the eve of a crucial battle.

On 13 February Hutton sent an appreciation to Wavell in which he stated that he had every intention of fighting east of the Sittang, but owing to the state of the troops they might be driven back to the river where he would fight hard to maintain a bridgehead until the arrival of 7th Armoured Brigade.

At the same time he impressed upon Smyth the importance of not withdrawing *behind* the Bilin River. Smyth, aware that one enemy division was pressing him from the front while another was making a flanking movement and heading for the Sittang, feared that the 17th would be destroyed piecemeal and he made a bold decision to withdraw behind the Bilin. There was nothing Hutton could do about it, but he visited Smyth at his headquarters and told him that there were to be no more withdrawals without his express permission.

Wavell was understandably furious and he conveyed his displeasure to General Hutton:

"I do not know what consideration caused withdrawal behind Bilin River without further fighting. I have every confidence in judgement and fighting spirit of you and Smyth but bear in mind that continual withdrawal, as experience of Malaya showed, is most damaging to morale to troops, especially Indian troops. Time can often be gained effectively and less expensively by bold counter-offensive. This is especially so against the Japanese."

Although Wavell had expressed his confidence in Hutton, far more powerful critics than Smyth were making their voices heard. Dismay and apprehension about the conduct of the war in Burma was growing in Delhi and London, and it came to a head in the middle of February when the Viceroy sent Winston Churchill an extremely strongly worded telegram expressing grave concern at the way in which events were developing:

"Our troops in Burma are not fighting with proper spirit. I have not the least doubt that this is in great part due to lack of drive and inspiration from the top." It was a view, said the Viceroy, that was shared by many others. They certainly included General Sir Alan Hartley who now feared that India was threatened.

The Secretary of State for India, Leo Amery, added his voice to those who thought something drastic needed to be done if Burma was to be saved and he sent a Most Immediate signal to Dorman-Smith: "Have heard doubts cast on Hutton's quality as a fighting leader. Have you any misgivings as to his being the right man? Your telegrams so far have been entirely appreciative."

Churchill, undoubtedly influenced by the fact that criticism of his own leadership had recently led him to seek a vote of confidence in the Commons, repeated the Viceroy's message to General Wavell, saying that the Chiefs of the Imperial General Staff wanted his opinion. If he agreed with the Viceroy's strictures he would send General Alexander to replace Hutton.

Wavell, still not fully recovered from his fall, stood by Hutton who had after all been his personal choice, although his support was somewhat qualified:

"I am very disturbed altogether at lack of real fighting spirit in our troops shown in Malaya and so far in Burma. Causes go deep, softness of last twenty years, lack of vigour in peace training, effects of climate and atmosphere of East. Conditions of fighting admittedly difficult but should not have been insuperable. Leaders of real drive and inspiration are few. I looked for one for Malaya and Singapore and could not find him. Hutton has plenty of determination behind quiet manner and will never get rattled but lacks powers of personal inspiration. At time I selected him reorganization of whole military machine in Burma was imperative. I knew he would do this excellently and considered also he would be resolute and skilful commander. I have no reason to think otherwise but agree that Alexander's forceful personality might act as a stimulus to troops. Dorman-Smith when I last visited Rangoon spoke well of Hutton and said he had impressed his ministers."

It was hardly a spirited defence. Even more tragic was the fact that Hutton helped to precipitate his own demise by having the courage to spell out the problems and dangers facing Burma. Replacing him, as everyone in their heart of hearts knew, was mere window-dressing. And no one was more aware than Winston Churchill that what was needed in Burma was more men and more up-to-date equipment and effective air cover. "But if we could not send an army we could at any rate send a man," he wrote.

In a Private and Most Confidential signal, Wavell was told that General Alexander would be arriving in Rangoon about 26 February and that it had been decided that General Hutton, in view of his local knowledge and the valuable services he had rendered, would remain as CGS. Hutton, however, was not to be told of the harsh criticisms that had been made, for the message concluded: "Please convey above decision to General Hutton emphasizing that change has been made on account of the proposed large increase in Burma army and that the services which he has rendered have been much appreciated by His Majesty's Government."

It was a cynical rider, but any qualms of conscience Wavell may have experienced were dispelled by an appreciation of the situation in Burma from Hutton which he considered needlessly pessimistic. It was not difficult after that to think that the arrival of General Alexander was the answer everyone sought.

While the wrangling went on and the rancour grew, Major-General Smyth was trying to achieve the near impossible – hold the Japanese on the Bilin.

"The fog of war" was a frequently used phrase in the first Burma campaign. In many instances it was totally justified, but there were also times when the fighting troops suspected it was a convenient excuse to cover up ineptitude and incompetence.

One, far from isolated, incident became the subject of much ribald humour in army messes and civilian clubs and was cited as a perfect example of panicky withdrawals when there was no real need.

Throughout their chequered history the British had always displayed a bewildering ability to laugh at their own follies, but what became known as "the Thaton train incident" was really no laughing matter, although people chortled over it.

When Major-General Smyth decided to concentrate his line behind the Bilin he moved his headquarters from Thaton, an important railway link about 25 miles west of Pa-an.

Smyth was having a conference with his brigade commanders when he saw to his horror the Rangoon express pass on its way to Thaton, which he now believed was held by the enemy. He personally supervised the laying of mines under the track and arranged for marksmen to be lined up to fire on the train when it returned, as he was convinced it would be packed with Japanese troops. Soldiers had their weapons at the ready, the engineers stood by to detonate the mines, and everyone's ears were straining to pick up the first faint rumble of the wheels. When it returned a few hours later there were no Japanese peering out of the windows, only Burmese refugees.

Smyth hastily halted the demolition parties and the train came to a halt. "The Japanese had been so flabbergasted by the unexpected appearance of the train that it had been loaded with supplies and new passengers and had started off on the return journey before they had gathered their wits," he said later.

The truth was even more astonishing.

When the 17th Division began to withdraw to the Bilin the KOYLI were the last to leave Thaton. They were informed that a train would be arriving some time around 10 pm which was to be loaded with stores and heavy equipment, including several days' rations for the entire division. As soon as the loading had been completed the battalion was to march to the river.

It was an unnerving time for the isolated Yorkshiremen. Ten o'clock came and passed and there was still no sign of the train. Lieutenant-Colonel Keegan, the Commanding Officer, kept glancing anxiously at the luminous dial of his watch. Midnight passed and there was still no sign of the train. Then, shortly before 2 am, a despatch rider arrived with the news that there had been a misunderstanding, the train would not be coming and the stores were to be abandoned and the battalion withdrawn immediately. Keegan needed no encouragement and an hour later the battalion, accompanied by a small party of Indian sappers, was making for the Bilin, blowing up bridges on the way. They made good progress and soon after dawn the men were surprised to hear the rattle of the cancelled train heading for Thaton.

When the driver found the village deserted he decided to abandon the train and made off into the jungle. However, the rattle of the train awakened two privates who had been sleeping off the effects of a stock of beer they had found when detailed to help with the loading. They clambered out from behind their hiding places to find themselves in sole possession of the village, an express train and a large amount of equipment, ammunition and food.

One of the soldiers, Private B. Bream, had never seen Yorkshire; he was an Englishman who was born in Burma and had enlisted when the battalion was stationed in Maymyo. Before that he had been employed by Burma Railways and had acquired a basic knowledge of engines. After considerable effort he managed to uncouple the engines, change the points and shunt the engine to the other end of the train. While he was busy with the engine his comrade loaded as much as possible of what he considered the most essential stores. A number of refugees also clambered aboard and it was only when they were seen leaning out of the windows of the carriages and waving as the train reached Bilin that the order to destroy the track was hastily countermanded and the soldiers told to leave their weapons.

Eve Curie heard the story when she visited General Smyth at his headquarters soon afterwards. She learned of the consternation aroused when it was realized that when Thaton was evacuated no one had remembered to warn the railway.

In fact a further two days elapsed after the evacuation before the Japanese occupied Thaton. Vital ground had been needlessly surrendered.

The course of injections recommended by Colonel Mackenzie must have been very effective, for when Hutton visited Smyth at his headquarters he saw no sign of ill health. Certainly Miss Curie was not confronted by a sick man. She found instead a comparatively young man with pleasant features who smiled easily, perhaps too much, and who was blasé about "victorious retreats". She listened as he explained the necessity for shortening the front by withdrawing steadily before making a stand. She had heard similar talk in France before the Germans overran it. But General Smyth attempted to allay her fears:

> "The battle of France was a swift retreat of mobile, partly mechanized forces, while the delayed action now fought in Burma is a slow-tempo one. Both the enemy and ourselves are compelled to use primitive tactics, primitive weapons, because of the terrain in which we operate. On the roads we can move with armoured cars, Bren gun carriers, and troop carriers, but when it comes to cutting across thick jungle there is nothing else to do but walk, and the combat becomes hand-to-hand."

She listened also to personal accounts of stubborn fighting and face-to-face combat from men who had survived the Salween battle, but they did nothing to reassure her. Everyone she spoke to insisted that Rangoon would be held, but far from dispelling her fears they increased them. She detected a lack of conviction and gained the impression that, without reinforcements and more air support, Burma would be lost.

Lieutenant-Colonel Keegan carried out an inspection of his new position on the Bilin with his company commanders and speedily realized that the battalion had an immense front to cover and was going to be stretched to breaking point. The river, far from being a major obstacle, was only a hundred yards wide and easily fordable. Added to that it was not very good ground on which to stage a defensive battle. There were only paddy fields interspersed with clumps of six-foot-high sugar cane which restricted the field of fire. The village of Danyingon, allocated to D Company under Captain E. D. Wardleworth, was even more difficult; it was dotted with large trees and surrounded by dense jungle.

Before setting off for a meeting with the C.O. of the 1st Battalion 7th Gurkha Rifles, Keegan addressed his officers, and uttered words that even the bravest soldiers heard with a thumping heart and a chill feeling of fear: the position was to be held to the last man and the last round.

A quarter of an hour later heavy bursts of machine-gun fire were heard in the direction of Danyingon. Keegan listened anxiously, hoping it was no more than a scare, for he knew D Company could not have taken up their positions, but as the firing increased in intensity he knew the battle had started in earnest.

At that precise moment Captain Wardleworth was riding his horse through the village studying the most favourable positions in which to deploy his men. The village seemed perfectly peaceful. He rode back and led his men into the village.

As they turned a corner they surprised a party of Japanese washing at a well who immediately took to their heels, but several were shot dead before they could escape. At the same time the Yorkshiremen came under heavy fire and dived for cover. A Japanese officer trying to rally his men from behind a bush was shot dead and several of his men were killed. Wardleworth then led a determined attack to clear the village but was forced to withdraw. He twice repeated the attack but each time failed. Undeterred he tried again, this time supported by four 3-inch mortars, but against such overwhelming odds there was little chance of success, and with no hope of reinforcements he was forced to withdraw with heavy casualties.

Corporal J. P. Howson, who remained in the village with his section of seven men in order to cover the withdrawal of one of the platoons after the first attack, was cut off. As the enemy approached from several directions his men hastily took cover under one of the stilted bungalows and prepared to fight it out.

By now enemy snipers had managed to sneak into concealed positions and Lance-Corporal R. G. Wood recklessly left his cover to try and pick some of them off from behind a tree. He took aim, fired and gave a thumbs-up salute before dropping dead.

From under a pile of charcoal Howson was picking off the enemy with every shot, while his men were also making each bullet count. Then, as the KOYLI mortars opened fire, Howson's men increased their tally as the Japanese were forced to retreat towards the bungalow in an attempt to escape the barrage. As the explosions crept closer further occupation of the hut became extremely hazardous and Howson pulled his section out and rejoined D Company, leaving the ground littered with dead Japanese, all shot from less than 30 yards.

It was a noisy prelude to one of the most savage battles of the campaign and one of the most futile.

Early next morning the 1/7th Gurkha Rifles supported the KOYLI in another attempt to occupy the village, but again they were repulsed after several hours of heavy fighting.

A further attack was made by the 4th Gurkha Rifles supported by mortars, but it was only a partial success and no further efforts were made to take Danyingon.

Meanwhile the Japanese were employing their customary flanking tactics. Position after position was stormed with a reckless disregard for casualties, although none of them really succeeded. The enemy made no attempt to launch a major attack on the British lines but were eventually able to achieve their object by tactically outsmarting the British.

Bren-gun carriers roared along the narrow roads pouring a murderous hail of fire into the concealed Japanese, while soldiers tossed grenades as fast as they could remove the pins. The enemy bullets made an ear-splitting din as they hammered against the armour and those Bren carriers which survived were pock-marked with holes.

The motorized transport was particularly vulnerable, confined as it was to the roads, and a party of Sappers detailed to demolish a roadblock was wiped out by enemy soldiers hiding only a few yards away. When ammunition ran out men engaged in hand-to-hand combat. Sergeant F. H. Clarke, a fiery, carrot-haired KOYLI, drove his bayonet into an officer who was so huge that when he fell he knocked the sergeant to the gound and he had great difficulty in withdrawing his bayonet. While he was on the ground Clarke was instantly attacked by three soldiers with swords. Company Sergeant-Major H. Houseley went to his aid with his bayonet and then the butt of his rifle. He was last seen cracking together the heads of two Japanese imprisoned in his powerful arms while six others hacked him to pieces with their swords. Not one man in that party survived.

The ghostly method of warfare with the enemy flitting like wraiths through the jungle was sometimes too much for men who liked to see their foe. Private G. Collins, roaring "Come out into the open, you yellow . . .", charged headlong into the jungle with his bayonet thrust in front of him. He was never seen again. Lance-Corporal J. Rowley crawled through the dense undergrowth to try and find his son-in-law, Lance Corporal W. A. Macdonald, the lightweight boxing champion of Burma, who was missing. He found him mortally wounded still cradling his Bren gun. He refused to be moved, but simply asked for some extra magazines.

At Battalion Headquarters Colonel Keegan ordered rations to be laid by the roadside for any men who might make their way back, but few did, and they gave heart-rending accounts of the brutality of the Japanese towards their prisoners.

As more and more of the enemy appeared it became clear to the men of B Company that they were cut off and attempts to get a message through to Battalion failed. Then Private W. Abbott from Hull volunteered to try and make it on foot. He set off at 8 am on 18 February on a trek that was to be hailed as an epic of endurance and personal courage. Without a compass to guide him he made for the sound of distant guns. His relief was unbounded when he saw two British trucks stationary in the middle of the road, and he broke cover and raced towards them only to be faced with a withering burst of fire from an unseen machine gun. One bullet crashed into his thigh knocking him flat. With a superhuman effort he managed to crawl behind a wheel of one of the trucks, but was forced to abandon his rifle on the way. The machine-gunner spotted it and knew he had a target that could not hit back and raked the lorry from end to end, splintering the woodwork and ripping the canvas to shreds. As Abbott hugged the ground, he saw empty .303 cartridge cases on the road, a Bren-gun magazine and a dead mule, and realized it was the scene of an ambush. When the machine gun momentarily stopped firing he slid from under the lorry and dropped into a ditch filled with Indian dead. Although losing quantities of blood he continued through the jungle.

When he eventually emerged onto the road he was relieved to meet some Burmans who seemed equally pleased to see him, and when he asked where the British were they pointed up the road and said there were many. As he paused to drink from his water bottle he saw one of them with his dah lifted above his head. Abbott automatically raised his hands to protect his face and the slashing blow practically severed the fingers on his right hand and badly injured his left. He lowered his head and darted between them and with rapidly stiffening fingers managed to pull the pin out of a grenade and roll it towards them.

He paused in the jungle to make two tourniquets out of a field dressing and a bandolier for he feared he was bleeding to death. The more badly injured hand he tucked into the neck of his shirt, the other grasped a grenade which his fingers soon froze round. From time to time he lapsed into unconsciousness, but he always rose and continued, his mind numbed to everything but the need to reach headquarters. He had lost all count of time when he stumbled upon a party of Gurkhas, and after receiving medical treatment insisted on delivering his message. He was placed on a stretcher and carried to Headquarters where he reported to Colonel Keegan.

Soon afterwards a Blenheim bomber was able to drop a message to B Company: "Abandon all heavy equipment. Withdraw to Kyaikto immediately."

It heralded what was soon to become a general withdrawal from the Bilin; by now the entire 17th Division was in a perilous position. Completely outmanoeuvred by the enemy, the British had been forced to attack repeatedly over ground of the enemy's choosing. All along the front the British and Indian troops had fought until they could hardly stand and they now faced the danger of being cut to ribbons.

Jackie Smyth was proud of the way in which his men had fought and died over the past few days, but he realized it had been in vain, and he signalled Hutton that his troops had fought to a standstill and he had thrown in his last battalion in an attempt to halt the enemy's flanking movements. He was aware of Hutton's insistence that there should be no more withdrawals but his own view was that the longer he remained there the more advantageous it was for the Japanese. A strong enemy force was heading for the Sittang and the crucial railway bridge.

When he received Smyth's message, General Hutton hastened to the front and, seeing how weak and exhausted the troops were, he gave permission for the Division to withdraw to the Sittang and issued orders that all transport should be got across at an early stage.

With understandable trepidation, Keegan gave the order to move and, as the battalion set off, bullets passed right over the heads of the men as the Gurkhas on one side and the Japanese on the other, engaged in a hectic exchange of fire. Eventually, to Keegan's amazement, the much depleted battalion reached the main road without encountering the enemy.

The KOYLIs described the march to Kyaikto as "absolute hell". It was blazing hot and there was no shade. The dust rose in thick clouds and the men marched with handkerchiefs over their mouths and noses. Water was scarce and Japanese aircraft bombed and machine-gunned them incessantly.

The motto of the KOYLI is Never Give Up, yet they felt they were being asked to do the opposite. As the Regimental History recorded: "The retreat was inexplicable to the men. So far as they could see the British had not been defeated, yet already they had retreated about seventy miles. As the C.O. made his way up and down the long column, men would say to him, 'When are we going to turn and have a crack at 'em, sir?'"

B Company, following the bulk of the battalion, arrived in Kyaikto in surprisingly high spirits considering how close they had come to annihilation. For much of the time they had moved along the same tracks by which the enemy were advancing, but they had only encountered them once and the outcome had been in their favour.

Ahead of the Company was No. 12 Platoon, led by Sergeant Steerment, and scouts reported that the village they were about to enter was occupied by the Japanese. Captain W. Baxter, who was with Steerment, instantly ordered three platoons to attack; unfortunately the one advanced before the other two were ready, and as the men broke from the jungle the enemy opened fire with every weapon they possessed at a range of fifty yards. Sergeant T. Wheeler was hit and Sergeant W. Johnson gravely wounded. Private G. W. Hall stood in the open and took deliberate aim with his Tommy-gun. A bullet hit him, then a second, followed by a third. He steadied himself and continued firing, calmly changing magazines when necessary. He was still firing when he sank slowly to the ground and died.

As the firing broke out Steerment and his platoon burst out of the jungle, and under cover of the then still upright Hall charged into the village forcing the enemy to flee.

The Company lost no time in reforming and continuing the march.

Steerment, however, remained behind with his seven men and the wounded. All but one of the wounded, Sergeant Johnson, were capable of walking and he sent them off with a two-man escort. A stretcher was made of bamboo and Johnson was placed on it, but progress was agonizingly slow as a path had to be hacked through the undergrowth to get the stretcher through, and after two hours they had covered less than a quarter of a mile. Steerment realized they would never reach Kyaikto, still fifteen miles away, and he decided to leave the wounded sergeant behind with a young corporal to look after him. He promised that a patrol would be sent back as soon as they reached the battalion. He was true to his word, and a patrol of Gurkhas in carriers set off, but the two men could not be found, and they were never heard of again.

The 1/3rd Gurkhas, who were acting as rearguard to the Division, also received a message that three KOYLIs were lying wounded in a village about eight miles away and Naik Panchu Ghale, with a party of eight men, was sent out to bring them back. He was told that if on his return his Company had withdrawn he was to make his way as best he could to Kyaikto.

After a long fruitless search for the wounded men, he returned and found that the enemy now occupied the area. After a short but violent encounter, he managed to extricate his men and lead them across country through the enemy lines. The next day his party was attacked and one man killed, while he was badly wounded in the stomach. Despite the agonizing pain, Panchu Ghale led his men, still carrying their weapons, to the lines near Mokpalin where he was placed on a truck with other wounded, while his small section rejoined the battalion.

Panchu Ghale's ordeal was just beginning. The lorry was ambushed but he managed to escape into the jungle with two other men and head towards the Sittang. Weak through loss of blood and in continuous pain, his progress was slow, and when he reached the Sittang he found the bridge had been destroyed. Undeterred, he walked up-river until he came across a native boat, and after crossing walked fifteen miles to Waw where he was picked up and taken to hospital in Pegu. Here his wound was attended to for the first time in six days.

Other units of the 1/3rd were meanwhile engaged in heavy fighting, and they reported that heavy casualties had been inflicted on a considerable enemy force many of whom were dressed as Burmans.

Captain Bruce Kinloch, who had been issued with a Lend-Lease jeep, had been racing from position to position with urgent orders and information about the enemy movements and the activities of fifth columnists and had just returned to help organize the rearguard when an enemy aircraft flew over.

"It came roaring low across the trees and I grabbed a Bren from one of the carriers and got onto it just as it banked. At first I held fire as I thought it was a Lysander. Then I saw a tell-tale red rising sun and I let fly with a whole magazine including tracer, which I could see pumping into the middle of the plane behind the pilot's cockpit."

Throughout 20 February the withdrawing troops passed through the rearguard and the Regimental History of the 1/3rd Gurkhas recalled the feeling at the time: "All day troops came back along the road through C Company. They were dirty, tired and thirsty, but by no means beaten. Their feelings were, 'If only the little . . . would come out into the open and fight, we'd soon knock hell out of them. When it comes to hand-to-hand fighting, we have them beaten every time.'"

After destroying the bridge over the Bilin, the Gurkhas followed in the wake of the Division. As they had received orders to travel light they had been forced to destroy or abandon much valuable equipment. While they marched, the route to Kyaikto was brilliantly illuminated with fires lit by Burmans to let the Japanese know the line of withdrawal.

General Hutton reported to Wavell that a serious situation had now arisen at the Sittang and as a result the loss of Rangoon was a possibility that had to be faced. He, therefore, requested that a convoy of seventeen ships heading for the port should be turned back to Calcutta as it would only result in the loss of valuable equipment. Only the 7th Armoured Brigade should be permitted to land. Wavell received the news with cold anger: he wanted to know why ships had to be turned back when every item of equipment was needed to fight the enemy:

"Why on earth should resistance on Sittang River collapse? You have at least four good brigades, no sign that enemy is much if at all superior and you have little if any air attack to face. Armoured Brigade should arrive today. What is the matter that these sudden and pessimistic reports are given?"

A flurry of signals followed. He could see no reason for the decision to practically abandon the fight for Rangoon and continue the withdrawal. "You must," he stressed, "stop all further withdrawals and counterattack whenever possible." He added a scathing line, "Has morale of troops and commanders collapsed?", but on reflection he deleted it.

At Kyaikto the KOYLI met the 2nd Battalion the Duke of Wellington's Regiment freshly arrived from India, the first British troops they had met during the campaign. The spick and span Dukes, freshly shaven and in clean well pressed uniforms, looked with a marked lack of respect at the grimy, tired Yorkshiremen and laughed rather derisively as they immediately set to work digging holes with their bayonets and dahs. The next day the Dukes were to appreciate how important that was if one was to survive.

On arrival in the forward area, Captain Tony Firth of the Duke's got caught up in a heavy stream of traffic bumping along the dusty road. "All starry-eyed I said to the battle weary officer in one of the trucks, 'Are we anywhere near the front line?' and he said, 'Don't be a bloody fool, *this* is the front line.'"

As the exchange of signals continued, Wavell ordered that immediate plans should be drawn up for a counter-offensive with the Armoured Brigade and all available troops east of the Sittang.

All was not yet lost. If Smyth could get the 17th Division to the Sittang intact and link up with the Armoured Brigade, the tide could be turned in his favour.

CHAPTER 10

"The trek through the forest was one long drawn out agony"
Bruce Kinloch

When the retreat to the Sittang began, the British commanders were locked in a bitter and acrimonious fight. Smyth, kept going by drugs and injections, was convinced that if he had been given a free hand the situation would not be so perilous. Hutton, written off as a failure yet forced to continue until he was replaced by Alexander, was expected to handle a campaign for which he was considered unfit. Understandably he felt bitter and resentful. General Wavell, haunted by the spectre of a series of disasters which had resulted in him being put out to grass in India, was beginning to have doubts about his ability to avert another defeat that would end once and for all his reputation as a military commander of stature.

Hutton was meanwhile brooding over his own "sacking". He felt personally let down and experienced a betrayal for having only done what he considered his duty. With Wavell so far away in Java he realized that he had not always been in a position to influence operations with the necessary speed and this had resulted in some unfortunate decisions. Hutton's problems were aggravated by the fact that he had to send all telegrams via Delhi which often took a week to arrive, while the same applied to the answers. He therefore felt it was his bounden duty to express his views on the situation as frankly and as honestly as possible. Having been Wavell's Chief of Staff he felt he could speak without reservation and he did, sending his telegrams Secret and Personal and not always showing them to his own staff. It was only later that he learned they were decoded in India and copies sent to the Prime Minister, the Chief of the Imperial General Staff, the Army Commander-in-Chief and the Viceroy. He only discovered this by accident when the C.I.G.S. sent him a personal telegram saying that Winston Churchill did not like the word *retreat* and would prefer the word *withdraw*. He also discovered that what had upset London and Delhi most was his considered opinion that Rangoon might fall, which made him a defeatist and alarmist.

"Of course the main factor affecting my supersession was the strange action of the Viceroy inspired no doubt by Hartley as Army Commander-in-Chief in telegraphing the Secretary of State suggesting my removal. There could be a number of explanations but the only logical one is that the Viceroy was persuaded by Hartley that the security of India was threatened. Certainly the Governor of Burma had nothing to do with it," he wrote later.

He was still, however, responsible for seeing that the army reached the Sittang intact, and to achieve that no time could be wasted in the withdrawal.

Smyth, who believed that too much valuable time had already been lost on the Bilin and permission to withdraw given too late, surprisingly decided to waste even more time. As the troops were tired and exhausted he considered it was unwise to break off contact with the enemy in daylight and the withdrawal was planned to take place under cover of darkness on the 19th–20th.

Hutton, aware that the Japanese were also heading for the river, emphasized the importance of sending all non-essential transport ahead so as not to hamper the withdrawal. Smyth held a conference with his brigadiers at which frank and outspoken opinions were exchanged, with Brigadier Ekin supporting Hutton's contention that all but the vitally essential transport should be sent ahead of the marching columns. He was also in favour of his brigade going on ahead so that there would only be two brigades on the inadequate road at the same time. Cowan agreed that it would certainly speed things up. Smyth, however, favoured the retention of as much transport as possible on the grounds that a large volume of transport would be uncontrollable in the bridge area as there was no effective form of traffic control available. Furthermore, as so much of the fighting efficiency of the division depended on transport and the wounded needed to be conveyed by ambulance, it was vital to retain as much as possible.

Although Brigadier Ekin thought the advancing enemy would by-pass Kyaikto, Smyth was reluctant to leave the area uncovered and two brigades, the 16th and 46th, were ordered to hold the area until the morning of the 21st. It was a costly decision for it meant that the bulk of the Division would be stationary for twenty-four hours. On the morning of the 21st the 46th Brigade took up position around the town while the 16th Brigade moved back about six miles towards the Sittang and took up position astride the railway. The History of the King's Own Yorkshire Light Infantry recalls the dismay experienced over the delay. "This halt at Kyaikto astonished and worried officers. With the Japanese moving steadily round the inland flank by jungle paths they felt it was vital to get back to the Sittang as quickly as possible, moving by night as well as day."

Through an unfortunate error of judgement the orders to withdraw were given in plain language over the radio and intercepted by the Japanese who were in a position to bomb, machine-gun and mortar the troops more or less at will, as there was only one track along which the army could withdraw.

It had been hacked through the jungle from Kyaikto to Mokpalin on the Sittang and was little more than a dusty corridor walled by high trees and scrub jungle. It was difficult enough for marching soldiers, but extremely hazardous for vehicles.

The withdrawal to the Sittang was a nightmare ordeal for men who had been fighting without respite for several days. The heat was intense under a cloudless sky and the dust thrown up by their boots and the wheels of the transport grinding along at two miles an hour completely obscured the track ahead and clogged the ears and throats of the soldiers. The men marched like automatons, seldom speaking as their throats were so parched. The Indians were better off than the British soldiers for they were able to wrap their pugarees over their faces and keep out the dust. Enemy aircraft flew low above the track, bombing and machine-gunning with deadly precision.

The progress of the column was further hampered by the enormous craters which pitted the road, presenting grave dangers to the drivers, and a large number of vehicles were so badly damaged they had to be pushed off the road and abandoned. Among them were ambulances packed with wounded who had to be hastily moved to other vehicles. The noise of the explosions caused the mules to career all over the place, their handlers clinging on like grim death to prevent them disappearing into the jungle.

The continuous low-level bombing was extremely unnerving for many of the younger soldiers who were experiencing it for the first time, but they stood up to it remarkably well and replied with light machine-gun and rifle fire. For an hour or so there was a welcome respite. Then the heavy throb of approaching aircraft was heard. As they swooped low overhead the troops halted and waved their topees in welcome; they were British and American aircraft and their markings were clearly visible. Seconds later the bewildered soldiers were diving for cover as machine guns opened up and bombs began to fall. A disastrous mistake had occurred; Rangoon had given the pilots the wrong bombing line and, instead of attacking the enemy, they were hitting their own troops. The whole of the 17th Division was caught in the murderous attack.

As the Hurricanes, Blenheims and Tomahawks attacked at tree-top level the men on the ground opened up with all available weapons thinking that the aircraft had been captured. The prolonged attacks were so intense that the slow-moving columns were brought to a halt and pandemonium broke out. Some of the Burmese drivers were so petrified they abandoned the ambulances and lorries filled with wounded and fled into the jungle. Mules carrying wireless sets stampeded and vanished into the scrub.

Bruce Kinloch recalled the costly error: "I remember lying on the ground with a .303 rifle and firing at Blenheim bombers which were flying low and dropping bombs on the column. Tired men were kneeling, scorched and blackened by the flames and smoke and crouching in the flimsy shelter of smouldering trees at the side of the track while streams of tracer bullets from the multi-gunned fighters scythed through the branches with a high-pitched tearing snarl that merged into a continuous ear-splitting crescendo of sound as the planes screamed over again and again just skimming the tree tops, straffing and bombing without a moment's respite. The earth heaved and shuddered under the muffled thud and roar of fragmentation bombs. The screams of injured mules ripped and torn by broken pieces of flying steel mingled with the groans and cries of sorely wounded and dying men. An ambulance was burning fiercely nearby, the Sikh driver cut in half by a machine-gun burst, the occupants dead. Two young Gurkha soldiers were standing solidly in the open behind the funeral pyre of the ambulance manning a tripod-mounted Bren gun and sending a steady stream of tracer bullets into the flickering guns of the howling fighters. All around them the grey powdery earth was leaping in tiny gouting fountains like erupting volcanoes as the bullets tore into the ground, until the three lonely figures were finally hidden in the mounting clouds of swirling dust. Miraculously they had not been hit, nor had they ever been attacked from the air before, but they had seen the ambulance and the cold rage that consumed them left no room for fear."

The attack continued for several hours and the losses in men and material were enormous. The gravest loss was the radio sets; it meant that communication during the coming battle would be more or less non-existent.

Attempts were made to convince the troops that the attack had not been carried out by R.A.F. and American aircraft, and it was even suggested that the bombers were Thai ones or Japanese 97 medium bombers which resembled Blenheims. As that did not explain away the markings, it was further suggested that they were captured aircraft. Cowan and Hutton knew the truth but did not think it would add to the men's morale to admit they were the R.A.F. and A.V.G.

Smyth observed the withdrawal with growing anxiety, aware that the Japanese, unhampered by wheeled transport, were moving swiftly and silently around his flanks and racing for the Sittang. He had only narrowly escaped capture himself when his temporary headquarters had been attacked and he had found himself standing with a drawn revolver ready to fight off the enemy. It was only the timely arrival of a Company of the 12th Frontier Force Regiment which had saved his headquarters from being overrun.

Some time before, the vital railway bridge spanning the Sittang had been prepared to take motorised transport and thousands of timber planks had been cut and laid over the rails, but by some oversight no guard rails had been erected. The bridge had also been prepared for possible demolition but, unknown to Smyth, the explosive charges had been removed while the planking was being carried out. A bridgehead defence had also been established consisting of odd units, some of which had been too severely mauled to be of much use in mobile actions. But the defence lacked depth and strength, and little attempt had been made to dig in, a fact which later aroused angry criticism from General Hutton who had laid down detailed orders for the defence of the bridge, stressing the importance of adequate forces being made available.

On the evening of 21 February Jackie Smyth inspected the defences and by nightfall the 48th Gurkha Brigade was bivouacked with Divisional Headquarters about two miles east of the river. As the first transport began to pass over the bridge the troops settled down for a meal and some much-needed sleep. For the first time in days Major-General Smyth experienced a feeling of relief; he might just have made it in time. His intention was for the bulk of the Division to pass through the bridgehead defence over to the west bank where he could expect to link up with the 7th Armoured Brigade.

Hutton, however, had doubts; he thought the withdrawal from the Bilin had taken too long and twenty-four hours lost in the Kyaikto area, which could well be the deciding factor.

Then, unexpectedly, a staff officer from Army Headquarters in Rangoon arrived at Smyth's headquarters with news that was to alter the entire strategy for defending the bridge. He announced that information had been received that the Japanese were proposing to make a parachute attack on the open ground on the west bank in order to seize the bridge from that side. He was not, however, the conveyor of entirely bad news for he told Smyth that the Armoured Brigade had arrived and, despite problems of unloading, would be in position within the next twenty-four hours. The 1st Cameronians and the West Yorkshires would also be arriving.

In Rangoon Hutton was becoming increasingly concerned at the situation which had developed at the river. He was also surprised to hear of the threatened attack by paratroopers. "One would like to know the identity of the staff officer who gave the warning of a possible attack," he commented later.

Meanwhile the transport continued to trundle over the bridge. At 3 am Smyth halted it just long enough for the 1/4th Gurkhas, supported by a company of the Duke of Wellington's, to cross in order to deal with the threatened parachutist attack. Soon afterwards Divisional Headquarters moved over to the west bank. Brigadier Hugh-Jones, who had been placed in charge of the bridgehead defences at extremely short notice, set up his headquarters on the west bank while a small Division Operational Headquarters was established a short distance away.

Once the Gurkhas had crossed the Transport started to move again, until it was suddenly halted by an unforeseen accident. A lorry driven too fast by an inexperienced driver overturned in the middle of the bridge and, because there were no guard rails, became jammed against the girders and two valuable hours were lost before it could be moved, enough time for several thousand men and vehicles to have crossed over. During the hold-up the six miles to Mokpalin became one vast traffic jam of often double-banked vehicles. The congestion was added to when the transport of the two rear brigades began to arrive.

Then Smyth made a move that was opposed by Cowan and disapproved of by Hutton when he learned about it. He set up his headquarters in a small railway station eight miles west of the bridge where the only communication with Hugh-Jones and Rangoon was through a very indistinct civil line.

With communications almost non-existent a state of near confusion prevailed and Hutton was so concerned at the way in which the withdrawal had been conducted and the preparations for the forth-coming battle that he sent an official to see Smyth which resulted in a further deterioration in their relationship. Smyth was so incensed that he sent a blistering signal to the Army Commander, dated 22 February:

"On my arrival at headquarters today I was met by a civil servant, Mr Richards, who said he had no knowledge of this area but had been sent to replace Pelly* in order to put some ginger into me and to impress on me the importance of not withdrawing my division.

"I cannot help regarding this as somewhat of a personal insult and my staff and commanders have done the same.

"If I have forfeited confidence to this extent I do beg of you to replace me at once. I have no personal ambitions as a soldier beyond doing my job to the best of my ability and there are plenty of other people who can take my place. Having delivered his message, Mr Richards asked me if I required him further. I replied that his presence at my HQ was obviously not condusive to any sort of harmonious feeling but that he must act as ordered by higher authority."

It was hardly the time for the two generals to fall out.
The day before, Wavell had signalled:

"You should draw up at once plans for counter-offensive with

* Colonel Raymond Pelly was a commissioner who greatly assisted Major-General Smyth.

Armoured Brigade and all available troops. If at all possible Sittang River must be re-crossed and counter-offensive made east of the river. In any event plans must be made to hit enemy and hit him hard if he ever succeeds in crossing. He will go back quick in face of determined attack."

The morning of the day in which he sent his angry message Major-General Smyth toured the area and inspected the 1/4th Gurkhas and visited a field ambulance on the east bank. There he stopped briefly to chat to Colonel Mackenzie, who had been so accommodating over his medical condition. He declined a cup of tea and set off on his return journey over the bridge. When he was halfway across, intense firing broke out from Japanese concealed in the jungle and within a few minutes all the medical personnel to whom he had been talking were either dead or captured. Among the few taken prisoner was Colonel Mackenzie.

The battle for the bridge had started and, although the outcome had yet to be decided, there was little doubt in the minds of anyone who had taken part in the retreat from the Bilin that it had been badly bungled, and as a result the enemy had a distinct advantage over the widely dispersed division.

Just before this, on the evening of 21 February, Major J. R. Doyle, second-in-command of the KOYLI who had been halted in the Kyaikto area, was ordered to take a reconnaissance party of twelve men to the far side of the Sittang and lay out the battalion position. They set off soon after nightfall and, knowing the enemy were not far off, each man carried a grenade in his hand ready to throw. The party arrived near to Mokpalin around 5 am, and soon afterwards they witnessed headquarters and the 1/4th Gurkhas cross the bridge. Doyle resumed marching and managed to hitch a lift on some vehicles which were following Divsional Headquarters hoping to get to the other side. Progress of the column was depressingly slow, punctuated by halts and stuttering advances. Then at 7 am, with the bridge less than a mile away, the leading lorries were caught in very heavy small-arms fire. The Japanese had cut the road, although they had not seized the eastern end of the bridge. But the greater part of the 17th Indian Division was now cut off from the bridge, the only line of retreat.

In the Kyaikto area the 16th and 46th Brigades began the exhausting march to the Sittang unaware that the enemy had already won the race to the bridge.

The Japanese 33rd Division had moved across country by hilly tracks and jungle, and by forced marches covered the distance from the Bilin in 56 hours. If the bulk of the 17th Division had not halted for almost an entire day when only fifteen miles from the bridge, the result would have been different.

CHAPTER 11

"Jackie, you dropped your Field-Marshal's baton into the
Sittang River"
General William Slim to Major-General Smyth

Jackie Smyth described the battle of the Sittang as "a dog fight in the
jungle", and no one who took part in it would quarrel with his
assessment, for men fought with animal savagery and died with little
idea of what was happening around them. Although it virtually decided
the fate of Burma it was short in duration, but time in the strict sense
had ceased to exist for the soldiers involved. Night or day made no
difference; the fighting was non-stop. And in its closing stages it
developed into an intense battle for survival with everyone's hopes
pinned on one thing: getting over the bridge to link up with the 7th
Armoured Brigade in order to fight a battle on more equal terms. The
weary troops, who were ambushed, shelled, mortared and bombed
almost every yard of the journey, had fought themselves to a standstill,
yet they responded to the rallying calls of their officers with magnificent
courage. Although in many cases they were out of touch with Brigade
and Divisional Headquarters, they were still confident they could make
the bridge, now such a short distance away.

Few commanders have faced a more bitter quandary than Major-
General Smyth as the attack developed. He was unable to pursue any
coherent tactical plan for the simple reason that he did not know what
was going on: the "fog of war" was complete. Feverish, wracked with
pain, and aware that he had forfeited the confidence of the Army
Commander, his judgement was understandably impaired. "Punch"
Cowan, the man closest to him, now realized just how ill he was and
stayed as close as possible.

Smyth was far from happy about the strength of the bridgehead
defences and felt they would have been much stronger and deeper if
only he had been allowed to withdraw from the Bilin much earlier.

99

Nevertheless, he still believed the bridge could be held and the army got over. But a series of blunders, some understandable, others unforgivable, more or less decided the outcome of the bloodiest and most confused battle in the campaign.

Brigadier Roger Ekins' 46th, gradually making its way to the river, was a brigade in name only, for it numbered less than 600 men. Brigadier John Keane Jones's 16th Brigade, also much depleted but in better shape, was making laborious progress to the river. Unfortunately they had no means of informing Divisional Headquarters of their whereabouts or progress and Smyth had no means of contacting them.

They now bore little resemblance to their original formations for their ranks included groups from other units which had lost contact with their main bodies. Soon afterwards the two Brigadiers decided that it would be far more efficient if they became one brigade and its leadership was decided by the toss of a coin which Jones won.

With an almost total lack of communication, the "fog of war" literally blanketed the battle area, and what could have been decisive victories were turned into unnecessary defeats. Nowhere was this more evident than in the strong points overlooking the vital east end of the bridge: Pagoda and Buddha Hills.

When the battle started, the bridgehead was manned by the 4/12th Frontier Force Rifles and the 3rd Burma Rifles with D Company of the Duke of Wellington's Regiment in reserve on the west bank in readiness to mount a counterattack should the bridgehead be threatened.

As the Japanese attacked, the Burma Rifles, their morale already at a low ebb, broke, and "Punch" Cowan, who was crossing the bridge at the time, was almost bowled over as the panic-stricken soldiers raced past him like a herd of stampeding cattle. Fortunately, the Frontier Force Rifles held firm and, led by Captain Sam Manekshaw, launched a determined counterattack.

2nd-Lieutenant John Randle, who had miraculously survived the near-massacre of the Baluchis despite his deplorable marksmanship, had been taken with the remnants of the Battalion by train to the Mokpalin area about two miles east of the bridge. There they remained for several days. He was placed in command of a composite company of Punjabis and Mussulmen, and it was not until the morning of the 22nd that the Battalion was ordered to head for the bridge and take up position on the west side. About halfway there they unexpectedly came under heavy fire from a Japanese machine gun sited in the Pagoda area. Although men began to fall around him, he pressed on, but one platoon, unnerved by the ordeal at Kuzeik, turned back.

On arrival at the bridgehead garrison Randle decided that the best thing he could do was report to the adjutant of the Frontier Force Rifles who ordered him to reinforce Captain Manekshaw's Company.

Soon afterwards he received orders to withdraw his company across the bridge to the area of a village about a mile to the west of it. "As we crossed we were fired on by some long range and inaccurate Jap machine-gun fire. I recall a splendid Sikh Subedar sitting in the middle of the bridge acting as F.O.O. to a mountain battery who was calling down fire on a large party of Japs we could see moving south down the river from several thousand yards to the north. I also saw the Dukes moving east across the bridge, little knowing that the next day I should be helping what was left of them out of the Sittang."

It did not strike him at the time, but later he reflected "how piteously unprepared the bridgehead garrison was".

"When one considers how important holding this area was to our forces, it was surely a major oversight that more was not done to prepare for what happened – proper trenches dug and wired, or panjis erected – they were bamboo stakes of varying lengths, put out in large numbers around any defensive position to cause injury to anyone approaching. The points were normally hardened by fire, which it was commonly believed made wounds more liable to infection. Fields of fire should also have been cleared with interlocking M.M.G.s and at least pre-registered defensive fire for the mortars. All the sensible requirements of such a situation. The 4/12th Frontier Force Rifles were a first-rate battalion, with a magnificent C.O., Colonel Donnie Edwards, but they were very weak after their battle at Moulmein and I don't think they had been there long. The failure to provide an adequate defence position was no fault of theirs. It would have been far better to have put my battalion to work there too, instead of sitting around in Mokpalin."

In the opinion of an admittedly "raw subaltern", Smyth could have despatched sufficient men, with adequate support weapons, to prepare a strong defensive position at the eastern end of the bridge without seriously weakening his forces at the Bilin.

"The unreliable Burma Rifles should also have been used in a reconnaissance role – as Smyth had wished – guarding the northern and north-eastern flanks of the division and reporting any enemy movements. Failure to take such steps resulted in the enemy being able to arrive without any warning and with complete surprise on what was the jugular vein of the Division. Failure to provide any flank protection was an elementary blunder. This failure was even more reprehensible in the light of the reports from a number of people in my battalion, including me, after we were seen off at Kuzeik, of large bodies of Japanese moving north, up the Salween rather than following up our withdrawal to Duyinzeik and Thaton."

The 1/3rd Gurkhas were harboured near the 2/5th Royal Gurkha Rifles about eight miles from Mokpalin when verbal orders were received for both battalions to withdraw to the bridge. Almost immediately they were caught up in the attack on the transport belonging to the 16th and 46th Brigades. The 2/5th were ordered to clear the high ground to enable the transport to move, and without mortar or artillery support did so with great determination, and although they suffered heavy casualties managed after three attempts to reach Mokpalin station.

Lieutenant-Colonel George Ballinger of 1/3rd and Ronnie Cameron of the 2/5th held a hurried council of war to decide the next move. The "fog", which Kinloch described as "a real pea souper", was such that neither knew what was happening at the bridgehead and assumed, incorrectly, that the enemy held both Buddha and Pagoda Hills, and decided that the 1/3rd should attack both under artillery cover, while the 2/5th held the higher ground at the eastern outskirts of Mokpalin.

Under supporting artillery the 1/3rd Gurkhas swarmed up the slopes employing blitz tactics which accounted for many of the enemy on the lower slopes. When they reached the top they encountered much stronger enemy opposition, but after a period of confused and ferocious hand-to-hand fighting the Japanese were driven back and two companies established a position at the top of the ridge. Two platoons under Captain A. H. McCrae actually gained the bridgehead, but it was a hollow victory. The Gurkhas had not known the 4/12th were still in position, thinking they had been forced to withdraw from Pagoda Hill in face of the artillery barrage.

It was a costly error; if the true position had been known and contact established, Brigadier Hugh-Jones might have been able to mount a joint attack and open the way to the bridge.

As the runners bearing messages were killed before they could deliver them, no one knew what the position was at the bridgehead. All that was known was that the Gurkhas were still fighting as hard as ever, although they were almost out of ammunition and Kinloch had to go back to Mokpalin to collect more. Kinloch who had taken over from the adjutant who had been wounded, said:

"At about noon Colonel Ballinger suddenly turned to me and said, 'Bruce, I would like you to go forward and try and find out what is happening to the forward companies'. I thought, well this is it, this is the end, literally a sentence of death, because I knew the whole jungle between us and the forward companies was crawling with Japanese. I tried to keep my emotions under control and I saluted and said, 'Yes, sir, certainly'. I had only gone a few paces when Colonel Ballinger called me back. 'I've changed my mind. I think it would be better if I went along with the Intelligence section. I'd like to see what's happening myself anyway.'"

Kinloch's sentence to death was commuted.

Colonel Ballinger set off with Subedar-Major Gagan Sing Thapa and a small party of men and encountered a runner from one of the companies who announced that their objectives had been achieved – the road to the bridge was open. Ballinger moved on and almost immediately came across a party of Japanese soldiers standing with their hands above their heads in surrender. One of them bowed low as the Colonel indicated they would be taken prisoner. Then without warning the Japanese flung themselves flat on the ground and machine guns opened fire from the surrounding jungle. Colonel Ballinger and several men fell dead. The remaining Gurkhas managed to escape and make their way back to Battalion Headquarters.

The enemy continued their attacks on the companies pinned down on the two hills, but despite the frenzied attacks the Gurkhas could not be dislodged.

Enough was known, however, to realize that they could not hold on without reinforcements and Major Bradford, who had assumed command, set off with Kinloch to the headquarters of the 16th Brigade. The railway station area was now under a two-pronged attack and the road was a shambles of jammed and burning traffic. But Brigadier J. K.

Jones had no men to spare and he ordered Major Bradford to withdraw his forward companies and hold a fresh position called O.P. Hill.

The condition of the 1/3rd Gurkhas was now desperate; there was a crying need for water and none of the men had eaten since the 19th. The forward companies were almost out of ammunition and fresh supplies were sent up by mules, accompanied by an N.C.O. with orders to withdraw to the new position. But he was unable to get through as the enemy had infiltrated behind them.

Immediately after dark the enemy launched attacks from all directions which continued throughout the night, but all were beaten off with grenades, Bren guns, rifles, pistols, bayonets and kukris. The Japanese adopted their customary terror tactics by employing tracers and firecrackers and these had unexpected results – a Mountain Battery, thinking they were distress signals, laid down a barrage on the pinned-down Gurkhas. Casualties were few but it hardly cheered the men who were finding it difficult enough to contend with a fanatical foe without being subjected to fire from their own side.

At Battalion Headquarters in a stretch of sunken road the Headquarters Company, plus A Company and two platoons of the 2/5th Gurkhas sent to assist in the defence of O.P. Hill, organized an all-round defensive position. Ammunition supplies were maintained by sorties to abandoned vehicles outside the perimeter.

That night, as the situation deteriorated, Brigadier Hugh-Jones strengthened the bridgehead with two companies of the 1/4th G.R. which now meant the defences were manned by the remnants of the Baluchi and Dogra Regiments, the 4/12th F.F.R., some 8th Burma Rifles, a company of the 1/3rd Gurkhas and a company of the Duke of Wellington's Regiment.

Although much of the defence still remained unwired, the positions around the bridge were considered to be quite strong. The enemy kept moving about all night and maintained incessant fire with mortars, grenades and automatic weapons and continued their harassing tactics with patrols which repeatedly bumped the defences. The jitter tactics led to a lot of panic firing and fire discipline in some sections was not all it should have been.

The Company of the Dukes were ordered to take up positions on Bungalow Hill just a little south of Buddha and Pagoda Hills; some time earlier they had been ordered to cross from the west bank and occupy it, only to be withdrawn soon afterwards. They realized it was a grave tactical error for it commanded an important position and should have been defended with the utmost determination. Now they had been ordered to reoccupy it. This they achieved without any opposition.

To the south a separate action was being fought. The 46th Brigade had halted near Meyon Chaung to enable the bulk of the Duke of Wellington's, as rearguard, to catch up. Ignorant of this, the 16th Brigade continued its march and a mile-long gap developed between the two brigades enabling the enemy to slip in and establish a road block. The 3/7th Gurkhas, the leading battalion of the 46th, immediately set about clearing it and soon afterwards the bulk of the brigade was caught up in a heavy mortar and artillery attack, and the ensuing battle quickly degenerated into a number of confused close-quarter encounters in which units became hopelessly mixed and progress to Mokpalin was brought to an abrupt halt.

Brigadier Ekin assembled a force of 500 riflemen and set off through the jungle in an attempt to skirt the road, but it was so dense they soon lost their sense of direction and became split up, and it was late evening before the bulk of the men reached the railway station two miles to the south of Mokpalin.

The move, however, had enabled the Duke of Wellington's and the 3/7th Gurkhas to avoid the block and reach Mokpalin Quarries and link up with the 4th Burma Rifles who had just arrived by train. Soon afterwards Ekin's force was again split up when trying to avoid another enemy column.

The bulk of the 2nd Battalion of the Duke of Wellington's Regiment, who not so long before had been fretting in Peshawar and reflecting that they had "missed the bus", were totally unprepared for the kind of fighting they were pitch-forked into. The only opportunity they had had of firing their hastily issued mortars and anti-tank rifles was over the stern of the ship carrying them to Rangoon, and within days of arrival they had been rushed to Kyaikto to support the withdrawal. They were itching for a fight and were under the impression that they were up against enemy who were "small uneducated men, with poor eyesight and incapable of shooting straight". They looked forward with relish to the task they had been given.

They scraped holes in the hard earth with bayonets and bare hands and prepared for the coming battle. They were subjected to continuous fire from snipers they could not see and they witnessed the unedifying spectacle of some Burma Rifles panicking after a jitter attack. Next afternoon they moved to a rubber plantation near Brigade Headquarters in readiness for withdrawal to the Sittang and were caught up in the straffing and bombing raid by the R.A.F. and A.V.G.

When the withdrawal continued the Dukes were again rearguard. The distance to the bridge was about eighteen miles along the one dusty track, and as the men were carrying full equipment they were quickly exhausted in the intense heat. The Brigade was soon caught in an ambush and the Dukes under heavy fire. In order to reach the bridge the troops were divided and the Dukes were sent through the jungle where they had to link arms to retain contact. They were constantly reminded of their thirst by the tantalizing clank of their empty water bottles, and they were reduced to chewing sugar cane to slake their thirst. Inevitably units were split up and lost contact with each other.

Among those who became separated was the Commanding Officer of the Dukes, Lieutenant-Colonel H. B. Owen who, with a small party, made his way to the river assuming that by the time he and his small party arrived the rest of the troops would be safely over. In total darkness Owen and his men crossed, but by the time he reached the other side he was completely worn out and had lost contact with the others. He found himself alone with his batman and decided to find some food and rest in a nearby village. As he was sleeping in a hut some Dacoits stabbed him to death, although his badly wounded batman managed to escape.

Meanwhile, the remainder of the Dukes managed to reach Mokpalin village only some two miles from the bridge where they were detailed to provide a protective screen for Brigade Headquarters. As it was so dark, Brigadier Jones decided to halt for the night and, anticipating surprise attacks, picketed the road to the bridge. Again the Dukes dug in with their bayonets and hands and were once more subjected to relentless sniping. Men who a short time before had been suffering from heat exhaustion were now freezing, for the night turned bitterly cold and they had no blankets or greatcoats, and had been without food and water for a considerable period. Sleep, however, was out of the question as a mountain battery maintained a continuous barrage. But the sound was comforting to the pinned-down men who calmly and patiently waited for dawn. With the bridge so near they knew that it would not be long before they were on the "right" side of the Sittang.

General Hutton was becoming desperately concerned about what was happening. A series of urgent messages were sent to Divisional Headquarters but they did not appear to be getting through. All he knew was contained in a progress report he had received from Smyth dated 14.00 on the 22nd:

> "Heavy fighting going on East side Sittang River. Enemy shelling our bridgehead with quite heavy guns and appears to be attacking strongly. So far have only got 1/4th G.R. over complete but oddments of other battalions are trickling in. Situation appears to be serious. Have no communication either 16th Infantry Brigade or 46th Infantry Brigade, but they are obviously very strongly engaged."

Hutton, in a message that got through, requested Smyth to meet him at a rendezvous halfway between Sittang and Rangoon. Smyth did not think it was an appropriate time to hold a conference, but he agreed to be there. When night came he left Hugh-Jones at the bridgehead and returned to his Operational Headquarters to have a meal and snatch a little sleep before setting off early next morning to meet the Army Commander.

For some time Brigadier Hugh-Jones had been increasingly alarmed at the failure of the two brigades to get through to the bridge and he was gnawed by fears that the enemy might storm the bridge and break up the concentration of the 7th Armoured Brigade which had landed at Rangoon. To avert this the bridge might have to be destroyed.

As reports spread that the bridge was about to be blown, every effort was made to contact the cut-off brigades. Horns were sounded, whistles blown, headlights switched on and off and voices raised in song and battle cries. All failed, although the nearest of the isolated troops were only 500 yards away. There was, however, one effective way of making contact — by patrol — but this was not resorted to, although it was suggested.

By now the tension was unbearable and several of the Burma Rifles deserted their posts and scuttled across the bridge in total disorder.

More stragglers began to arrive, confirming Hugh-Jones's worst fears; perimeter defences were being overrun, recaptured at bayonet point only to be lost again.

Before he settled down for a brief rest, Smyth had sent "Punch" Cowan to talk things over with Hugh-Jones, and he had returned conscious of how touch-and-go the situation now was. Cowan was not comforted by the knowledge of just how strong the enemy forces were, for a Japanese officer had been shot and a signal plan for two divisions had been found in his possession which indicated that the enemy was in far greater strength than had been realized. Doubts began to assail him; the retreat from the Bilin should have been made earlier and with greater speed; Smyth should not have established his own headquarters so far from the bridge. He had expressed his doubts about the wisdom of this, but Smyth had not agreed with him.

At 2 am. Brigadier Hugh-Jones summoned Captain Richard Orgill, Malerkotla Sappers, the officer responsible for preparing the bridge for demolition, and asked him if it could be successfully blown during daylight, but the engineer was unable to give him any guarantee.

The possiblity of the bridge having to be destroyed had occurred to General Hutton some time before and he had issued orders for engineers to prepare it for demolition. He had also foreseen the importance of providing adequate water transport to enable troops to cross over: 300 sampans had been bought and two power-driven vessels had been sited near the bridge, and ramps built on either bank. But Colonel A. E. "Tuffet" Armitage, the C.R.E. of the 17th Division, had ordered their destruction in order to prevent them falling into enemy hands when the first attack was launched. So if the bridge was blown the second line of evacuation no longer existed.

But an even worse shock was the discovery that the bridge was not even prepared for demolition; the explosives had been removed by the 1st Artisan Works Company to enable the boarding of the bridge to be carried out safely, and the Sappers who were responsible for the job in the first place had been withdrawn for other duties, a decision which mystified Hutton when he heard about it. "I have never discovered who, if anyone, gave orders for the Sappers and Miners to be withdrawn from the bridge," he insisted.

It was, therefore, a remarkable achievement that it was blown at all. Smyth, until shortly before his death, was still under the impression that the work had been carried out by Hutton's Sappers.

It was, in fact, an eleventh-hour job which was tackled with immense bravery and coolness by a handful of men from the Malerkotla Sappers and Miners.

The bridge over the Sittang consisted of eleven spans each of 150 feet, but when an inspection was carried out it was found that only the centre one had been prepared for demolition and that not very thoroughly. The boxes which had been prepared by the Artisan Works Company were no longer in position and the explosives had been removed and stacked away.

Captain Richard Orgill was summoned by Colonel Armitage and told to have the bridge ready for demolition by the evening of 22 February. Orgill inspected it and decided that at least three spans would have to be blown, and he assembled a party of officers, N.C.O.s and fifteen sappers to carry the explosives and prepare the charges. Men from the Artisan Works Company were also enlisted to retrieve the explosives which were stored in safe places. The party worked throughout the night, and by 10 am at least one span was ready and Orgill assured Armitage that the rest would be completed by 6 pm. Throughout the hours of daylight the men were continually sniped at and bullets regularly clanged against the girders. But casualties were minimal, which was surprising as some of the men were working astride girders high above the river and a sitting target for any marksman.

Colonel Armitage, who had gone through a very harassing period, did not impress the hard-working Malerkotlas with his enthusiasm. Lieutenant Bashir Ahmad Khan recalled: "Colonel Armitage, who was only seen once, in a much disturbed and tired condition, left everything to Captain Orgill."

Faced with numerous technical difficulties which included a shortage of cable fuses and explosives, Orgill decided that the actual firing point would have to be on the bridge itself, some distance from the west bank.

Before the work was completed, Brigadier Hugh-Jones withdrew the bridgehead forces and instructed Orgill to be ready to blow. The firing party took up position, but the order was not given.

Then at about 2 am on the 23rd Hugh-Jones again consulted Orgill and asked him, if the bridge was not destroyed in the dark, could it be done in daylight. The captain said he could not give him a complete assurance but he would have a try.

Lieutenant Roy Hudson, who helped to prepare the bridge, who was to have been "firing officer" until he was relieved and who is one of the two surviving officers of the unit, listed a catalogue of blunders that made the disaster that followed inevitable:

The tactical mistake in not making sure the 17th Indian Division was over the bridge; the failure to check that the bridge was not ready for demolition and, when this became apparent, the dilatoriness of the C.R.E. in not correcting it until it was almost too late; Brigadier Hugh-Jones asking Orgill the wrong questions; Major-General Smyth considering it more important to leave the bridge site to attend the meeting with Hutton instead of remaining at a Forward Command Post until the battle was decided.

Some time between 4.30 and 5 am, Orgill was told by Hugh-Jones that he had decided the bridge was to be destroyed as soon as the bridgehead forces had been withdrawn. Lieutenant-Bashir Ahmad Khan was given the unenviable role of being in charge of the firing party and three sappers prepared a firing pit under the abutment wall from which he could operate the exploder. "A Gurkha officer, in charge of a Vickers gun, was stationed in the middle of the bridge to provide covering fire and give the final order. He gave the order and withdrew his gun team, leaving the bridge deserted except for a handful of men entrusted with the task of destroying it."

At 4.30 that morning "Punch" Cowan received a telephone call over a bad line from an "hysterical" staff officer of 48 Brigade informing him that the bridge could not be held for another hour and seeking a definite order to blow or not. Cowan asked if Jonah – the nickname for Jones, the Commander of the 16th Brigade – was safely over the bridge and he was told, yes. He immediately woke Major-General Smyth and passed on the message and it took him less than five minutes to give the go-ahead, leaving the actual time to the discretion of Hugh-Jones.

Smyth then despatched an urgent signal to Hutton:

"Now clear that bulk of division have ceased to exit. Have so far only got over the bridge two formed battalions but odd troops continue to arrive. Obvious that bulk of tpt (*sic*) have been lost. Am still holding bridge but must blow very early hour today when it is considered that all who can do so have crossed."

He then set off for his meeting.

Hugh-Jones immediately began to withdraw the bridgehead troops. Orders that the bridge was to be destroyed had arrived on the east side at about 0330 hours and the troops were told to take off their boots and make their way as silently as possible over the bridge. Colonel Edwards and the Frontier Force Rifles were almost the last to go. Remaining behind were the two sections in the sandbagged emplacements on the bridge. Then a telephone message came through that the sappers were still not quite ready and the remaining troops were told to hang on. For fifteen minutes, unknown to the enemy, all that stood between them and the bridge were two sections of troops.

Lieutenant Bashir Ahmad Khan recalled, "After lighting the safety fuses I jumped into the firing pit and exploded electronically. The electric circuit worked. The explosions were enormous and nearby trees lost their leaves and our little fox hole was filled with water." The time was 5.30 am.

Two spans toppled into the river while a third was badly damaged. Immediately a deathly silence blanketed the battlefield. Stranded on the "wrong" side of the river was two-thirds of the Division, just when they were in sight of the bridge.

As dawn was breaking "Punch" Cowan went to survey the scene of devastation and half an hour after the explosions he was holding a conference with Brigadier Hugh-Jones and Colonel Lentaigne when an Indian officer swam across with an urgent message in code marked "Jonah to Punch" – "I am attacking the bridge at first light". It was in response to a message from Cowan that had reached the troops at Mokpalin. "Friends waiting to welcome you at east gate."*

Cowan recalled, "When Brigadier Hugh-Jones read the signal he broke down and I then put Lentaigne in temporary command of all troops on our side of the Sittang."

---

* Controversy still exists over the message that was received just prior to the demolition. The Official History states that when Cowan asked if "Johah" was over the officer mistook it for Brigadier Hugh-Jones. Cowan, however, was adamant that there was no such mix-up, for Hugh-Jones was invariably referred to as Noel.

CHAPTER 12

"There is no doubt that the battle of the River Sittang was nothing less than a disaster"

Lieutenant-General Hutton

The three shattering explosions were clearly heard above the crack of rifles, the chatter of machine guns and the crump of mortar shells, and a bright tangerine glow suffused the sky. The troops fighting doggedly towards the Sittang did not need to be told what it meant; the bridge had been blown and their only avenue of retreat cut off.

Captain Bruce Kinloch heard the detonations with mounting anger. "We had been sacrificed, abandoned and left to our fate for reasons which in the circumstances we just could not comprehend. A few minutes after the explosions a complete and eerie silence fell on the battlefield. Not a sound could be heard. It was literally a stunned silence. It was a silence of mounting fury and disbelief, of seething resentment and anger. My own fury was not directed at the enemy but at our own senior commanders who had been responsible for blowing the bridge. We felt the senior commanders had panicked and let us down."

The lull in the fighting was short-lived. A solitary shot rang out and immediately the battle was resumed with undiminished ferocity while aircraft appeared overhead and resumed their straffing.

Kinloch's thoughts echoed those of most of the men who felt that panic from the top had robbed them of achieving their objective. "I was determined I was not going to be taken prisoner. I felt this was the end, that I was going to die; I was quite certain of it."

It was an attitude most of the Gurkhas shared, but coupled with the resignation was a fierce determination to take as many Japs with them as possible.

Although the battle area was relatively small the lack of communications meant that the Gurkhas defending the area around the bridge had no idea how many troops were stranded on the "wrong" side, and Kinloch decided the only way to find out was to drive to Mokpalin. On arrival he was relieved to find that the bulk of the two brigades were still holding a horseshoe-shaped line of defence. There he managed to obtain some water and one biscuit each for the Gurkhas who had not eaten for five days.

Brigadier Jones could not see the bridge, but he had heard the explosions and promptly abandoned his plan for a dawn attack on the bridge, and, realizing that a crossing during daylight was courting disaster, decided to hold his positions until night, then gradually thin out so that it could be made under cover of darkness. He hoped that this could be completed by the following morning. Meanwhile he detailed all men who could be spared from the fighting line to gather material for the building of rafts and floats.

He also gave orders for the 1/3rd Gurkhas, supported by a company of the Duke of Wellington's, to hold their positions near the bridge until the wounded and the remainder of the troops had crossed. The 2/5th Gurkhas were to hold the high ground to the east.

Soon after Kinloch returned to the battalion the Gurkhas were once more in action when about thirty Japanese soldiers were spotted marching along the railway line between O.P. and Pagoda Hills and only 150 yards from Battalion Headquarters.

"We waited until we had a good opportunity and then we opened fire with L.M.G.s and Tommy-guns and the result was quite dramatic, because we killed most of them and the survivors rolled down the bank into the jungle. This was followed by a very strong attack on our flank which again resulted in heavy losses to them. The mortars which we had managed to scrounge out of the transport provided very accurate fire indeed on the Japs and we reckoned this was one of the hardest single blows we gave to them on the Sittang," said Kinloch.

Those who had already reached the east bank of the river began to strip in readiness to swim the swollen river. Weapons were thrown into the water as there was no possible chance of getting across burdened with a rifle and ammunition. Many of the men removed their boots for added buoyancy, although the wiser ones tied them round their necks knowing they might need them for the gruelling march that lay ahead.

Within minutes the river was covered by a mass of bobbing heads. Men were swept away never to be seen again. Many became exhausted when they were half-way across and were drowned. Cramp claimed many more. Others decided to let the current do the work and allowed themselves to be carried downstream until they were beached. Non-swimmers sat dejectedly on the bank contemplating the options available, either fight to the last or be taken prisoner.

During the withdrawal the British soldiers had seen that when it came to personal courage the Gurkha had no equal. But at the Sittang they found that they did have one fear – water – for few had learned to swim. They saw them eyeing the roaring water and debating silently with themselves whether it would not be better to die fighting than try to get across. The British soldiers and the Gurkhas' own officers owed them too much to abandon them, and they did their utmost to get as many over as possible. Improvised life-jackets were made of empty petrol cans which were lashed round the chests of the Gurkhas with puttees, while swimmers gave up their berths on rafts. Even the doors of houses were utilized and kept afloat with water bottles.

On the "safe" side, John Randle was supervising a party of men who were helping exhausted swimmers ashore. "On the way I passed Brigadier Hugh-Jones, ashen-faced and in a state of collapse, being physically supported by Lieutenant-Colonel Donnie Edwards of the 4/12th Frontier Force Rifles. Three weeks later I was in a hospital ship going up the Irrawaddy and I saw Brigadier Hugh-Jones again – his hair had gone white with the shock of it all."

The greatest suffering was endured by the wounded who knew they had no chance of reaching the other side by their own efforts. The Regimental Aid Posts and ambulances were packed with men suffering from the most appalling injuries, many of which were already septic. The desperately overworked medical officers did what they could with the limited facilities. Orderlies applied crude field dressings to wounds which needed hospital attention, while doctors carried out hasty amputations in conditions that would have shocked critics of field hospitals in the Crimea.

In a situation where everyone could have been forgiven for adopting an "every man for himself" attitude, there was a remarkable and moving display of self-sacrifice among those who had escaped un-scathed. They accepted without demur that the wounded should have priority, and they took the injured men down to the bank without a thought for their own survival. Those who were unable to walk were dragged along the ground on blankets, carried or supported by comrades. The majority, however, had to make their own way as best they could, and a long procession of crawling, hobbling and tottering men was soon winding its way slowly to the river.

The KOYLI were still in position when daylight broke. The jungle around them was swarming with unseen Japanese who kept up a relentless attack.

Morale had slumped and an air of panic had set in among the men who were sorely tempted to make a dash for the river. Colonel Keegan knew that such a move would be disastrous and he decided to set an example by strolling casually from one company to another offering a word of comfort or cracking a joke. He kept it up for several hours, and the sight of his rotund figure looking so composed and relaxed had an electrifying effect on his men, who immediately shed all thoughts of abandoning their posts and prepared themselves to fight to the last round. Many died holding the position, but their stubborn resistance enabled a large number who would otherwise have been trapped to get through to the river. As the Regimental History records, "Any man who was there will tell you that if only the rest of the division had stayed put, the Japanese would have been whacked."

Meanwhile the Gurkhas and the company Duke of Wellington's were still fighting vigorously and holding their positions around the eastern end of the bridge. They were desperately thirsty and hungry, for the lorries containing the rations had been looted and all that had been recovered was a case of biscuits and a few loaves. Around midday it was decided to evacuate the wounded to the river, and this was supervised by Lieutenant Sundaram, a young Indian doctor, whose dedicated care of the wounded and reckless disregard for his own safety was rewarded with an M.C.

Throughout the day the Japanese tried to infiltrate the 1/3rd Gurkhas position but were repulsed. Then in the afternoon there was another tragic error on the part of the R.A.F. A force of Blenheim bombers attacked the bridgehead positions and straffed the Battalion

Headquarters. As a result of the intensive bombing, Brigadier Jones decided to alter his plans – instead of waiting till 2030 hours to withdraw the bulk of his men he advanced the time to 1430 which meant a crossing in daylight, the one thing he had been anxious to avoid.

At Mokpalin the battle had continued unabated, with Japanese fighters swooping down at treetop height to machine-gun the hemmed-in troops, while mortars maintained a non-stop barrage.

The enemy launched attack after attack, but the defences held, apart from some Burma Rifles who broke and made for the river. The four mortars of the KOYLI fired until all the ammunition was expended; even then the crews, with total disregard to their own safety and in defiance of all safety regulations, continued to fire dud shells at the enemy.

Some ammunition belonging to a Mountain Battery caught fire and exploded, immediately attracting the attention of enemy bombers which dropped their loads right into the heart of the fire.

The fighting continued until the order to begin the withdrawal was given at 2.30 pm.

Earlier, Colonel Cameron had reconnoitred the river bank and found a suitable track to the river near a fishing village not far from a spot named Farewell House. But, apart from two small dug-out canoes, there were no boats, and there was little bamboo along the bank with which to make rafts, which meant that material would have to be carried down from the Mokpalin area.

Just as the withdrawal was about to start, enemy mortars hit an ammunition dump and the fire quickly spread to the transport, much of which contained ammunition, which was clogging the road. To Cameron this presented encouraging possibilities; if the entire column was set on fire it would provide a perfect barrage to cover the withdrawal. Every available man was fallen in while Cameron hurriedly explained his intentions. Then he described the route to be taken to the river. As they passed through the bazaar every man was to help himself to as much bamboo as he could. Once they reached the river bank rafts were to be assembled while swimmers were to give every assistance to non-swimmers.

Lieutenant-Colonel Charles Bagot, MC,
Gloucestershire Regiment

O. D. Gallagher of the *Daily Express*

Leland Stowe of the *Chicago Daily News*

Lieutenant-Colonel Tony Mains, 9th
Gurkha Rifles

CQGM George Biggs, MM,
Gloucestershire Regiment

Sir Reginald Dorman-Smith with three Chinese generals

Major Bashir Ahmad Khan, Royal Indian
Engineers

Captain John Randle, Baluch Regiment

The Sittang Bridge

Major-General J. G. Smyth, VC, MC

Major-General D. T. C. (Punch) Cowan, DSO, MC

Men of the 7th Hussars with their 'Honey' tank

The faces of the soldiers were grim and determined as they started their hazardous journey, but there was no sign of panic. By then most of the transport was burning and the ammunition exploding at regular intervals. The inferno of flame and noise which provided such excellent cover was still raging more than an hour later. But by the time the rearguard troops had reached the embarkation area – a small stretch of beach opposite Farewell House and downstream of the bridge – it was obvious to Cameron that the cover of burning lorries and exploding ammunition would not last until everyone was over. The congestion was steadily mounting and a large number of the rafts were still uncompleted. While the Subedar-Major chivvied the weary raftmakers into greater activity, Jemadar Dhirbahadur Guring and a volunteer from the Jats who were still holding the Farewell House area headed back towards the enemy and set fire to a long line of bamboo huts which soon provided replacement cover.

Shortly afterwards, Lieutenant Sundaram reported that all but five of the casualties were either across or on their way. He was just putting the finishing touches to a raft made from bamboo, petrol tins and empty water bottles when two KOYLI arrived supporting a badly wounded Colonel Keegan whose luck had finally run out.

Cameron was faced with a harsh and heart-breaking decision; the raft could only carry two men, but would support three on either side if they were capable of clinging one with one hand while swimming with the other. One place was allocated to Colonel Keegan and another to a Gurkha who, although badly concussed, was likely to recover. Space was also given to another Gurkha with a shattered arm, but who was capable of clinging on with his other. The remaining places were given to a 1/3rd Gurkha who had provided the petrol tins, an officer of the 1/7th Gurkhas, Jemadar Dhirbahadur, Lieutenant Sundaram and Lieutenant-Colonel Cameron. Two Gurkha officers and a rifleman had to be left; even in more favourable conditions it was extremely unlikely that they would have survived. Cameron, who was the only swimmer, launched the precarious raft with the assistance of Lieutenant Sundaram and their effort encouraged many waverers to set off on their own, among them fifty or more non-swimmers.

It took more than two hours to propel the raft across, but as soon as it was beached Lieutenant Sundaram volunteered to return to fetch the two Gurkha officers and rifleman.

Among the last to reach the river were the KOYLI who carried their wounded through the blazing village and were extremely relieved to find the enemy was not showing any great desire to pursue them. As they passed through the village they tore down planks and uprooted anything else that was suitable for raft-making. The men retained commendable discipline as they waited to cross, and some passed the time throwing abandoned arms and equipment into the river.

Major Doyle, the adjutant, who had been shot through the groin and was bleeding profusely, straddled a stout bamboo pole and managed to get across with the assistance of Lance-Corporal A. Porter who kept a watchful eye on him from astern.

Feats of incredible courage and endurance were commonplace but few equalled the efforts of Captain E. D. Wardleworth of the KOYLI. After having a shoulder wound dressed, he made his way to the river with the wounded and remnants of his company, then swam over to find a boat in which to ferry the wounded. He found one, plugged the hole in it and brought it back. Having handed it over he swam back again to organize rescue parties.

Captain R. Howden, in agony from a shattered leg, was lifted tenderly into the boat and when he was settled several more wounded were helped aboard, together with some non-swimmers, and the boat was cast off. But it sank when only fifteen yards out and Howden, despite his wound, swam back to the bank. The boat was salvaged and patched up and the party set off once more, with Howden baling with his hat and non-swimmers clinging to the side. Eventually it reached the west bank where Howden was placed on a door and carried along the railway line until an engine was found and he was placed on the coal in the tender and driven to Waw. Three days later, when he arrived in Mandalay, his leg was amputated, as gangrene had set in.

Private D. A. Price, who was suffering from multiple shrapnel wounds, made a raft of some pieces of wood and fishing poles and, with five non-swimmers clinging to the side, pushed it across the river. Price could hardly stand when he stepped ashore, but someone handed him a bottle of beer which he nonchalantly opened with his teeth, drank, and then walked barefoot the 25 miles to Waw.

The Dukes had fought with a tenacity that was in keeping with their proud tradition but they had suffered grievous casualties. Many admit they would not have made it to the river but for the personal example set by Major "Bull" Faithfull who had taken over as C.O. following the murder of Colonel Owen.

Faithful, an International and Army rugby player, a superb boxer and an outstanding swimmer, walked along the river bank where his men stood in nervous and uncertain groups studying the swirling current and literally bullied and coaxed them into taking to the water. There was nothing to it, he roared. And they believed him.

Tony Firth and a KOYLI private made a raft of bamboo, stripped down to their vest and pants and carefully lifted a wounded soldier aboard. "We swam and pushed the raft ahead of us and when we reached the far bank I was glad I had kept my .45 pistol for there were a lot of evil-looking Burmans around with their dahs, which they were not using for domestic purposes."

Firth managed to get aboard a train which was taking men of the 17th Division to Pegu where it was proposed to rearm and re-equip them in order to renew the battle. "I sat next to the C.O. of the Jats, shaking with fever and clad only in a GS blanket, who told me that the Jemadar with him was the one who had found the body of our murdered C.O., Lieutenant-Colonel Owen. The Jemadar said he had taken a suitable toll of the villagers."

Throughout the whole of the night men continued to arrive at the west bank in twos and threes and in small parties, when any hope of reorganizing on the spot was out of the question and they had to make their own way as best as possible towards Waw, the fit carrying the wounded.

Still gallantly holding their positions near the bridge, the 1/3rd Gurkhas and the attached Dukes heard the sound of heavy firing and explosions from the direction of Mokpalin and prepared themselves for another attack. But when nothing happened Major Bradford and Captain Kinloch decided to drive there and find out what was happening. When they got there they discovered the sound had come from the burning lorries and exploding ammunition; the troops had withdrawn.

Major Bradford decided the time had come to pull out and head for the river; the mules were released and the Battalion formed up and headed due west through the jungle. The river was reached without incident. Some 800 yards below the bridge they came across the wounded and a few stragglers who had still not crossed, and a defensive perimeter was formed near a cliff while parties were detailed to prepare rafts.

Kinloch studied the bridge through his binoculars. "I could see clearly that only the two middle spans had been blown and they had settled down in the river forming part of a V and it looked to me that it should be possible to get control of the bridgehead on our side and it wouldn't be too difficult in the darkness to get men to run along the bridge and clamber across the broken spans. So I thought I would go and have a look.

"It was all very quiet, strangely so, and I wandered carefully along the bank to see what was around me, but all I could see were corpses bobbing in the current at the edge of the river and the odd soldier, mostly Indian sepoys and the odd British rank, wandering about rather vaguely with shell shock. I eventually got to the actual bridgehead where there was a sandbagged position. From that point there was a track leading to Pagoda and Buddha Hills and I decided to walk up and find a spot we could move to. I carried my binoculars round my neck on a short strap with two Mills grenades with the pins flattened for ease of withdrawal in the canvas case. I left my Tommy-gun behind, but I did have my .38 Smith & Wesson with which I was a pretty good shot in those days. I strolled up the track leading to the pagoda; there was jungle on either side and after about 100 yards I came across a very large tree. In the shadow of a fork I could see what appeared to be the outline of a British steel helmet. Then I realized we had evacuated the area and I whipped out my pistol and challenged just to make sure, and the head disappeared. I ran straight up to the trunk, crouched against it and as cautiously as I could peered round the left-hand side. I found myself facing, literally face-to-face at a range of about five feet, a Japanese officer wearing a peaked cap, leather boots and a sword. I reached into my binocular pouch, removed a grenade, pulled the pin out with my teeth, counted four and as the smoke started to go from it rolled it in a bowling action round the tree. There was a pause, followed by a gasp and the scutter of feet, then a shattering explosion. There was a brief silence and then from every direction light machine guns opened up on me. Japs hidden in the jungle had been waiting for me to walk into a trap. Just to make things worse the heavy Vickers machine guns which had been set up on the other side of the river to cover any last crossers opened fire. I did 100 yards in eight seconds flat."

Despite the presence of the Japanese he was still not convinced that the bridgehead could not be taken and when he returned to the Battalion he suggested to Major Jack Robinson, the officer commanding the Duke of Wellington's, that he could clear it with two platoons. The Gurkhas were too exhausted to be asked to tackle it. He readily agreed and Kinloch advanced with the two platoons along the river bank until the bridgehead was almost reached. One platoon occupied the sandbagged position, while Kinloch and a young soldier crawled up the almost sheer bank of the railway cutting. "He was just that much quicker and more enthusiastic than I was, and obviously far less cautious, because he was crawling fast with a grenade in his hand with the pin out. He got to the top just ahead of me when there was a whip-like crack of a rifle shot and I saw him turn round and slither past me with his eyes wide open, and he said as he went past, 'They're just over the top, sir'. Then his hand opened and the grenade with the pin out rolled down among troops below. I don't know how many casualties it caused, but we hugged the bank as a veritable hail of mortar bombs, grenades and machine-gun and rifle fire poured down on us and on the platoon in the sandbagged position. All the time I could hear the bubbling sound of the young lad dying; he had been shot through the chest and his lungs were filling with blood."

The two platoons were forced to retire to the river bank where men had been organized into raft-making parties. But most of the rafts proved quite useless and sank when launched with a heavy loss of life, and it was decided to stop for a while.

As most of the Duke of Wellington's could swim, they parted from the Gurkhas and decided to make their own way across the river. Major Jack Robinson was convinced that the bridge could still be crossed. He had earlier inspected it and found that only one span had been completely blown and in this section there was a gap of only twenty yards and a small party had been sent to try and work their way over by sliding down the near girder, crossing the gap and clambering up the far girder; but fire from the enemy had been intense and few had succeeded. A second attempt had fared no better, but in the dark a fresh attempt might succeed. He detailed men to collect as much rope as possible to form a life-line between the broken spans. But not enough rope could be found so he, with Corporal A. Fox and Lance-Corporal R. Roebuck, swam the 1100 yards to the west bank and returned with more rope. They completed the life-line under continuous fire from Pagoda Hill and as soon as it was dark the company, including non-swimmers and some 500 Indian and Gurkha troops who had joined them, successfully reached the far bank. Throughout, Robinson, Fox and Roebuck remained in the water to encourage the non-swimmers.

A considerable number of 1/3rd Gurkhas, however, were still stranded on the river bank and it was decided that an attempt should be made to recover some boats which had been spotted through binoculars on the far side; if these could be retrieved some sort of ferry service could be organized. Captain Kinloch, Lieutenant Barney Darley and Lieutenant Mackenzie, an officer from the 21st Mountain Battery who was attached to the Battalion, volunteered to make the crossing.

"We made a tiny raft out of bits of wood lashed to water carriers with rifle slings, which was just big enough to carry our clothing and pistols, and when darkness fell we started to swim over," said Kinloch. "It took us something like an hour and a quarter to get across. We then started looking for serviceable boats, but those we found were riddled with bullets or had had the bottoms chopped through to prevent them falling into Jap hands."

After considerable searching they found a large boat – a sampan, complete with paddles – which they managed to get to the east side. It was quickly loaded with wounded and Kinloch and Mackenzie took it back over. Then Kinloch, with Lieutenant Headley from the Burma Rifles and a British private, took the boat back to collect more men. When the boat was full it was taken back by Headley and the B.O.R., while Kinloch remained behind to discuss the next move. With just one boat available it was obvious that only the wounded could be evacuated and a conference was held at which it was agreed to move the troops along the bank and lie up in the jungle and attempt to cross the next night.

As Kinloch and Darley had left their boots on the far side and were in no fit state to march in the jungle, it was decided they would wait for the boat to return and cross with the remaining wounded.

"When dawn broke we saw thankfully that there was a heavy mist lying right across the river which hid it from the Japs and acted as a smoke screen. We moved down and caught sight of the boat appearing out of the mist, and we loaded the rest of the wounded and crossed over. One or two were in a very bad state, and I remember one poor Gurkha rifleman with his brains literally oozing out of the back of his head, and I went so far as cocking my pistol and pointing it at his head, but just at that moment I heard the creak of bullock carts and the doctor arrived so I held my fire."

Kinloch and Darley decided to return with the sampan and collect enough men to retrieve some boats which had been reported to be on the west bank some distance downstream. In this way it was hoped to rescue the rest of the battalion. Tragically, before the plan could be put into operation firing was heard from the east side and through his field glasses Kinloch saw large numbers of enemy troops swarming out of the jungle. In desperation some of the Gurkhas dived into the water and tried to swim across under intense fire.

Major Bradford and the remainder of the Gurkhas put up a short but stout resistance until it was obvious that they faced certain annihilation if they fought on. Knowing that the thought of surrender was abhorrent to the Gurkhas as long as they still had some ammunition and their kukris, Bradford turned apologetically to Subedar-Major Gagan Sing Thapa and said, "I'm afraid we shall have to surrender". The Subedar-Major disagreed. He had been a soldier for thirty years and had no intention of surrendering to a pack of diminutive Japs. For the first and only time in his service he deliberately disobeyed an order from a British officer. As a smiling Japanese officer walked up to Bradford to disarm him, Gagan Sing roared a Gurkhali obscenity and fired his revolver at the Jap. The officer immediately shot Bradford, mortally wounding him. A Gurkha Naik then shot the Japanese officer through the head while the Subedar-Major turned his revolver on himself and shot himself through the heart.

The remainder of the battalion were marched to Mokpalin station where the officers and men were separated before being taken into captivity.

Kinloch and Darley observed the tragic scene through their glasses and, not knowing that some of the Gurkhas had managed to cross the bridge with the Dukes, assumed that they and the seventy men who had been ferried over were the sole survivors. The two officers set off across country with a party of about thirty men from different units to try and locate the division.

Kinloch said, "With the help of two Burma riflemen we managed to get some food from a village; the first meal that many of the men had had for several days. Very tired and weary, and moving across the paddy fields in extreme heat, most of us wanted to sleep on our feet. I remember stepping into a thorn bush and feeling a stab in my leg; I wondered how on earth there could be a thorn bush in a paddy field. Then I looked down and saw a two-foot-long snake coiled round my left leg, its teeth sunk into my ankle. Anyway, Barney very gallantly sucked the wound which was all he could do. My leg swelled up quite a bit, but I managed to keep going through the night. Eventually at about 2230, having marched for nine hours, a voice with a broad Glaswegian accent suddenly came out of the darkness, 'Halt, who goes there? What's the password?' 'I don't know any . . . password,' I said angrily. That obviously convinced him that I couldn't possibly be Japanese, so he allowed us through.''

For his gallantry at the Sittang, Kinloch was awarded an immediate Military Cross.

For several days men continued to straggle into Waw and it was obvious that the 17th Division had ceased to exist as an effective fighting force. When there was little or no hope of further survivors turning up, a roll call was taken which revealed the immensity of the disaster. Some 5000 men had been killed, were missing or had been captured. All that remained of the original division were eighty British officers, sixty-nine Indian and Gurkha officers, and 3335 other ranks. Between them they could only muster 1420 rifles, fifty-six light machine guns and sixty-two Tommy-guns. A number of guns had been lost, along with most of the transport, while most of the survivors had no boots and possessed no clothing other than what they stood in.

The 1/3rd Gurkhas and the 2/5th Gurkhas had suffered such severe losses that the two battalions were amalgamated under Lieutenant-Colonel R. T. Cameron and were called the 5/3rd Gurkha Rifles. The KOYLI could only muster eighty officers and men, and the Duke of Wellington's about 400. For a short time the two battalions became a composite battalion called the King's Own Dukes. The 1/7th and 3/7th Gurkhas became the 7th Gurkhas while the 7/10th Baluch, 5/17th Dogras, 4/12th Frontier Force, 3rd, 4th and 8th Burma Rifles were linked and commanded by Colonel Edwards.

Because the losses had been so high the various brigades were also restructured. The weary and tattered remnants withdrew to Pegu where strenuous efforts were made to re-arm and re-equip them for the fighting that lay ahead. There a desperate search was made to collect every available weapon and the arms were even removed from local police stations. Some men found that they were expected to face the enemy with pre-South African War carbines. Understandably they were highly critical of Major-General Smyth and Brigadier Hugh-Jones who they believed had panicked and blown the bridge too early.

Smyth shrugged off their criticisms in a manner that did nothing to alleviate their resentment. By some odd process of reasoning which they found incomprehensible, he implied that they owed their survival to the destruction of the bridge.

After his meeting with Hutton, Smyth returned to Headquarters. "Almost immediately after the bridge had been blown the firing died down and the Japanese pressure was relaxed. They had failed in their object of capturing the bridge and had suffered heavy casualties, particularly in the bridgehead area, and at once they started to withdraw and move up river to effect another crossing, but the Sittang was broad and swift and I realized we had gained an invaluable respite.

"Unhindered, except for a little desultory rifle fire at long range, some 3000 of our men on the far bank were able to swim or raft themselves over. I was able to drive my divisional car close to the river bank without a shot being fired at me."

The men who had managed to get across would not have described the firing they encountered as desultory.

In fact the bridge was not as vital as Smyth considered it to be, for the Japanese, who were not dependent on motorized transport, merely headed up-river and forded it. It delayed them, but the loss of time was more than compensated for by the knowledge that the retreating army was nowhere near as formidable as it had been before the disaster.

Ironically it took the *Daily Express* Military Reporter in distant London to put the bridge in its proper perspective. "At this time of the year the river is at a low level and with the Japanese weight of numbers, as well as their skill in crossing water, the Sittang might prove a fairly easy obstacle.

CHAPTER 13

"I suddenly began to see that a scapegoat would be required for the Burma disaster"

Sir John Smyth

Major-General Smyth was virtually alone in thinking he had made the right decision to demolish the bridge. General Wavell made no attempt to disguise his anger:

"The battle of the Sittang bridgehead on February 22nd and 23rd really sealed the fate of Rangoon and lower Burma. From reports of this operation which I have studied I have no doubt that the withdrawal from the Bilin river to west of the Sittang was badly mismanaged by the headquarters of the 17th Indian Division, and that the disaster which resulted in the loss of almost two complete brigades ought never to have occurred."

It was still debatable that the fate of Burma had been sealed, but there was no question that Smyth's brilliant career had come to a tragic end, a fact of which Smyth was blissfully unaware as the 17th Division was reorganizing at Pegu.

On 25 February he sat down and wrote a confidential letter to Hutton:

"My dear General,
    The medical board held on me on 11.2.42 whilst agreeing that I was quite fit to carry on, recommended that I should be given two months' leave as early as I could be spared. As my division has now been so much reduced in numbers . . . I am writing to ask if I could have that leave as early as you could spare me. I should have hated to have asked for it whilst active operations were in progress or had there not been a really efficient substitute in Punch Cowan ready to

step into my shoes. I have, however, had rather more than an ordinary strain and do feel very much in need of a rest.

"I have also had to conduct a series of withdrawals since I have been in command of the division which are always lowering to the morale of troops and I feel they would perhaps do better under new management. The war is going to be a long one and I hope that you may, if you do not think I have done too badly, change me for someone in India where I can have a bit of a rest and be ready for an active command again."

It was an ill-timed letter. Hutton was hardly in the frame of mind to deal with requests for leave from a man who had sacrificed two-thirds of his division. Hutton did not reply to the letter but went to see Smyth and on his return to Rangoon sent a signal to the Military Secretary in Delhi informing him of Smyth's request:

"I visited him yesterday and he appeared well and cheerful. I made no suggestion that he was to blame for recent reverses. This is not the moment to spare people to proceed on leave and I must assume that he has lost confidence in his ability to command and should be relieved. Propose to appoint Cowan and despatch Smyth to India forthwith."

General Wavell, fuming at the way events had developed in Burma and aware that Rangoon was now directly threatened, and depressed by Hutton's pessimistic predictions, flew to Rangoon.

He went directly to Hutton's headquarters where he insisted Rangoon should be held until reinforcements had arrived by air at Magwe. Shortly afterwards he cabled the C.I.G.S. stating his intentions and concluded rather tersely, "Cowan succeeds Smyth, who is definitely a sick man, in command of 17th Division". Just prior to that Smyth had been told by Army Headquarters to proceed to India on a month's leave.

It was a pity that Smyth was not allowed to do so for it would have prevented the bitter controversy that arose and continued until all the principal characters were dead.

But when General Wavell arrived in Burma, he was in a furious temper and Hutton recalled their meeting at Magwe with a bitterness that still burns through the written words. "It was the only time I have seen him completely lose control of himself. He stormed at me in front of the Governor, the A.O.C. and a number of officers and civilians in a most excited way and I felt that the only dignified thing to do was to make no reply."

Apart from the Sittang disaster, Wavell was greeted with a signal from Smyth which advised an immediate withdrawal from Pegu. Without delay the two generals drove to Hlegu, halfway between Pegu and Rangoon where Smyth had established his headquarters and was in the process of handing over to Cowan. The Commander-in-Chief was in no mood to tolerate another withdrawal and he made his views abundantly clear: Rangoon was not to be given up without a battle, and the most aggressive battle possible both in the air and on the land.

An even more unpleasant, and for Smyth disastrous, interview took place between him and General Wavell, the contents of which can only be imagined.

It took place in private, and afterwards Cowan saw Smyth sitting with his head in his hands and shaking. He turned to the man who had replaced him and said, "My career is finished". Cowan tried to convince him otherwise, but Smyth replied, "You do not know Wavell". In the middle of the campaign Smyth had been sacked.

Smyth, sick and in pain and utterly worn out, was told he would be going to India and space was available in General Wavell's Blenheim bomber. It was a flight of agonising torment for the soldier who had set off for Burma with such high hopes. It was not a direct flight as Wavell had to stop at Lashio for a meeting with Chiang-Kai-shek and the two soldiers sat at opposite ends of the aircraft without exchanging a word. Smyth interpreted the stony silence as a perfect example of Wavell's inability to communicate. The truth was less palatable, but no one tried to disillusion Smyth, for, as Cowan put it, "Wavell remained mute because he was disgusted with Smyth and thought he had let the side down".

The next day they continued the flight to Calcutta, still at opposite ends of the Blenheim and in total silence. The two men were never to exchange another word throughout the remainder of their lives.

At the airport Lieutenant-General Sir Harold Alexander, as calm and unruffled as usual, was greeted by Wavell who whisked him away for a briefing. Smyth, who knew him well, was not allowed to speak to him. It was an added humiliation, for Smyth felt he could have offered some useful advice which would have helped him in the daunting task that confronted him in Burma.

There was no doubt at all what Alexander was told, for soon afterwards Wavell sent a signal to Hutton reiterating his determination to hold Rangoon at all costs. Hutton disagreed. "I certainly felt then, and still feel, that if he had had his way the whole Army and a large number of civilians would have been captured in Rangoon by the Japanese. In fact by holding up the evacuation and ordering Alexander to counterattack at Pegu he very nearly achieved that result," he wrote later.

The dejected Smyth saw his luggage unloaded from the Blenheim and dumped on the tarmac and he was told the C.-in-C. wished to complete the remainder of his journey to Delhi on his own. Wavell strode past him without exchanging a word or a glance.

Smyth had to survive a plane crash before he eventually arrived in Delhi where even greater shocks awaited him. Next morning a letter from the Military Secretary was delivered to him by personal messenger informing him that on the orders of General Wavell he was to be deprived of his rank of major-general forthwith and retired from the army. He was further instructed to inform the C.-in-C. in which country he wished to reside.

Then some vinegar was rubbed into the wound when he was told to explain to General Wavell his reasons for requesting leave when his division was in action. He did so, and shortly afterwards was charged with a series of offences which stood justice and fairness on their head.

He was accused of proceeding to Burma while unfit and of asking for leave when he had been passed fit for active service.

Bitter and resentful, he blamed Hutton, "who was fighting for his military life", for his downfall. In fact Hutton was sympathetic. "He still had an open wound and his state of health must have been known to a number of senior officers in India, including General Hartley the Army Commander-in-Chief and possibly to some of my own staff, though nobody felt it was his duty to tell me."

In his opinion the Military Secretary and the medical authorities had a duty to inform Wavell of his condition.

Smyth tried desperately hard to remedy what he considered a gross injustice, but nothing could shift Wavell and he was "bowler-hatted".

Feeling he had been made a scapegoat, Smyth approached the Military Secretary and pointed out that, as his thirty-year-long career had not been exactly undistinguished, he should be allowed to seek an interview with Wavell, but Sir Alan Hartley strongly advised him against it as nothing could change Wavell's mind.

He was a far sicker man than he realized (a medical board later found he was suffering from paroxysmal tachycardia, the after-effects of his fissure operation, acute dyspepsia and malaria) and he was sent to Simla to recuperate. There his health steadily deteriorated.

Ill as he was, he rushed to the support of Hugh-Jones when he heard that he was blaming himself for his sacking. He wrote to Hutton asking him to assure a deeply distressed Hugh-Jones that his action in blowing the bridge had not resulted in the ruin of his (Smyth's) career and his own reputation being tarnished.

"Hugh-Jones is, as you know, a very highly strung person, and I am sure he will get well quicker if he knows there is nothing in the idea he has got hold of."

Smyth commented briefly on his own health and said he had now been classified at Category D and the doctors did not consider he would ever be completely fit again. "With this I do not agree, but I realize now that I was as ill as my ADMS said I was in Burma and a great deal worse than I myself realized. I am sorry for your sake that I was not in top form."

Unfortunately, no amount of reassurance could help Hugh-Jones shed his sense of guilt and the strain affected him mentally and physically to such an extent that long after many had forgotten the Sittang he asked to be tried by court martial. A few days later he committed suicide by walking into the sea.

Smyth suffered a complete breakdown in health which he bore with immense fortitude for several years. His reputation was partially restored when he was later made an honorary brigadier for outstanding services. He also carved a new career becoming a Member of Parliament and a distinguished author and broadcaster. But he could never erase the Sittang from his mind and he kept returning to it like a terrier to a bone despite the counselling of old friends like Cowan who urged him to forget it and concentrate on the new life he had made for himself.

No one disputed the fact that Smyth had been faced with an

agonizing decision; what angered them was his repeated insistence that the blowing of the bridge had not destroyed his division. "The Japanese immediately drew off and I was able to get some 3000 men over the Sittang by raft or by swimming."

Cowan commented, "Dear Jackie must claim that. In actual fact it was Brigadier Jones who organized it, and was the last to swim for it."

Hutton, tired of the repeated accusation that the disaster would have been avoided if Smyth had been allowed to fight the campaign as he wanted to and on ground of his own choosing, wrote, "It is obvious that if he had been left a free hand he would have scuttled back across the River Sittang as quickly as possible, after perhaps token resistance on the Bilin River."

Before the campaign ended Wavell and Hutton were also to pay the price of failure and the ill will that built up between the senior commanders was undignified and brought little comfort to the men who had left so many of their comrades in unmarked graves in the jungles of Burma.

CHAPTER 14

"They watched Sir Reginald Dorman-Smith's government disintegrate through sheer inability either to make policy or administer"

Fred Eldrige, Public Relations Officer to
General Stillwell – *Wrath in Burma*

It is now necessary to look back in time for, despite General Wavell's determination, the fate of Rangoon had virtually been sealed *before* the Battle of the Sittang. The port on which supplies to the army depended was already doomed as the 17th Division was moving back from the Bilin, although desperate and dishonest efforts were made to try and convince the population otherwise. As the situation on the battlefront was worsening by the hour the Daily News Bulletin, issued by Major Cook on 18 February and which appeared in a prominent position on the front of the *Rangoon Gazette*, announced:

"Well informed quarters are not inclined to admit any question of an immediate evacuation – or even a distant threat to Rangoon at present. . . . Our forces are in very good heart and are only anxious insofar as they are counting the days until the time comes for an advance."

The real truth of the situation lay buried in an announcement in the same issue that the next day nine banks were to close their doors and move to Mandalay. The few shops still open had also erected barricades which had an uncomfortable air of permanence. Even so, efforts were still being made to retain some semblance of normality and people continued to gather in the clubs at night.

Lady Dorman-Smith continued to visit the sick in hospital, confining her own misgivings to the pages of her diary. The day before Major Cook's comforting message, she recorded that she had helped her married daughter Pat to pack as many as possible of her wedding presents and get them aboard a train for northern Burma. The next day she wrote, "Told tonight that everyone is to leave Rangoon. We may move off at a few minutes notice. . . . It all seems so terribly tragic – this awful 'scorched earth' policy and the wastage of so much."

Two days later she and her two daughters were ordered to be ready to leave for Maymyo. She packed an album of precious family photographs and "Got a small trunk full of clothes and a few oddments out the dining room and was ready by lunch".

That same day the first stage of the evacuation was announced when the E flag was hoisted. The E referred to the windscreen stickers which had been issued to essential personnel and anyone who was unable to display one would have his vehicle requisitioned or put out of action. But many people chose to ignore it and hung on to their cars, aware that the possession of an automobile might make the difference between death or survival when the time came to leave. It was not always courage that induced many to remain; rumours abounded that the evacuation had been started because, with the imminent arrival of troop reinforcements and squadrons of aircraft, the city would be defended street by street, and the skies above cleared of enemy bombers and fighters.

For some time Sir Reginald Dorman-Smith had been under intense pressure to proclaim martial law, but he had stubbornly resisted on the ground that such a step would have a disastrous effect on the morale of the civilians. The day after the hoisting of the E Flag at the personal request of the C.O.C. Rangoon was placed under military command, but by then it was too late to halt the plunge towards total anarchy. Law and order had already collapsed.

The intransigence of the Governor was bitterly resented by the army and Lieutenant-Colonel Charles Bagot, who found himself largely responsible for maintaining law and order, was particularly incensed. The disinclination of the Government to give the military authorities full control added nothing but difficulties in dealing with a rapidly deteriorating situation and restricted the activities of the forces in matters of security.

Confusion and misunderstanding, he commented, arose between responsible civilians and the military, particularly among those whose businesses were at a standstill and who were in need of a definite policy and clear orders to guide them.

The lack of any coherent policy resulted in a complete lack of confidence in the authorities and many people made private arrangements to leave, a decision which aroused anger and derision among those who were determined to stay and see it through to the bitter end.

A mass exodus started comparable to those which had followed the first air raids. The evacuation order had come so suddenly and with such abruptness that many people moved out abandoning all the possessions they had acquired over a lifetime of service. Many left without even bothering to lock their doors.

The débâcle was an open invitation for roving bands of itchy-fingered Burmans, hoodlums, thieves and pro-Japanese saboteurs to indulge in a wanton orgy of looting, arson and violence. They roamed the near-deserted streets smashing down the doors of the houses of the well-to-do British, seizing everything that attracted their attention. Scott Market, the most famous of Rangoon's shopping centres, was razed to the ground. As the fire service was barely functioning the fires quickly spread, especially in the native quarters where the houses and bazaars were mainly wood.

Men of the Gloucesters armed with rifles and Tommy-guns patrolled the streets shooting as many of the looters and arsonists as possible, but they were too undermanned to control the hundreds who seemed intent on destroying the city. For days the corpses of the shot men lay in the roads, attracting swarms of bloated flies. A check on their ammunition made the Gloucesters realize that they could not have accounted for so many dead; the marauding gangs were shooting each other with weapons and ammunition stolen from houses and from the stockpiles in the docks.

While the equipment-starved army was doing its valiant best to halt the Japanese advance, the docks were piled high with everything they so desperately needed. Soldiers were dying for lack of much-needed medicine and drugs while looters were smashing vast quantities of them stolen from chemists, from warehouses and from the huge consignments destined for China.

As more and more responsibility fell on the shoulders of minor officials who had remained at their posts, disastrous decisions were made with the best of intentions. The most tragic was made by a young Indian Civil Servant, Mr J. Fielding Hall, who had recently been appointed Judicial Secretary. Concerned that they would starve, and pestered by the staff clamouring to leave, he issued written orders for hundreds of criminal and civil lunatics, lepers and convicts to be released from the asylums and prisons. It was a humanitarian gesture which had disastrous consequences. Many of them joined the looters and fire-raisers, adding to the mounting chaos and disorder. Some committed murder and appalling sex crimes. Wild-eyed lunatics ran through the burning, smoke-filled streets screaming incoherently. One was seen standing in the middle of a main road directing the stream of evacuating traffic. Many of the lunatics who had known no other home refused to budge from the asylum gates and merely covered their terror-stricken faces and bore the ferocious beatings of the wardens with silent resignation. A number of the lepers had been incarcerated so long they were unable to take advantage of the unexpected freedom and simply sat down in the middle of the road hoping that someone would come along and help them.

Orders were also issued for all the reptiles and wild animals to be released from the zoo which added to what was already a nightmare situation.

Too late Mr Fielding Hall realized that he had consulted the wrong file, that the Evacuation Instructions had been altered so may times that he had issued the wrong orders. He took it so much to heart that he shot himself.

Violet Kelly and Miss Maxfield, still tending the sick and wounded in Rangoon General Hospital, hurried from bed to bed assuring their patients that there was nothing to get alarmed over.

Then the hospital received an order from the Governor to leave Rangoon. "We could not possibly leave our patients uncared for," said Miss Kelly, "and so a few of us decided to remain. However, when some of the young nurses said they wanted to remain we persuaded them to leave as we felt responsible for their safety." No official arrangements had been made for the evacuation of the hospital staff, although they were all on the list of essential workers who had been assured that they would be looked after if the time ever came for Rangoon to be abandoned. Eventually, by dint of some harsh words and gentle persuasion, they were taken to the railway station in buses and lorries which Miss Kelly and some senior colleagues had managed to purlion and put aboard a special train for Mandalay.

Remaining at the Rangoon General was a skeleton staff which had four wards containing seventy patients to look after. They could only be cared for by the remaining sisters working a long shift system.

As the situation worsened, Miss Maxfield and one of the army surgeons called on the Governor to see what could be done to improve things and, shortly after their return, Sir Reginald arrived at the hospital and visited the wards, chatting to every patient and asking them how they were getting on.

To Violet Kelly's surprise he confided that he had never issued any order for evacuation and was greatly relieved that the senior staff had refused to abandon their charges. It occurred to her that someone must have used his official seal without his consent or knowledge. Not everyone in Rangoon was as dedicated as the senior staff at the hospital, and more than one European managed to be evacuated on the strength of false documents.

The improvised routine at the hospital soon broke down for unexpected and unforeseen reasons. "The Casualty Department was flooded with people who had drunk themselves unconscious: either from depression or looted alcohol," said Miss Kelly.

The same day a more serious problem arose. The servants refused to continue working as they had not been paid for some time and were in a belligerent, unco-operative mood. Far from upraiding them Miss Kelly sympathized. "Poor things, they had been so loyal since December 23rd."

After many heated exchanges and bustling to and fro between various government officers, the Medical Superintendent managed to obtain a cheque for 60,000 rupees, but when he tried to cash it he found the banks had transferred their money to Mandalay. "Good fortune came at the last moment when the owner of a large store came to the rescue; he was only too glad to supply cash for the cheque," said Miss Kelly.

No sooner had the wages problem been settled than there came another sudden change of plan; having been told to remain they now received orders to have all the patients ready to leave by train that afternoon.

In the ensuing panic one thoughtless person went off with the stores and equipment earmarked for Miss Kelly and Miss Maxfield who were due to follow the main party by road. After a hastily snatched meal the two women managed to scrounge a few basic supplies, having been warned to leave as quickly as possible as looting and sabotage were rife throughout the city, and the culprits were being shot on sight.

The hospital servants and their families numbered more than 500, far too many to be accommodated on the overcrowded trains, so they were sent to the harbour to embark on a Calcutta-bound ship where a woman added to the complications by giving birth to a baby. "Some of them went to the docks as often as five times only to be told there were no more ships for Calcutta," said Miss Kelly. "Then, as an added problem, we learned the person in charge of evacuation had run away leaving thousands of people stranded."

To allay their fears the stranded servants were assured that they would now be evacuated by rail, and they waited with mounting apprehension as the promised lorries failed to turn up. In desperation some of the servants and their families decided to start walking. It was a farcical situation, for in the docks there were several hundred Lend-Lease lorries. Fortunately someone provided one and a shuttle service was laid on until the last person was safely away.

The Sisters who were to have followed by road some time later then received a military order announcing a further change of plan: they were to leave at once. "I only had time to add two walking sticks and a golf umbrella to my few belongings," said Miss Kelly, "and it meant we were unable to take a lot of the medical equipment we had collected."

So the small convoy of private ambulances and an ancient bus set off. "Great towering columns of black smoke were rising in the sky from four different places where fires were raging," said Violet. But they were not too downhearted; they were assured that the Japanese had been pushed back. "It was just one of the many false rumours that were circulating."

Joan Morton, who had stuck so nobly to her post, was told when she reported for duty that all the women were to be evacuated up-country immediately. "We were given the choice of either leaving that afternoon in an R.A.F. convoy by road, or next morning by air, when we would only be allowed a very small amount of luggage."

She discussed it with her husband who was busy trying to curb the looting and outbreaks of arson, and he decided it was better to leave at once. "There was absolute chaos at headquarters, everyone was running to and fro, and no one could tell us where to go or when the convoy was leaving."

She said farewell to her husband leaving him standing on the steps of the house trying to fight back tears, as she called to the driver, "Go quickly". It was the last time she saw him.

Finally the dozen vehicles set off on what was to prove a nightmare journey. "The dust was appalling and progress very slow. There were so many halts that cars would race to the head of the column to see what was causing the hold-up."

Usually it was the result of an accident on the road which was choked with fleeing people, many of whom were on foot. "Going round one bend in the road, we found to our horror that a lorry had gone right over the edge into a deep kud about thirty feet deep. It was full of Indians who were lying about in a terrible state, either dead or seriously injured. Those who were conscious were screaming and yelling their heads off; it really was a nightmare. The R.A.F. chaps were wonderful, lifting the lorry off those trapped underneath, and carrying those who could not walk up on to the road, where they were laid out in rows alongside the dead. A woman doctor in the party tried to relieve their pain with morphine injections."

The injured were then put aboard the already grossly overcrowded lorries and driven to a nearby village hospital. It was not an ideal solution but all that could be done in the circumstances.

After a long and exhausting journey dogged by continuous mishaps they arrived at Magwe airfield, but several days elapsed before they were able to board a plane for India.

On the day that the E Flag was hoisted the 7th Armoured Brigade, comprising of 7th Queen's Own Hussars, the 2nd Royal Tank Regiment, the 414th Battery Essex Yeomanry, Royal Horse Artillery, and the 95th Anti-Tank Regiment, arrived. Disembarking at the same time were the 1st Cameronians and the 1st West Yorkshires who had been hastily despatched from garrison duty in India. On them were pinned the hopes of holding Rangoon and keeping the vital Burma Road open.

The 7th Hussars had formed part of the renowned "Desert Rats", the victors at Sidi Barrani, who had taken on Hitler's crack panzers and fought them to a standstill at Sidi Rezegh. Now they were expected to do the same in Burma.

As the seven ships bringing the brigade and its equipment docked, the men leaning over the guard rails were greeted by a picture of frightening devastation. Huge deserted warehouses stood unguarded, their doors thrown wide open. Cases of champagne and crates of beer lay alongside stocks of ammunition, rows of lorries and mounds of food. Fires burned in every direction, and high pillars of black smoke towered above the city.

There was not a dock labourer in sight, and the troops had to turn to and unload themselves. In the *Birch Bank*, which carried tanks, lorries, ammunition and stores, the ship's crew taught the soldiers how to operate the winches and donkey engines.

When night came the troops ignored the dangers of air raids and switched on the ships' lights and continued working throughout the hours of darkness. Within forty-eight hours the ships had been emptied, a remarkable achievement for men unskilled in the difficult task of off-loading heavy equipment.

As soon as the tanks were ashore the men started getting them ready for action, a slow and messy job for the guns had been coated with mineral jelly for the long sea voyage.

As the first troops moved away from the dock area, unbelievable scenes confronted them. Lunatics prowled the streets, ferreting among the foul-smelling rubbish dumps in search of anything edible. Wild dogs gnawed at the dead and flocks of vultures descended to tear at the unexpected harvest of carrion. Unmilked cows with swollen udders rummaged among the refuse for particles of food and bellowed in misery for want of water. Looting was rampant and seemingly uncontrollable. The Rev Neville Metcalfe, Chaplain to the 7th Hussars, was about to sit down on a convenient log when he noticed that it was observing him with a malevolent eye – it was one of the alligators freed from the zoo. Soon afterwards he spotted a fully grown boa constrictor curled around a branch above his head.

With so many temptations on view it was understandable that the soldiers felt entitled to help themselves. The Gymkhana Club was looted of 100 cases of liquor, and there was no doubt in anybody's mind that the newly arrived troops were the culprits.

Corporal Alexander Morrison, a driver with the 7th Armoured Corps, and just a few days short of his twenty-second birthday, took one look at the shops and reasoned that it was pointless to let thieves have the lot. "I walked into a jeweller's shop which had been left wide open.

Everyone had evacuated completely, so that apart from a few natives the town was dead. I picked up the best wrist watch and put it on. I also took a solid gold cigarette case and lighter. I thought the Japs would have taken them anyway."

Neither were the officers averse to helping themselves. Morrison, who drove a Humber staff car belonging to a Lieutenant-Colonel, attached to the 13th Light Field Ambulance, found it was filled with cigarettes and whisky marked "Property of the Colonel."

"I must admit I helped myself to the hard stuff now and again when the Old Man wasn't looking. He used to mark the level of the whisky in the bottle with a pencil on the label, but I got round that by rubbing his mark off with a piece of rubber padding from my tin hat and substituting my own lower down."

Morrison had joined the army in 1936 when he was sixteen by adding two years to his age. At seventeen he had experienced his first action and killed an Arab terrorist. Regrettably, like many young regulars, he had been encouraged to look down on natives. As a driver in the Middle East one of the first pieces of advice he had been given was, "If you run over an Arab, make sure you kill him."

Now he was witnessing the folly of such counselling in burning Rangoon.

The task of maintaining some semblance of law and order fell largely upon the Gloucesters, but it was made doubly difficult by the unmilitary demands continually made upon them. Colonel Bagot was repeatedly frustrated by having them "milked off" for jobs that any civilian could have undertaken. They helped in the hospitals, unloaded ships, and performed the most distasteful tasks to prevent pestilence breaking out in the filthy, foul-smelling city. He was particularly incensed when he had to provide an escort of one warrant officer and fifteen other ranks to accompany Lady Dorman-Smith and her family to Maymyo.

The police were of little use for they refused to go out at night when they were most needed, and there was justified suspicion that they actively engaged in looting themselves and were openly amenable to bribes.

Major Tony Mains was entrusted with the onerous task of seeing that the evacuation was conducted in an orderly manner. His job was not made any easier by the obstacles that were placed in his path by some officials, including a senior police officer. One confidential report said, "He did everything in his power to subvert the other police officers and to prevent co-operation between them and the army."

The problems of evacuation were almost insurmountable as space aboard ships was extremely limited and the only other main route out of Rangoon was by rail.

Earlier on, in order to retain as many essential services as possible, the remaining personnel in hospitals, government departments and the Port Trust, had been given a solemn pledge that they would not be abandoned at the last minute. It was a promise that was becoming harder and harder to honour; it led to indignant protests that Europeans were being given an unfair priority, and it did not take long for the "privileged evacuees" notices which appeared on some carriages to be distorted into "whites only". It was true that some Europeans did expect, and sometimes got, preferential treatment, but generally those responsible for allocating accommodation on the few trains were scrupulously fair and gave as much attention to a lowly hospital servant who had stood by his post as someone in a more senior position or higher social strata.

Tony Mains could have become a rich man overnight, but he ignored all attempts to buy a seat, and he was not averse to using brute force to ensure there was no queue-jumping.

The major problem confronting him was that there were only two rail routes out of the city: one which everyone was anxious to travel on was direct to Mandalay and was largely reserved for the "privileged evacuees". The other was a shuttle service to Prome. Understandably Mandalay was a much more attractive proposition being at that time well out of range of the Japanese. To give the senior railway officers greater authority and to halt the desertion of the mainly Indian drivers and firemen, the railways were militarized and one of the more senior officers, Mr C. R. Brewitt, was given the rank of Lieutenant-Colonel and appointed Deputy Director of Railways in the Rangoon area. He and his officers were responsible for keeping the trains running, Mains for overseeing embarkation.

Major Mains' small force of soldiers was poorly equipped for the task. Apart from a few shotguns capable of firing scatter shot or a single bullet, and a few pistols, most of the men had to rely on lathis – stout bamboo poles with brass tips. He ought to have been able to call upon the railway police but they were conspicuous by their absence and their Superintendent had been among the first to leave the city.

The impatient crowds which jammed the station refused to accept that the lack of staff and the almost complete absence of Indian coal coolies prevented trains being run more frequently, and they were deaf to explanations that the already overworked engine crews were also doing the stoking, and in addition to evacuating civilians still had to provide the army with vital supplies which were being backloaded. The sole thought in everyone's mind was to get out of Rangoon as quickly as possible.

The train to Mandalay, the No. 1 Up-Mail as it was called, invariably attracted large crowds who were prepared to force their way aboard. Without a public address system it was difficult for Mains, with only a hand megaphone, to make himself heard above the incessant din, so he instituted a crude but effective system to ensure that all who were entitled to travel were given space on the train. Each party had to have someone in charge, and when he was allocated space it was his responsibility to see that boarding was conducted in an orderly manner. Anyone who tried to crash the barriers forfeited his place, and that threat alone usually proved an excellent deterrent. If that failed they received a hefty bang on the head with a lathi. Passage on a train was, however, no guarantee of survival. One of the last trains to leave was ambushed by dacoits and the occupants robbed and many murdered.

The measure of the problems confronting Mains can be gauged from the fact that one of the most unpleasant incidents was caused by members of the Rangoon City Police, most of whom were Indians. They should have been occupied in helping to maintain law and order in the city, but they were determined to get away, having heard of the terrible reprisals being exacted by the Japanese against the police who had remained at their posts in Tavoy.

On one occasion Mains was alarmed to see that a hundred policemen had congregated at the station and were threatening to storm the barriers. All that stood between them and their objective was himself and five men of his Field Security Unit. His megaphone appeals had no effect on the unruly rabble who, on their way to the station, had indulged in an orgy of looting and were weighed down with all kinds of linen in addition to their personal belongings. Not only were they determined to get aboard, they were determined to hang on to their loot, even though luggage was strictly limited. As the mood of the deserting policemen grew uglier, Mains ordered his men to use their lathis, much to the annoyance of Mr R. G. Prescott, the Commissioner of Police, who happened to arrive on the scene. He angrily demanded to know why his men were being beaten. Far from being intimidated by the presence of a senior officer, Mains calmly asked him to explain why he allowed his men to loot and to turn up unannounced. It created a frigidity between the two men which did not make for a harmonious working relationship.

Equally disgraceful scenes were taking place among the vast numbers of well-to-do people hoping to sail to Calcutta. On three successive days the office of the Agent of the Government of India in Burma was under siege from crowds seeking berths. A black market in tickets was the inevitable result and the Government was forced to take over the sales. Once again there were allegations of corruption and bribery and the accusation that Europeans were given preference when it came to saloon accommodation. In order to prevent ships being rushed and uncontrollable crowds assembling in the harbour where they presented perfect targets for the bombers, a camp was established near the racecourse for those already possessing tickets and would only have a short time to wait, but twice it was besieged by thousands of fit and able men demanding passage. Many of them refused to leave and the camp quickly became filthy, polluted and uninhabitable.

Although Eve Curie was fulsome in her praise of the fighting soldiers she met on the front, she had little respect for the civilians she met in Rangoon: "I felt, perhaps foolishly, that I could have taught them a lot about their own country; that just because I had been through the blitzkrieg in London, I knew England better now than they did themselves – I mean that England of 'blood, sweat and tears'. When I passed near stiff civil servants sipping their gimlets in a club, when I talked with officers who still believed it was smart to wage a war as one would run a dull business and to speak of patriotism with their tongue in their cheeks, I felt like saying to every one of those men: 'Hey, mister! Your clock has stopped, and you must put it right.'"

CHAPTER 15

"I can see nothing in sight which can save Rangoon"
Sir Reginald Dorman-Smith

The day after the start of the evacuation all newsmen were ordered to leave Rangoon and the Governor broadcast to the country that the city would become another Tobruk. "When he spoke he knew damn well that Rangoon was completely untenable . . . so did every radio listener," said Leland Stowe.

Whatever slim hopes Dorman-Smith may have had had been shattered by the news of the Sittang disaster, but General Wavell still insisted that the city *could* hold out and the enemy pushed back by the newly arrived tanks and infantry. Furthermore, Alexander would be arriving soon to put a bit of backbone into the army and launch a counterattack.

General Hutton was in an invidious position and acutely conscious that whatever he said or did would be wrong, for he was merely a "caretaker", having forfeited the confidence of London and Delhi for his pessimistic views.

Sir Reginald was in a similar position. His broadcast merely echoed Churchill's and Wavell's opinions. Like Hutton, he had issued repeated warnings about the true position, but he had been ignored. Now he was conscious of being the butt of every club joke in Maymyo and Mandalay. Every setback in recent weeks, and the neglect of the years before he assumed office, were placed on his doorstep.

As the disorganized and routed 17th Division was falling back, a signal in secret cipher marked Most Immediate was issued from Army Headquarters which revealed how critical the situation was. The military had taken over the city which now had few police, no fire or ambulance services, conservancy or labour. Although the telephones were still working, the army was manning the water and power supplies.

At the same time Hutton received a caustic signal from General Sir Alan Hartley informing him that Burma now came under his command. "Rangoon must be held if humanly possible to do so. I am sure that you are considering every possibility in the way of offensive action towards this end."

A clearly rattled Hutton replied:

"I have never given you or anyone else the slightest indication of any intention to abandon the fight for Rangoon and protest most strongly at the implication. I have said quite correctly that I did not feel certain Rangoon could be held. . . . Possibility of offensive action has always been in my mind but it is impossible to ignore the realities of the situation on the spot which have so far been concerned with active defence against superior numbers with very limited resources pending reinforcements. Practically everything I have said has been actually borne out by events, but the unpleasant truth is never popular."

Hartley replied, "No implications were meant or intended. I am well aware of your great difficulties and of your gallant efforts to surmount them." It was an empty assurance as far as Hutton was concerned, for he was convinced that Hartley had played a major role in getting him replaced. General Hartley had taken charge of Burma when A.B.D.A. command was disbanded, but it was not long before General Wavell was once again in command.

Sir Reginald Dorman-Smith was by now reconciled to the fact that Rangoon would never be another Tobruk and he told his family in Maymyo that the time had come for them to leave for Lashio.

His wife recorded her reaction: "Completely thunderstruck. Rang up Reg and told him that it would be fatal if I go – so he left it to me to decide but that others must go. Can't understand the suddenness of all this."

Four days later the Governor sent the following message to the Viceroy:

"This is the last message I will send from Rangoon until we have recaptured it. From my information received today from commanders who have fought the Japanese it would appear that nothing short of a seasoned army corps could retrieve the Sittang situation. Our troops have fought very well but they are worn out. Whole consensus of opinion here is that mere brigades could not alter the situation. Having heard all available evidence I have decided, in order to continue any organized resistance in Burma, Rangoon will have to be evacuated tomorrow. 1200 hours February 28th the signal goes which means that all remaining essential workers depart except demolition squads. Unless some miracle happens I propose to start demolition at or about 7 hours on March 1st, Burma Daylight Saving time. I appreciate the fact that any decision I will make will probably be wrong, but it is now essential to make decisions. I bitterly regret that we must go from here."

He went on to say that he intended to leave the city soon after the demolition order was given.

General Wavell, who had now reverted to Commander-in-Chief India, decided, in view of the depressing messages from the Governor and Hutton, to fly to Rangoon immediately. With the vast distances that separated them and the time it took for signals to arrive, Delhi found it difficult to accept the reality of the situation and held blindly to the view that Rangoon could and must be held. When Wavell arrived in Rangoon he impressed upon Dorman-Smith and Hutton that the city *must* be held. He still under-estimated the fighting qualities of the enemy and the speed with which they could move; furthermore, the "miracle" that Dorman-Smith hoped for would materialize in the form of General Alexander. In addition, Chinese troops would be entering the battle.

Captain Kinloch, who had been appointed Liaison Officer to the 17th Division, was given the job of driving General Wavell round the various units and seeing as many formation commanders as he could. "The General was taciturn and appeared very morose, scarcely reacting to the sight of a Major in the 4/12th Frontier Force Rifles who was standing up in the turret of a tank which had just gone through one of the many enemy road blocks. Sticking out of his neck, like a golf tee, was the sharp end of a .256 bullet from the rifle of a Japanese sniper. Undoubtedly he was a brave man, but as a leader he inspired neither confidence nor respect, let alone affection. He was inarticulate and totally lacking in charisma."

Soon after leaving Burma he sent out a signal to Hutton:

"Hang on hard. Rangoon must not be given up without battle and the most aggressive battle that our means allow on ground and in air. Enemy cannot be really strong west of Sittang for some time yet and you have one hundred tanks."

Hutton replied:

"I realize of course that I may be said to have failed but the task was I think one in which, with the resources available, failure was inevitable. The only thing that might have turned the scale would have been an exceptional commander for 17 Division, but he would not have had his troops under him long enough to make much impression. The presence of the unreliable Burma Rifles, one or two weak Indian battalions and the absence, till the later stages, of any British battalions in the Division made Smyth's task very difficult. Owing partly I think to his health he did not do justice to his reputation."

When the army took over, Colonel Bagot was appointed Military Governor and Mains his deputy, but neither positions were officially approved as the Governor considered the titles derogatory to his authority, so Bagot became Military Commandant and Mains his Assistant.

So Martial Law was never, in fact, proclaimed, although a curfew was ordered which was not imposed for the simple reason that it was not necessary; apart from the essential "last ditchers", only looters, released criminals and lunatics occupied the city.

The biggest trouble spot had been the main market where the pickings were plentiful and easy, but this was soon brought under control when Mains gave the order to open fire and five were killed and several wounded.

"News of our action must have spread rapidly amongst the criminal elements because mob looting never occurred again, only isolated instances. Arson was another serious problem and one which we never really mastered, with the result that large portions of the city were burnt out," said Mains.

As alcohol had played such a prominent part in inflaming the crowds and rendering many of the newly arrived troops incapable of carrying out their duties, Mains was determined there would not be a repetition when the next batch of reinforcements arrived and he gave orders for all the liquor in the bonded warehouses in the docks to be destroyed.

A much graver problem was the corpses which still littered the docks and streets; fat and bloated in the heat, they presented a serious menace to health. In normal times the disposal of the dead was a task undertaken by the sweeper class, but they had all fled and it was unthinkable to ask Indian troops to do it. So the task fell to the British troops in Field Security. Mains set up a special squad which consisted of a small van manned by two British soldiers smothered from head to toe in disinfectant, while the actual task of handling the bodies was meted out as punishment to looters who had been caught red-handed. As the administration of justice had ceased to exist, it was a wiser and more humane way of treating criminals than shooting them on sight as he was entitled to do. After criminals had done a stint of such unsavoury chores they were released. It was impossible to detain them as the prison staff had gone and there was no means of feeding them.

As more and more men arrived in Rangoon to replace equipment lost at the Sittang, a system of "permits to loot" was introduced. Although highly irregular, it was a brilliant example of British compromise, and the system was administered in a scrupulously fair and semi-official manner. A permit was issued to replace equipment lost through enemy action and parties were escorted to one of the stores and warehouses and allowed to help themselves.

The plight of the Sittang survivors was extremely acute; they were short of virtually everything from knives and forks to soap and toothpaste. But ideas varied considerably as to what constituted essential equipment.

Bruce Kinloch, detailed to collect as much as possible for his men, found Rangoon "a total shambles", but still stocked with everything "from aero engines to crates of drink". But the sight which impressed him most was that of a grand piano lashed onto the top of a 7th Hussar tank.

John Randle arrived in the city with a three-tonner to collect what he could for the Baluchis. "It was an eerie feeling as the streets were entirely deserted. There was the odd dead dog and abandoned vehicle and parts of the Syriam oil fields were burning and the smoke blotted out the sun. But it was not the scene of total devastation I had been led to expect. I met some Royal Marines pouring whisky into the docks and one said, 'We're not going to let those buggers have it', meaning the Japs."

Randle obtained his permit and was duly warned that it only entitled him to military equipment.

Tony Firth, a signals officer with no equipment, found himself on a similar mission for the Duke of Wellington's and, apart from collecting the basic needs of the men, he acquired some candles and several wooden boxes which were later filled with shutters and adapted for sending signals in morse.

Evacuation was imperative, but the final decision was deferred until the arrival of General Alexander. Everyone knew what his orders were and the intense political pressure he was under, but few doubted that, once he had personally taken stock of the situation, he would realize that his mission was impossible.

CHAPTER 16

"I had time to pack only two suitcases and a tin box"
Sir Reginald Dorman-Smith

Winston Churchill was desperately relying on General Alexander to
give his reputation a much-needed fillip by saving Rangoon. An
uninterrupted series of setbacks and disasters had had a demoralizing
effect on the British people and another reverse did not bear thinking of.
The Battle of the Atlantic was not going well. The German warships
Gneisenau, *Scharnhorst* and *Prince Eugen* had cocked a snook at the Royal
Navy by sailing to safety through the channel. The loss of Singapore
had, in his own words, been "the worst disaster and largest capitulation
in British history", while events in Burma had soured Anglo-American
relations. On the other side of the Atlantic there was a growing
despondency at the apparent willingness of the British to surrender an
Empire which they had so tenaciously built up over the centuries.
Coupled with that was the deep concern over the Burma Road which
Roosevelt considered so vital to the Allied cause. If Rangoon fell it
would literally be the end of the road. On top of all that, Russia was
clamouring for a Second Front.

General Alexander was riding high on a crest of popularity not shared
by other commanders. His personal gallantry was beyond dispute, and
he had proved his ability in the field by his brilliant work commanding
the rear-guard during the Dunkirk evacuation. Alex also had the
advantage of looking the part. He was remarkably handsome in a
dashing, cavalier way and always impeccably dressed, with his cap set
at a slightly rakish angle.

He set off on his forlorn mission grimly determined to carry out his
orders, and when he met Wavell he was again told that Rangoon must
be held at all costs. Sir Reginald's plans to abandon Rangoon were
halted.

He arrived in Rangoon on 5 March and immediately met Cowan and

Hutton to discuss the defence of the city. Cowan's 17th Division had now been reinforced by the 7th Armoured Brigade, and the 63rd Indian Infantry Brigade was disembarking, but within a short time he accepted how critical the situation was. The Japanese had crossed the Sittang in force and were thrusting their way between Cowan's Division and Major-General Bruce Scott's 1st Burma Division. He realized he had two options open to him; either he could try and close the gap between the two advancing Japanese divisions or abandon Rangoon; but his orders were perfectly clear, and he countermanded Hutton's orders for a further withdrawal and ordered the 17th Division to attack in a north-easterly direction towards Sittang, whilst Bruce Scott was to attempt to drive southwards. He also visited the battalion headquarters of the Gloucesters and impressed upon Bagot that the city would not be abandoned. Bagot made no audible comment, although he mentally dismissed the assurance as "a pipe dream".

But within a short time General Alexander was almost ready to concede that there was no way of holding on to the city and he would have to agree with Hutton's policy of denial and demolition; if the 17th Division encircled at Pegu was to be saved from annihilation, an immediate withdrawal was imperative. The enemy was now hammering at the doors of Rangoon.

During this trying period Bagot's neck had permanently assumed the look of a cooked lobster. For weeks he had had to look on impotently as the army suffered defeat after defeat, and he had been scathingly critical of the optimism of some of the commanders which he dismissed as, "Bliss born of the most regrettable ignorance of their profession". Having been an eye witness to the disintegration of the city he was never under any illusion that it could become another Tobruk; and when Hutton repeated that Alexander intended to stand and fight he retorted, "What with? Ink bottles and pens? You may feel suicidal, sir, but I am going to fight my way out with the troops under my command and I suggest, with all due deference, you and your staff come with us."

Bagot had finally become convinced that Rangoon was doomed when the Chinese arrived in large numbers and began to remove as much Lend-Lease equipment as they could. At the same time Americans and British started to destroy some of it. Bagot decided he would help himself to as many vehicles as possible and he detailed his adjutant to go to one of the lorry parks and help himself, but on arrival he was warned off by Chinese armed with Tommy-guns. Undeterred, the adjutant returned at nightfall and took seventeen Dodge chassis before the heat from burning vehicles forced him and his men to withdraw. The Pioneer Corps of the Regiment worked non-stop constructing bodies for the lorries. In a similar manner eight scout cars were obtained and 3-inch mortars fitted to them. Company by company the Gloucesters entered the arsenal near Rangoon and helped themselves to clothing and automatic weapons and machine guns, two Italian Breda guns and 1000 shells. The wheels of the guns were changed for jeep wheels and locked onto the back of jeeps to provide mobile artillery. By methods that could not bear too close a scrutiny, the Gloucesters also got hold of a large amount of equipment which included twenty-one anti-tank rifles. Their fire-power was strengthened still further by machine guns, mortars and grenades from a detachment of the Burma Rifles which had been disarmed after mutinying and shooting their British officer.

Bagot had no qualms at all in reversing the "poacher turned gamekeeper" adage and he instructed his men to collect everything that would help them survive the ordeal that lay ahead. Two launches indispensable for crossing rivers were 'borrowed' and hoisted aboard three-ton lorries to the strains of the Eton boating song. Bagot also realized the importance of good health and water testing equipment was purloined along with stocks of cholera vaccine from the refrigerators of the now near-empty hospitals.

By the time the order to evacuate Rangoon came, the Gloucesters had 128 vehicles, which included several jeeps, twenty motor cycles, twelve carriers, eight armoured cars, water tanks and petrol bowsers. So, although weak numerically, they were strong in fire power and transport.

George Biggs recalled, "I went down to Rangoon for the last time with a 3-ton truck to see what I could get before the Japs took over the city. Everywhere was a shambles. . . . I loaded up a good quantity of goods which I thought would be useful, among which was thirty choice cured York hams, and the same amount of Christmas puddings."

The time had also arrived for the Governor to leave. With news so sparse, incredible stories circulated in Mandalay and Maymyo about his panic departure, none of which were true. He was accused of running for it to save his own skin, and leaving the "last ditchers" to fend for themselves. And, whereas most people had evacuated with only a handful of possessions, he had piled his Rolls Royce with every imaginable luxury, including his collection of gramophone records and pet monkey. Even worse, he had packed all his ceremonial uniforms, when most refugees had been forced to flee in what they stood in.

It was not until after the war that Dorman-Smith deigned to answer his critics. "I had time to pack only two suitcases and a tin box. In the box I placed all my diplomatic regalia as a privy councillor – the two coats (blue silk encrusted with gold lace and embroidery), silk breeches, stockings, cocked court hat with its crest of ostrich feathers, gold shoe buckles and sword. To me those uniforms meant as much as the regimental flag does to a regiment.

"As the only councillor in the Far East, I was determined that Emperor Hirohito was not going to get my court dresses to hang up on show in his palace. On the first stop 200 miles out of Rangoon I decided to burn them, but there was no time. The Japs were after me. So I gave the box to Colonel Richmond, my military secretary, who took it some distance and then had to entrust it to the headman of a jungle village. He gave the man a gun and told him what the box meant to me, and said, 'Look after it. We will be back.'"*

Alexander's decision to try and hold Rangoon and restore the situation on the Pegu front proved a disastrous one and the delay caused almost resulted in the capture of himself and the entire army. The counterattack was doomed from the start and heavy casualties were inflicted on the British troops, especially the untrained 63rd which was thrown straight into battle and more or less disintegrated.

As the Japanese swept towards Rangoon Alexander now had one object in view – to withdraw and hold Upper Burma. And as the army prepared for what was to become the longest and most terrifying withdrawal in the long history of the British army, the signal was given for everything to be destroyed that would be of assistance to the enemy.

The possibility of having to resort to a "scorched earth" policy had been envisaged when Japan first entered the war and Leslie Forster, a former engineer of Shell-Mex and an expert in demolition, had been flown out to draw up the necessary plans. He was described by Dorman-Smith as "the greatest saboteur in history", having previously destroyed the oil fields in the Dutch East Indies. He was ably assisted by

* Three years and six months later, when Sir Reginald returned to Burma, the box was handed back to him.

Walter Scott, a young Royal Engineers captain, who had also established a reputation as an explosives expert with the retreating B.E.F. in France.

General Alexander reluctantly gave the signal "Red Elephant" at midnight on 7 March, which meant demolition would start at 2 pm. Dead on time a series of violent explosions rocked Rangoon like an earthquake. One of the first targets was the total destruction of the Burmah Oil Company's vast installation at Syriam.

Some time before, Forster and Scott had laid tons of explosives throughout the refinery and drained 150 million gallons of oil, petrol, kerosene and high octane aircraft fuel from the gigantic storage tanks to create a secondary blast. At 2 pm the electric circuit was fired. Tanks disintegrated and machinery and metal sheets were hurled high into the air. Within a short time a great pall of dense black smoke soared thousands of feet into the air. It resembled a total eclipse, as the sun was blotted out. A tidal wave of fire flowed down to the estuary of the Irrawaddy destroying everything in its path.

"When we were 42 miles out of Rangoon we could see a pall of smoke 18,000 feet high – testimony to Mr Forster's efficiency," said Sir Reginald.

A further series of explosions immediately followed the first. Tony Mains was sitting with Prescott in his headquarters when the fan suddenly stopped and they heard an enormous bang which signalled the end of the power station. Similar ear-shattering explosions announced the destruction of the sewage works and other vital installations.

The telephone exchange was demolished soon afterwards, having been kept operating until the last possible moment. One of the few buildings spared was the Shwe Dagon Pagoda, the most sacred Buddhist shrine in Burma, its gold dome, standing as high at St Paul's, reflecting the glow of countless fires. Buildings, shipping berths, workshops, warehouses and mills were destroyed and locomotives immobilized.

More then 1000 Lend-Lease trucks and jeeps were splashed with petrol and set on fire by members of the American Military Mission. Very close to 70,000 tons of American materials destined for the Chinese was standing in the docks; some of it was destroyed, but a lot remained to fall into the hands of the enemy.

"Bobbie" McLean-Brown, the dock official, already a legendary figure following his efforts after the first air raids, added to his reputation by destroying all the usable boats in the river before the floating inferno from the refinery made further efforts unnecessary or impossible. With a handful of Indian labourers he went from wharf to wharf setting fire to storehouses and their contents, and dynamiting machinery. He then secured a tug and went round the harbour altering the position of buoys marking the safe channel and other navigational hazards such as sandbanks and mud flats. When his task was almost completed he saw troops hurrying along the water front, and he turned to his party and said, "Good, our boys are still there. We've got plenty of time." Then a Lockheed Hudson bomber flew low overhead and dropped a canister which ignited a red flare when it landed on the water. He retrieved it and found a scribbled message: "Go to Akyab immediately – the Japs are here – get out."

The troops he had seen ashore were Japanese. Even then he continued with his work of denial, sinking several more vessels before forming an armada of small boats and cramming them with "last-ditchers" and ferrying them to three merchant ships waiting downstream to take them to Calcutta. By then they were being pursued by boats containing Japanese and hostile Burmans and he aimed the bow of his tug at one and sliced it in half.

Major Tony Mains, who had been told that he and his men were to be evacuated by sea, learned at the last minute that they would have to go by road. A young naval Lieutenant, who was wondering how he could get away, was invited to join Mains' party and in gratitude he informed him that there was still some beer in the Port Trust Club which was still cold as the refrigerator had been operating until the power station was blown. "We parked our vehicles in front of the now deserted fire station, collected chairs from inside and proceeded to sit on the pavement and drink our beer, more as though we were in some Continental café instead of being in the eerie position of the last inhabitants of a deserted and partially destroyed city," recalled Mains.

George Robertson, the young Anglo-Burmese R.N.V.R. Lieutenant, was also stranded as he had been up country when his entire unit had been evacuated earlier. "I went to the deserted navy headquarters and found the place had been ransacked and looted. I went to my room to find that everything I owned had been stolen. I had nothing but the clothes I was wearing."

Having nowhere to stay in the abandoned city, he called on his elder brother John, a customs officer, who was living in the Boat Club at the Royal Lakes, to warn him and his colleagues to pull out without delay. "We welcomed the timely warning," said John Robertson, "and our immediate action was to have a celebration, and we joyfully set about opening the crates of beer that had been submerged in the lake to keep cool."

At first light they loaded what they could into some commandeered Lend-Lease lorries and set off up country. George did not accompany them for he heard that the *Heinrich Jensen* had returned to the port to evacuate the demolition squads, and he went and reported to her commanding officer, Captain K. S. Lyle R.N., and explained that instead of taking passage to Calcutta he would like to go up-country in search of his mother.

George Robertson just managed to keep one jump ahead of the Japanese as he made for Bhamo to find his mother. "In Bhamo I offered my services to the Chinese, telling them I was a naval officer and if they could use my services I should be glad to join them. They had several truck-loads of arms and explosives but were short of drivers and were only too glad to accept my offer. I drove the truck beyond Myitkyina, taking my mother with me. Eventually some friends managed to put her aboard the last plane from Myitkyina."

Shortly afterwards he lost touch with the Chinese group but managed to team up with some army officers who had been detailed to destroy the suspension bridge about fifty miles north of Myitkyina. When the task was completed he began the long trek to India. It took him three months to reach Calcutta.

From Maymyo the Governor made a desperate radio appeal aimed particularly at Burma officials: "At this hour there is only one unforgivable sin, the failure to have the courage and conviction to take a decision. You may wish to defer your decisions to a higher authority. But you are close to the front and are in vital positions. Do not, therefore, worry about referring to anyone. Act, provided your decision is calculated to embarrass the enemy and contribute to our war effort; I will back you, right or wrong."

Some responded, but sadly there were those who, after a life of colonial administration in which red tape and countless files and endless meetings had sapped all initiative, were incapable of making any decision. Instead they stayed in the clubs of Mandalay and Maymyo, continually lamenting the lack of guidance from the top.

CHAPTER 17

"Men were dying like flies, and soldiers were digging holes to
roll them into"

Corporal Alexander Morrison

To appreciate General Alexander's sudden realization that Rangoon
could not be held it is necessary to look back in time and follow the
misfortunes of the hard-pressed army in the Pegu area.

The miracle that was hoped for by the arrival of the Armoured
Brigade was as much a last straw as the belief that one man, in the
embodiment of General Alexander, could alter events. But the sight of
the Stuart tanks, known to their crews as 'Honeys', had an immediate
morale-boosting effect on the tired and dispirited survivors of the
Sittang. They were further encouraged by the arrival of two splendid
British infantry battalions, the 1st Cameronians and the 1st West
Yorkshire.

Although great efforts had been made to regroup and re-equip the
17th Division, the men were still short of most things; they lacked Bren
guns, Tommy-guns and, just as important, clothing, for many had
arrived nearly naked. In a climate where sunstroke took a regular toll a
hat was a basic necessity, but even these were hard to come by, and the
troops displayed remarkable ingenuity in fashioning headgear out of
palm leaves, strips of cloth and puttees.

Despite their sorry plight the arrival of the tanks and infantry served
as a tonic and they were soon ready to engage the enemy once more.
It was just as well, for the fighting at Pegu was to be ruthless in the
extreme.

The crack 7th Hussars, with their distinctive cross-belt, were
renowned for their dash and elan; as cavalry they had demonstrated it
at Waterloo, and more recently in the Western Desert. But it was soon
clear to them that they were about to be engaged in a type of warfare
totally alien to anything they had experienced. Instead of wide open

spaces with plenty of room to manoeuvre, they were being asked to fight in terrain entirely unsuitable for their tanks and against an enemy who moved with incredible speed along uncharted jungle tracks made known to them by hostile Burmans. Before the first shot was fired they were to discover that it was a very strange war indeed. When they arrived at Pegu with 414 Battery, Royal Horse Artillery, headquarters were established in an abandoned girl's school, where they enjoyed iced drinks and hot baths, and, but for the presence of the Sittang survivors, could have been forgiven for thinking they were far from the front line. To their amazement they found that there were still people in Burma who did not know there was a war going on. 'A' Squadron, seeking somewhere to harbour for the night, thought they had come across a small village until a saffron-robed priest with a shaven head appeared and asked in perfect English, if they were on manoeuvres.

"No, we are fighting a war," said the Squadron Leader.

"Ah, well, have a cigar," was the astonishing reply.

The priest then proceeded to bless the tanks.

They needed some divine protections, for shortly afterwards they were engaged in a battle that was as ferocious as it was confusing, and the 7th soon had an opportunity of exploding the myth that the Japanese were invincible when three Stuarts encountered three enemy tanks in a clearing. Two were immediately knocked out and the third, which was abandoned, was towed in triumph back to H.Q. From then on the 7th Armoured were to fight alongside men who frequently had to resort to the bayonet and the kukri, who adopted methods that were employed at Agincourt; panjis – sharpened bamboo stakes – were driven into the ground and concealed with foliage. Although the tanks were never able to operate as their crews would have wished, they nevertheless fought with great skill and tenacity. But for them the army would never have been able to withdraw to India as it did.

While Rangoon was in its death throes, the situation in the Pegu area was as follows:

The 48th Gurkha Brigade consisted of the amalgamated 5th/3rd Gurkhas, the 1/4th and the amalgamated 1/7th and 3/7th; the West Yorkshires, still to be blooded, occupied the north-west of the town, while the Cameronians were in the town itself, guarding the bridges over the river and the railway. The 7th Hussars covered the roads at the northern end. There were insufficient forces available to complete the perimeter and men were warned not to go anywhere without their arms as a British Officer had had his throat cut by hostile Burmans and a 7th Hussar had been hacked to death with a hoe.

On 2 March General Wavell arrived and gave a pep talk which did not go down too well; the next day the Japanese air force began a softening up process. Two days later Pegu was again attacked and set on fire. At dawn the Japanese were seen moving towards the railway station from the north-west. Tanks, supported by the West Yorks and Cameronians, moved in quickly and dealt with the enemy, inflicting heavy casualties. The Scots attacked the enemy through a red haze of hate; earlier a patrol had been ambushed and their naked bodies were later recovered by their comrades; they had been tied to trees, their feet several inches above the ground, and bayoneted in the chests, groin and stomach.

It was now abundantly clear that, no matter how hard the infantry and tanks fought, there was little hope of holding Pegu and the order was issued to prepare for withdrawal to Taukkyan. The Japanese moved swiftly and once again employed crude but effective road-block tactics which cut off the line of withdrawal.

The 63rd Indian Infantry Brigade, which had recently arrived in Rangoon, was already on its way to help relieve the pressure on the hard-pressed forces at Pegu. But they were mainly raw recruits and hardly any of the officers or men had ever seen a mortar, Bren gun or anti-tank rifle. Their initiation in the use of these new weapons had been over the stern of the troopship. They also suffered a shattering blow before they even saw the enemy; a reconnaissance party consisting of the Brigadier, his Brigade-Major, one of the battalion commanders and two other commanding officers had gone ahead to see at first hand what the situation was. On the way back the party was ambushed and everyone was either killed or badly wounded. In one incident the 63rd Brigade had been deprived of its leaders. Even so they fought magnificently, but they were no match for the Japanese.

The Stuarts were virtually confined to the roads as the open ground was latticed with deep ditches, known as bunds, which halted them in their tracks. In the sweltering heat the four-man crews endured agonies of discomfort in the cramped turrets.

Corporal Alexander Morrison said, "The tank gunners saw little to fire at although they were under constant attack. We just did not know where the shots came from. We were fighting an unseen enemy."

But if the tank men experienced the extreme fanaticism of the enemy, unlike the Commander-in-Chief, they awarded him unstinting respect for his fighting qualities, if not his ethics. At Pegu a Japanese officer on horseback charged a tank, clambered aboard and attacked the commander with his sword, forcing him to grab a hammer and beat his hands until he fell off. When he fell into the road the tracks ran over his legs, but he still drew his pistol and continued firing at the retreating Stuart propped up on one elbow. Another Squadron was attacked by a screaming horde with grenades attached to the ends of poles, who ignored the blistering hail of fire from the Brownings and Tommy-guns to run right up to the turrets, often killing themselves with their own grenades.

In engagements that resembled the mad bayonet charges of the First War the officers were invariably to the fore. Lieutenant-Colonel Cameron, in command of remnants of the 1/3rd and 2/5th Gurkhas, was hit in the leg by a sniper's bullet, and, although unable to walk, continued to command from a stretcher and later a carrier. As long as he was visible there was not the slightest sign of faltering among his men, and for his inspired leadership he was awarded a DSO. Lieutenant-Colonel Joe Lentaigne of the 1/4th led several bayonet charges, bellowing orders and encouragement through a mouthful of shattered teeth.

The carnage in men and material was indescribable. The roads were jammed with burning lorries, tanks and ambulances. The cries of the dying and wounded rose above the din. Corporal Morrison, who thought he was immune to the spectacle of human suffering, having already seen so much, was horrified by what he witnessed.

"In a plantation there was a clearing between the trees where dozens of badly wounded men lay on the ground in rows as there were not enough stretchers to go round. On one side there was a canvas sheet between a couple of trees where a surgeon worked all night with an oil lamp sawing off arms and legs. Men were dying like flies and soldiers were digging holes to roll them into. There were several bodies to each unmarked grave."

He had driven the Colonel there to see that as many of the wounded as possible were evacuated. "The final vehicle was being loaded with the last of the wounded who stood any chance of surviving the rough journey ahead. All that were left were the dying and immovable, the hopeless cases, rows of them. The medical officer was going round giving each man an injection of morphine. On one side of the clearing lay half-a-dozen corpses and as I watched about a dozen large vultures, massive birds, over three or four feet high, were tearing them apart and eating them.

"Four medical orderlies drew lots to see who would remain behind with the wounded and await his fate at the hands of the Japs. By the sound of things he wouldn't have to wait long."

As three officers climbed into the Humber Morrison was told to drive off. "We left one lone figure, a young medical orderly, who stood to attention and saluted us. I thought, 'What a hell of a situation to leave one man in.'

"From time to time a lorry or an ambulance received a direct hit, but a tank quickly pushed the whole mess off the road, leaving room for the next vehicle to pass. Here and there along the bloody stretch of shell-torn road was a burning tangled mess of what had once been an ambulance or lorry, and the air was heavy with the smell of burning flesh."

Many who survived the holocaust of Pegu speak of one remarkable man in tones of true reverence: the Reverend Neville Metcalfe, Chaplain to the 7th Hussars. The respect was not in deference to his cloth, but his incredible heroism which was responsible for saving the lives of so many of the wounded. He could and did fight the good fight with all his might and his attitude was summed up by his own words, "Service comes before services." A firm believer of the dictum that God helps those who help themselves, he had filled his car with minor comforts from abandoned shops in Rangoon – cigarettes, beer, chocolate, razor blades, soap and toothpaste – and these he liberally dispensed among the hard pressed soldiers at Pegu.

Early in the battle at Pegu a heavily defended road block had prevented him from rejoining his own unit and he attached himself to the Regimental Aid Post of the West Yorkshires and the Cameronians. The Regimental Aid Post was under constant and intense fire and one of the two doctors was killed by a sniper's bullet and an ambulance destroyed by a mortar bomb. In addition to helping the doctor attend gaping wounds and shattered limbs, Metcalfe set up a small canteen and, with the assistance of his driver, Trooper Mansell, succoured the wounded with hot tea and biscuits. As the enemy seemed determined to wipe out the post he volunteered to transport as many of the wounded as possible in his car to the hospital at Pegu. This meant jettisoning the results of his looting, but two soldiers saw that it was fairly distributed among the remaining wounded. No sooner had he completed one trip than he returned for more casualties, often under heavy fire.

The Red Cross did not mean a thing to the Japanese – in fact it was an invitation for destruction. The overcrowded hospital was under constant attack and a bomb destroyed one wing. Throughout the night he helped the medical staff patch up the mangled and broken bodies that kept pouring in. Whenever he had a moment to spare, he complied casualty lists.

Then some tanks arrived and it was announced that Pegu was to be evacuated that night. The tanks would smash through the road blocks in order that the wounded could follow on behind.

Metcalfe insisted on staying until the very end, burying as many of the dead as he could. When the moment came to leave he sat beside the driver of the last ambulance as it pulled out of Pegu and made for Hlegu Road.

He was told that as soon as his ambulance crossed the sole remaining bridge the order would be given for it to be blown up, but halfway across the ambulance broke down. Metcalfe jumped out and ran up the road and persuaded the driver of the only other vehicle in sight to back onto the bridge and give the ambulance a tow. After an agonizingly long time the engine of the ambulance fired and he ordered it to set off after the withdrawing convoy.

Despite urgent entreaties from his driver he remained behind with a detachment of Cameronians who had been detailed to demolish the bridge, as he had seen a number of destroyed tanks and lorries with bodies hanging out of them and was anxious to recover their identity discs for the benefit of the next of kin.

His own lorry was then hit by a mortar which blew him into a ditch crowded with Cameronians, at which point he wisely pocketed his Bible and picked up a dead man's rifle and joined the Scotsmen who were preparing to clear the last road block. Although under heavy and accurate fire, the rearguard made their way along the ditch until they reached the roadblock which presented a sickening scene of carnage and destruction. All around were burned-out lorries and other vehicles, surrounded by dead and dying men. Again he collected as many identity discs as possible. Eventually the rearguard managed to reach Hlegu some twenty miles away. It was a particularly hard slog for Metcalfe who had lost his boots in the explosion and had to make the journey barefoot.

Denied any air cover worthy of the name, the withdrawing troops were bombed incessantly by enemy aircraft which roamed at will, while on the ground they were subjected to a merciless bombardment from artillery and mortars and contintually harassed by unseen snipers. Yet miraculously they managed to break out, although the price was sickeningly high in dead and wounded.

Corporal Morrison recalled picking up a leaflet dropped from the air;

"You are now completely surrounded. You are outnumbered one hundred to one, lay down your arms, give yourselves up and you will be well treated. Why fight? You cannot win."

The 'Old Man' gave a derisory gesture and told him they would fight back to back if necessary, but they would never surrender.

His attitude summed up that of the rest of the infantry and tankmen and for several hours the battered army leap-frogged its way towards Prome. Weary as they were, the British, Indian and Gurkha troops prepared themselves for the fight to retain Middle and Upper Burma.

CHAPTER 18

"The whole British Force from Rangoon, and with it General
Alexander and his headquarters, would have been destroyed
had it not been for the typically rigid adherence to the letter of
his orders by a Japanese divisional commander"

Field-Marshal Slim.

As the Rangoon force withdrew along the Prome Road, it resembled a
mechanical, slow-crawling centipede. From front to rear it measured
several miles. Thick clouds of dust rose in the air as the column of
lorries, ambulances, Bren-carriers and tanks ground along a road never
intended to take such a volume of traffic. Trudging alongside on the
verges were lines of sweat-grimed soldiers who had little idea of what
was going on or where they were heading. In the background burned
the funeral pyre of Burma's greatest port.

If they were ignorant of what was going on, then so was General
Wavell, for on the day the denial programme was carried out he cabled
Alexander:

"Understand from naval authorities decision taken to evacuate
Rangoon. Cable most immediate reasons for this very grave step
which affects whole course of war in East. Has battle taken place?"

The new Army Commander's reply was blunt and forthright: the
counterattacks had failed with heavy losses and his main task was to save
his army from destruction and hold as much of Upper Burma as possible.

Meanwhile the 17th Division, with the 16th Brigade as rearguard,
was falling back from Pegu to link up with the Rangoon forces on the
Prome Road.

Owing to years of parsimony and the vested interest of the railways
and the Irrawaddy Flotilla Company, the road system in Burma was
totally inadequate to meet the needs of a modern army in retreat. There

Major-General Bruce Scott

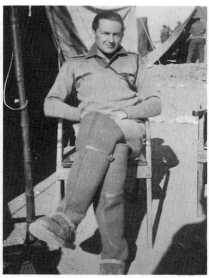

Captain Tony Firth, Duke of Wellington's Regiment

Captain Bruce Kinloch, MC, 1/3rd Gurkha Rifles

Captain Mike Patteson, MC, 7th Hussars

Refugees from Rangoon on the road to Prome, January, 1942

Million-gallon oil tanks ablaze at Yenangyaung

Corporal Alexander Morrison

The Rev Wilfred Crittle

Stanley Farrant Russell on his way to visit a patient

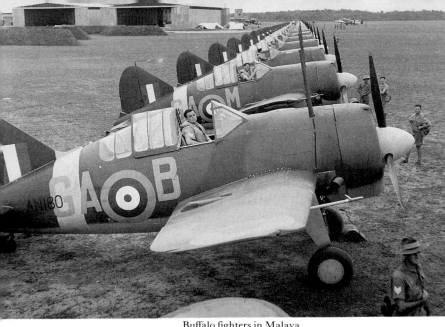

Buffalo fighters in Malaya

The five British officers of the 1/3rd Gurkha Rifles who arrived in Imphal in May, 1942.
Left to right: Captain McGilchrist, Colonel Thornton, Captain Kinloch, Captain Macrae,
Captain Darley

were only two possible routes out of Rangoon that could take motorized transport: the first went through Pegu up the Sittang Valley to Mandalay, the second went through Tharrawaddy and Prome along the valley of the Irrawaddy. Between the two valleys lay the Pegu Yomas, a wild area of jungle-clad hills with no lateral roads for two hundred miles.

The route chosen by Alexander for the Rangoon force was the one along the Irrawaddy Valley, along which the 17th Division was also moving.

For some twenty miles out of Rangoon the two routes followed the same road to Taukkyan where they then forked at Milestone 17, the right fork went to Pegu, the left to Prome.

Unless the withdrawal was accomplished with clockwork precision a gargantuan bottleneck was inevitable. And that is precisely what happened when the Japanese established road blocks in the Taukkyan area. In a short time the entire Burma Army, apart from the 1st Division, was bottled up in a long stretch of the Prome Road.

By his rigid adherence to orders, Alexander had exposed the whole of the army to destruction or capture. But by one of those strange quirks of fate the army was saved by the same rigid adherence to orders on the part of General Sakuria, commanding the Japanese 33rd Division.

As the Rangoon garrison passed the village of Taukkyan heavy firing was opened on the leading vehicles. Blocking the road was a tree trunk and some 40-gallon drums of highly inflammable oil and tar speared to the ground with steel spikes. Almost immediately a tank which went forward to reconnoitre was hit and set on fire. Within an area of a square mile the Rangoon force became bogged down in a bumper-to-bonnet jam of double-banked vehicles.

The tank crews, their backs bronzed from the desert sun, calmly clambered out of their turrets to light cigarettes and brew tea. Gunners rested near their field and anti-tank guns. None moved off the road and deployed to battle positions. British soldiers, Gurkhas and Sepoys, worn out by days of fighting, slumped down by the roadside only too glad to ease their cramped and aching legs. To add to the confusion the army was further hampered by the presence of thousands of refugees and countless civilian vehicles.

The road block at Taukkyan was in fact one of a series of obstacles extending over a considerable length of the road and affecting not only the progress of Alexander but also the 17th Division. The entire army was stretched out in a 40-mile ribbon of road.

The block had first been sighted by a carrier force led by Captain John Christison of the Duke of Wellington's Regiment which had been patrolling the road north of Taukkyan to make sure it was clear for the garrison force. About three miles from the village they were ambushed by a party of Japanese who were setting up a road block. The first carrier managed to smash through it, but the second crashed and although the Baluchi Captain driving it managed to escape into the jungle the two soldiers with him were killed. Christison's carrier received a direct hit from a concealed gun which killed one of the crew. Christison and the remaining soldiers continued to fight on until they too were killed.

The Rangoon garrison could not have been trapped in a worse position. On one side of the road was dense jungle, on the other a rubber plantation, and from both sides unseen snipers were able to maintain a continuous and accurate fire on anything that moved.

A concentrated air attack would have been disastrous but fortunately there were only sporadic raids which were met by a hail of fire from small arms and Bren guns fired from the hip or resting on the backs of comrades.

"I remember," said Bruce Kinloch, "seeing General Alexander sitting in a camp chair, his head in his hands, helpless to do anything until the road block had been broken. Jap planes bombed the road junction and an enemy recce plane skimmed the tree tops while tracer shells from our Bofors light ack-ack guns pumped away at it. One shell blew a enormous hole, some three feet in diameter, through the port wing, but somehow it still managed to fly on, staggering like a winged goose. There was a distraught R.T.O. near hysteria as he tried to control the traffic at Taukkyan, who drew his revolver and threatened to shoot me if I tried to force my jeep through the traffic jam. I had an urgent message to deliver to the General I told him, and I saw his finger quiver on the trigger as I was unkind enough to laugh at him – poor devil, he was near breaking point, but I was telling the truth."

It seemed incredible that an entire army could be halted in its tracks by such a primitive obstacle but such was the terrain that it was almost impossible to destroy the block with artillery fire. Yet somehow or other it had to be forced.

Colonel Bagot, leading the column, had a feeling that the task would fall to his men. His intuition was right. A senior staff officer, escorted by two motor-cyclists, careered up the road and halted by the side of the Gloucesters' commanding officer. The moment Bagot had thought about for so long had now arrived; instead of being burdened with all the unsavoury chores, his men were going into action for the first time. The staff officer told him that his men had been assigned the task of clearing the block. Bagot, no man to shirk a challenge but nevertheless a realist, pointed out that he only had one rifle company available and would like C Company, which was protecting Army Headquarters, to be released in support. The staff officer refused his request and told him to "get on with it" as the column was "in a hurry to get on". He would have some artillery and tank support. It was, he insisted, merely a question of pushing up the road as the enemy did not consist of more than a patrol. With that the staff officer disappeared.

Bagot was joined by one of the tank commanders and an artillery officer and together they surveyed the block and the burning tank which had been knocked out trying to break through. Having studied the scene, the artillery officer explained that his 25-pounders could not smash the block as the trees were too dense. A position might, however, be found some way back from which fire could be brought to bear on a small area, but the problem was that there was no observation post from which to study the effect. The tank commander was adamant that no more tanks should be endangered; the anti-tank guns would have to be knocked out and the road block cleared by infantry; then the tanks would follow. Bagot refrained from saying that what he was being asked to do was contrary to everything he had been taught in peacetime, when it was automatically assumed that in such action the infantry would rely on the support of other arms. All the essential aids of success had been denied him and he thought it was a decision that merited 'bowler-hatting', "The maxim 'economy of force' had been reduced to a farce," he reflected bitterly.

Private H. J. Hale saw his C.O.'s neck redden. "Then the colonel turned and shouted, 'To hell with the tanks. The 28th are going forward and remember the 28th does not know how to retreat. Go up there and don't come back.'"

B Company advanced with a platoon on either side of the road and a third in reserve on the left. Since the block itself did not amount to much in the way of a physical obstacle, Bagot assumed it was defended by a strong force and he ordered two mortars to shoot up the area while two Bren-carriers would advance on either side. The first carrier would crash through, followed immediately by the second. The enemy would then be forced to betray their whereabouts and covering fire could immediately be provided. Having announced his plan of attack, Bagot clambered aboard the first carrier to lead the assault.

As the carriers raced up the narrow road Japanese soldiers hiding in the undergrowth opened up with tracers, and two platoons of enemy soldiers scurried across the road. Bagot knew that the one small patrol he had been told to expect was a gross underestimation. Enemy mortar shells began to rain down in front of the block and the second carrier received a direct hit which killed the entire crew. Bagot speeded up and smashed into the block, but in doing so one track hit the side of a culvert which slewed it round at right angles and brought it to an abrupt halt. Less than 40 yards away in a clearing an anti-tank gun supported by fifteen enemy soldiers was clearly visible. A burst of machine-gun fire from the carrier soon dispersed them, but the anti-tank gun fired almost simultaneously, killing everyone but Bagot and Philatoff the driver. B Company walked into a withering hail of machine-gun and rifle fire while the platoon on the left was caught in an ambush and completely encircled when only fifty yards from the block. Another platoon made a wide circling movement and almost reached the road obstacles when it was attacked by a large enemy group. The platoon advancing on the right side of the road also ran into heavy and devastating fire from well-concealed snipers.

Bagot and the White Russian slid into a ditch and managed to get back. Bagot ordered one platoon to advance again and try to secure the wood on the right, while another was sent to try and take the other side.

Having located the site of the anti-tank gun, it would have been a relatively simple task to clear it if all four companies had been available to him but A Company had been detailed to provide cover for the Rangoon demolition squads, and C Company had been on duty guarding the airfield and had not yet caught up with the main column. Because the losses had been so severe and there were no resources available, a patrol was hastily made up which included signallers and stretcher-bearers to make a direct assault on the anti-tank gun. Two of the party were immediately shot in the back by Burmans concealed in a nearby house; the patrol returned the fire, killing all the occupants.

Then, when the patrol passed a small sandpit, they were again fired on by a party of mixed Japanese and Burmans armed with automatic weapons. They were quickly silenced by a well-lobbed grenade, but concealed snipers continued to take a heavy toll. One enemy party opened fire at a range of less than twenty yards and the Gloucesters went in with the bayonet and the enemy broke and fled into the jungle. But fire immediately broke out on all sides and the Gloucesters realized too late that they had been led into an ambush. They hurled grenade after grenade at the unseen enemy, but the undergrowth was so dense that several hit branches and bounced back. But they still managed to kill a large number of enemy and after several similar sorties the Japanese retreated, but by this time the small party of Gloucesters had been reduced to three men and Bagot decided he must contact the 9th Platoon and call upon it to make one more desperate attack on the anti-tank gun. But before this could be put into effect the platoon was heavily engaged by a large enemy force which they fought off for over half and hour, by which time the Japanese were once more well established. Nothing, it now seemed, could prevent them from breaking through to the unprotected tanks.

Bagot was determined that this would not happen and he detailed several men to form a screen between the enemy and the road, at the same time extricating the wounded. One of the platoons which had returned was also sent forward to resume the battle at the road block, and when the Headquarters Company arrived two more platoons were formed from the administration staff. One, under Captain Middleton West, the adjutant, closed in on the anti-tank gun but was caught in a burst of concealed machine-gun fire. Although mortally wounded, Middleton West helped to get some men into a jeep but they were all killed before they could get clear.

The Gloucesters had fought without respite for four and a half hours against an entire Japanese battalion and by nightfall all the officers of B Company were casualties, and only six N.C.O.s and fourteen men were left, while the admin platoon and battalion headquarters had been reduced to about one third. Against such superior odds there was nothing Bagot could do but wait for his other two companies to arrive.

With so much at stake it was surprising that a stronger and more determined effort was not made to break through. The Gloucesters had fought an epic battle, but the situation demanded more than sheer courage.

As there was still a little light remaining it was decided to make another attack. An Indian battalion was placed at Bagot's disposal and he not unnaturally asked for artillery and tank support. When this was refused he called for volunteers to man two carriers to support the Indians. Among those who stepped forward was Philatoff who had taken part in the first assault. Colonel Bagot got in beside him. The two purloined Breda guns and the rest of the Gloucesters' mortars had now arrived and together they plastered the entire wood and started a huge fire. As soon as the bombardment ceased the carriers raced up the road and at the sight of them bucketing along with all guns blazing the Indians charged, cheering at the top of their voices, only to be met by machine-gun fire and a mortar barrage. The second carrier was hit and burst into flames and Private Philatoff who was in the leading carrier with Bagot, although wounded twice, collected the wounded from the carrier at the road block and drove them through a mass of machine-gun and mortar fire to safety. He was awarded the Military Medal.

The sight of the carriers being hit had a demoralizing effect on the Indian troops and the attack petered out.

When darkness descended Bagot made his way back and reported personally to General Alexander.

Major Tony Mains recalled, "The most unruffled man in the whole set-up appeared to be the Army Commander himself. He was sitting quite imperturbably in a Burmese house, with nothing to lighten the darkness except a few oil lamps, apparently completely unconcerned that his command of the Army in Burma appeared unlikely to last more than a few days."

Alexander, who was not to escape criticism for his handling of the situation, listened attentively to Bagot and decided to march a battalion of Gurkhas through the night round the flank on the west and attack the block from behind at first light. They would be supported by the relatively fresh two battalions of Gloucesters, who had been following behind the main column, who would mount a frontal attack. This time there would be artillery and tank support.

Throughout the night the Japanese continued a relentless sniping and several attempts were made to infiltrate the British lines, but they were all thwarted by mortar fire and grenade attacks from small patrols.

As daylight approached, enemy activity slackened and when dawn came the area around the road block was pounded by the guns of the

12th Mountain Battery. When the barrage lifted a troop of tanks and a company of the 1/11th Sikhs made for the road block. To their utter amazement it was deserted. The Japanese had gone.

No one was more relieved than the Army Commander who, fearing his army would be cut to ribbons or taken captive, had been preparing to issue the order "every man for himself" and let them disperse and fight their way through the jungle.

The Japanese had missed a heaven-sent opportunity of ending the war there and then, but the road block which so nearly ended in calamity was not deliberately set up to trap Alexander; it was part of a wider plan to seize Rangoon without having to fight a major battle. General Sakurai, anxious to seize the port's facilities and oil, ordered his troops to abandon the road block and continue their march on the port. Apart from his rigid adherence to orders, the Japanese commander was under the false impression that the British forces were not retiring but heading towards the city to reinforce it. A disaster on the same scale as Singapore had been avoided by sheer luck. Alexander could not believe his good fortune. Kinloch said, "I remember seeing him leap into a staff car and roar off up the Prome Road when the news came through that the Japs had abandoned the road block and marched across the paddy fields towards Rangoon".

Hampered as they were by the long column of refugees, the soldiers still halted their vehicles and gave a lift to those who were finding it hard to continue. Even the tanks had elderly men and women clinging precariously to the side of the turrets and many of the refugees owed their survival to the improvised taxi service.

With hindsight General Wavell realized that he had asked the impossible of the new Army Commander and signalled, "Well done. Responsibility for position in which you and troops were placed is wholly mine and I congratulate you all on determination with which you have extricated yourselves. Much regret casualties."

When the first Japanese troops entered Rangoon they had to clamber over the debris to hoist the Rising Sun over the railway station. The greatest port and the business heart of Burma was theirs, but it looked as if it would be a long time before it could be of any use.

The refinery still burned and would continue to do so for several weeks. An R.A.F. Hurricane flew over the city on a photographic mission, but the pilot reported that he was unable to go below 18,000 feet, and all his camera could record was a vast yellow and red blanket that obliterated the whole area.

The 'last-ditchers' had done all, and more, that was asked of them, yet the sad but harsh truth was that the denial policy was not as effective as everyone thought. The port area extended over such a vast area that in the time available it had been impossible to destroy everything. In addition to vast amounts of raw materials, the Japanese were presented with millions of dollars' worth of Lend-Lease equipment. After a hurried inspection the Japanese realized that enough of the port facilities remained to maintain a far bigger army than they would ever need.

As the army withdrew, Hutton, who had been sent to Maymyo, where headquarters had been established, was finding his position more and more untenable. Although he had been superseded by Alexander he had been asked to remain as his Chief of General Staff and had become critical of Alexander's strategy. "At the time I felt very strongly on this subject and it was largely on this account and my disagreement with the conduct of operations at Prome that I asked to be relieved as C.G.S. to Alexander," he wrote later, adding, "As will be understood I took very little part in the issue of orders for the counterattacks. At the time I blamed Alexander for these suicidal orders and it was only later that I realized he was loyally carrying out Wavell's instructions. My position was really an impossible one. I was the same rank as Alexander, who was promoted acting General, although I did not know it in April and except at Army Headquarters everyone thought I was still in command. I naturally got very tired of explaining that I was not. Fortunately Alexander and I were already very good friends and there was never any friction between us."

When General Wavell visited Maymyo Hutton again mentioned that his position was impossible and when convenient he should be replaced by someone of more appropriate rank. A Brigadier was sent to take over but Hutton was asked to stay on for the time being. Hutton believed that Alexander had suggested to Wavell that he be asked to stay on, but this only made his position even more anomalous, for although Hutton took great care not to interpose himself between Alexander and his Brigadier General Staff, the Army Commander continued to discuss the campaign with him, and he found himself "a fifth wheel to the coach".

Alexander finally agreed to him returning to India where he completed his report and took some leave. Although it is jumping ahead in time it is appropriate to complete the story, for General Hutton was to take no further active role in the Burma campaign.

His report led to some acrimonious correspondence and discussions with General Wavell, for Hutton pointed out that his warnings of the probable fate of Rangoon, considered alarmist and pessimistic, had been borne out by events, and Wavell, by his action in delaying the third stage of the evacuation scheme, had almost caused the entire army to be captured. "This would have been a disaster comparable to the surrender of Singapore but with far less excuse. The effect on India, Great Britain, the Chinese and the Americans would have been incalculable. Wavell never, however, indicated any point at which action by me could have averted the inevitable, nor in fact has anyone else."

Hutton hoped he would be given an active appointment; instead he was asked by the Viceroy to coordinate the military and civil war effort in India. He accepted but made it clear that he still considered himself eligible for a fighting appointment. But when he mentioned it to the Viceroy he was told to put it out of his mind. "No doubt he had discussed the matter with Wavell."

The bitterness still burns through the pages of the personal memoir written many years after the war had ended. "Wavell could no doubt have found me military employment in India before he himself was displaced as C-in-C. He could also have pressed my case more strongly with the authorities at home, but I realized that my seniority and the P.M's prejudice against anyone who he felt had failed him was an obstacle, but the real obstacle was no doubt Wavell himself."

CHAPTER 19

"The next morning we moved to where we had been before this useless venture had begun"

War Diary of the 7th Hussars

As the army continued its fighting withdrawal there must have been times when Alexander felt he was moving down an endless tunnel which would never provide the faintest glimmer of light. Although his army was grossly under strength in men and materials, he was still expected to inflict a major defeat on the enemy, but no matter how hard and how valiantly his soldiers fought, nothing, it seemed, could stem the Japanese advance. His spirits soared, however, when he learned that his request for an additional corps commander had been granted, and the man chosen by Wavell to fill it was Lieutenant-General William Slim. In a time of great adversity no commander could have asked for a better or more reliable deputy.

No two men could have been more dissimilar than Alexander and Slim. In appearance Alexander, the aristocrat, was the Arab thoroughbred to Slim's Shire horse. Slim had enjoyed none of the advantages of birth and background which so many considered essential in order to attain high rank in the army. He was a rarity who gave substance to what most rankers considered an empty soporific, namely that every private had a Field-Marshal's baton in his knapsack.

Slim was a "soldier's soldier" in every sense of the word. He had enlisted as a private, been made up to lance-corporal, and "busted" back to private, been discharged as medically unfit after being badly wounded, yet somehow or other had rejoined and won an M.C. and D.S.O. as a young subaltern in the First War. During his chequered career he had been an office boy, a schoolteacher and a foreman in an engineering works. With his broad, jutting jaw and powerful frame he resembled a prize-fighter, but behind the pugnacious exterior were the brains of a remarkably astute strategist.

Slim was serving in Persia when he was summoned to India by Wavell and his departure for Burma was so hurried that an Indian tailor had to sit up all night making him three khaki bush shirts, three pairs of slacks and shorts, his own personal baggage being somewhere between Bagdad and Bombay.

Slim, never a man to shirk a challenge, knew from the outset that he was confronted with a mountainous task, but his confidence received a severe jolt when he landed in a Lysander at Magwe airfield. There was no response from the ground when permission to land was sought, and when the aircraft touched down the airfield was deserted. Aircraft were parked around the perimeter, but there were no guards; the control section huts were empty, and the pilot could not get anyone to answer the telephone. Eventually the man on whom so many hopes were pinned managed to hitch a lift in a Burma Rifles lorry which took him to the R.A.F. Wing H.Q. about three miles from the airfield. As Slim recalled, "Although I knew warning had been sent from India, I never discovered whether I had really been expected or not. It was a strange arrival, and not too reassuring as to either the standard of staff work in Burma or the safety of our precious aircraft."

Slim's command was the newly formed Burcorps which consisted of the 17th Indian Division under "Punch" Cowan, the 1st Burma Division under Major-General Bruce Scott and the 7th Armoured Brigade under Brigadier John Anstice.

Slim wasted no time. The morning after his arrival he flew to Prome where he met General Alexander and his two divisional commanders. In some respects the briefing had the air of a regimental reunion, for Slim, Cowan, and Scott had all served in the same Gurkha battalion and had been close friends for twenty years. Slim could not have chosen two men in whom he had more trust, or whom he would rather have worked with.

The 17th Division was some thirty miles south of Prome, while 1st Burma Division was at Toungoo, some eighty miles to the east and on the other side of the Yomas, holding the Sittang Valley. The Chinese V Army was due to take over in the Toungoo area, and as soon as they did Scott was to join Cowan and the Armoured Brigade.

Slim made a tour of inspection and spoke to as many troops as possible, doing his utmost to boost their morale. The tank men impressed him greatly but he noticed that there were also a considerable number of badly shaken troops. He made an immediate impression, for he was able to talk to the British soldiers in their own barrack-room jargon, to the Gurkhas in Gurkhali and the Indians in Hindustani.

With a characteristic lack of fuss he set up his headquarters in the deserted Prome law courts where his personal office was a judge's room lined with dust-gathering legal tomes. His first task was to decide on the overriding object of the campaign. This was no simple matter, for Slim had not received any clear-cut order as to policy, and even at the end of the campaign he was still not sure. The only thing that was certain was that somehow or other the initiative had to be wrested from the enemy.

It was not false optimism. There had been successes, admittedly on a small scale, which showed that man for man, and given the right circumstances, the British and Indian troops were more than equal to the Japanese.

Major 'Mad Mike' Calvert, later to become one of Wingate's best known column commanders, and the recipient of two D.S.O.s, had led a daring river raid on the town of Henzada and inflicted heavy losses on a force of hostile Burmans led by Japanese officers.

Calvert had been growing more and more frustrated at the Bush Warfare School in Maymyo and was anxious to take a more active part in the war that was being fought by others. With some of the officers and men who had been trained in guerrilla tactics and sabotage, he formed a commando unit to operate behind enemy lines. All were volunteers and included British, Australian and Indian troops, most of whom had been recruited from the Maymyo hospitals where they were recovering from wounds received earlier in the campaign or men who had lost touch with their units. There were men from the Dukes, KOYLI, Cameronians and Gloucesters. Calvert made incredible demands on the courage and stamina of his remarkable little force and got it.

Around the same time, in a spirited action at Letpadan, the Gloucesters had routed a formidable force of Japanese. After attacking with grenades, rifles and Brens, they had chased them through the streets and into the jungle at the end of their bayonets.

Alexander signalled Bagot, "My heartfelt congratulations to you and all ranks. A splendid show and just what I wanted. You have set a fine example of enterprise and proved that we can defeat the Jap at his own game. Chief was delighted."

Slim wished to repeat those successes on a grander scale but he knew that his chances were summed up by his own surname; his forces were gravely under strength with little or no likelihood of reinforcements, while the disposition of his corps left much to be desired.

Prome was held by the 17th Division which was still reeling from the defeat at the Sittang and the subsequent fighting; Bruce Scott's 1st Burma Division was heading towards Prome as fast as possible but he was aware that speed itself could be counter-productive; little would be achieved if his force arrived piecemeal.

Prome meantime became the target of a series of air attacks. The bombers usually arrived around breakfast-time and departed leaving large areas of the town burning. Fire-fighting was greatly handicapped by hostile Burmans who added their own fires to those caused by the incendiaries. On top of that there was the problem of the thousands of refugees who crowded the streets and river wharves waiting to cross the Irrawaddy. Cholera and malaria were rife and the water had become so polluted that there was a risk of it spreading among the troops.

Much more serious, however, than the air attacks on Prome was the series of raids on the airstrip at Magwe. On 21 March a powerful force of bombers and fighters attacked the vital airfield still occupied by the R.A.F. and A.V.G. and in the space of 24 hours six raids were made by an overwhelming force of two hundred and fifty medium and heavy bombers. When the first wave came over no warning was given and twelve Hurricanes were dispersed around the airfield. The unease Slim had experienced on arrival was fully justified. Some managed to take off and destroy four enemy aircraft, but most were damaged. By the next day only three P40s and three Hurricanes were airworthy. A high price had been paid for the failure to provide pens and dispersal areas. The A.V.G. Commander announced that as there was no adequate warning system he had no option but to withdraw those of his planes which could still fly to Loiwing.

The final attack was made by a force of fifty bombers in two waves with a strong fighter escort which resulted in the destruction of almost all the aircraft. The few still airworthy took off for Akyab, followed soon afterwards by Burwing H.Q. and squadron personnel, who headed for Lashio and Loiwing. The next day the Japanese attacked Akyab with the same devastating results and the airfield was abandoned, which meant Slim had no air cover.

With no opposition, the enemy planes could indulge in pattern bombing, all emptying their bomb bays at the same time. The troops took it all with remarkable stoicism, but they were bitter about the hurried and undignified departure of the R.A.F. and there were outspoken accusations that they had panicked.

Soon afterwards Slim became the recipient of more bad news. The Chinese defending Toungoo were in danger of being overrun by a much stronger enemy force. Although the Chinese were fighting stubbornly, the burning town was completely surrounded and being subjected to merciless attacks from the air and by artillery and infantry. The Chinese were lacking in just about everything but courage, and the enemy was made to pay for every blood-stained yard of the burning town.

Chiang Kai-shek urged Alexander to launch a counterattack in the Prome area in order to relieve the pressure on his army in the Toungoo area. Slim was under no illusions that Burcorps could do little to remedy the situation, but orders were orders. The order to counterattack was, he suspected, based more on political considerations than military reality.

Chiang Kai-shek had never totally committed himself to the defence of Burma for he mistrusted the British and had grave doubts about their fighting qualities. His attitude was understandable; he had witnessed nothing but a series of disastrous withdrawals.

On the other hand the vacillating Chinese leader was far from reliable himself; he seemed incapable of reaching a firm decision on anything, and when he did he invariably changed his mind. And when Chinese troops commanded by the crusty American General "Vinegar" Joe Stilwell were placed at Alexander's disposal, the commanders were reluctant to obey any orders until approved by the Generalissimo, which again entailed interminable delays. Neither were matters helped by the casual manner in which officers went about their task. No one questioned their fighting ability but they lacked efficient organization and time meant little or nothing to them. If they were ordered to attack at a certain time but failed to meet the deadline, they simply put back their watches.

Slim doubted whether he could do much at such short notice but he asked Cowan to do his best. The omens were not all bad for at the time that Slim received his order the Gloucesters had carried out a bold strike and taken Paungde, a big village thirty miles from Prome, killing a large number of the enemy.

George Biggs, who was providing covering fire for B Company as it advanced across an open paddy field, said, "If I had not seen it I would never have believed that the men advanced in open order as if on training in peacetime; no one faltered unless killed or wounded."

As the Gloucesters were virtually isolated, Cowan ordered them to withdraw, but he then received orders to mount a counterattack and he decided to do so with a striking force consisting of one battery of artillery, tanks and three infantry battalions – the Gloucesters, the Dukes, Cameronians and West Yorks, commanded by Brigadier John Anstice.

The counterattack never got off the ground and achieved little but to add to the long list of casualties. Ten valuable tanks were lost and nearly 410 officers and men killed or wounded.

Once again the infantry did all and more than was asked for; outnumbered and outflanked they inflicted enormous losses on the enemy. But a withdrawal was inevitable and the tanks once more roared to the rescue, bringing out the infantry, many of whom were badly wounded.

Then Brigadier Anstice received another setback when he was told that the town of Shwedaung on the main road ten miles south of Prome was in the hands of the enemy. Even worse, enemy troops were infiltrating behind him, so Cowan ordered him to withdraw. But this was easier said than done for at Shwedaung the Japanese had set up a series of road blocks.

Shwedaung sprawled across both sides of the main road for about two miles in length and a mile in depth. As there was no other road capable of taking transport the road blocks would have to be smashed, and Anstice ordered his advance guard to storm the road block at the southern end of the town while infantry attacked the northern outskirts.

The men who had fought at Paungde had marched hard and long under a pitiless sun to reach Shwedaung where they halted only long enough to collect water and eat some emergency rations, but when they were ordered to try and dislodge the enemy at the road blocks there was no hesitation. A Battery of 25-pounders hammered at the blocks for 15 minutes before the assault was launched. The fighting was again at close quarters and was so confusing it was almost impossible for anyone to form a coherent picture. Enemy snipers seemed to be concealed in every tree and house and cunningly sited machine guns and mortars in every bamboo grove. One platoon of the Dukes lost all its five non-commissioned officers in the same number of minutes.

It was almost a repetition of the road block at which General Alexander and most of his force had narrowly escaped capture. Trapped behind the obstacles were the headquarters of the Armoured Brigade, the tanks, most of the infantry and some 300 vehicles of all descriptions.

In addition to the enemy, the troops had to maintain constant vigilance against treacherous Burmans who adopted the guise of friendship in order to betray them. A harsh reminder of this occurred when a detachment of Marines, Commandos and Burma Military Police were sent to occupy the nearby village of Padaung. The villagers welcomed them and provided food, but as they were eating a force of enemy troops who had been hiding in the village opened fire. Although the small detachment put up a spirited fight they were hopelessly outnumbered and many were killed. Twelve British soldiers and Marines who were badly wounded were captured and kept alive until the following day when the Japanese used them for bayonet practice to impress the natives.

At the same time the British troops encountered several hundred troops wearing the distinctive blue uniform of the Burma National Army. Although led by Japanese officers, they were a harsh reminder that not all hostile Burmans were loot-hungry dacoits; many were motivated by a true patriotic zeal and fought with a reckless fanaticism, thinking themselves invulnerable to bullets. When their casualties mounted they became more circumspect.

In desperation Anstice decided to launch a night attack on the road block by tanks supported by artillery, a task that would have been difficult enough by daylight.

Lieutenant Mike Patteson, who had won an M.C. at Sidi Rezegh, and Lieutenant G. Palmer, were chosen to lead a small force of Stuarts. Many died in the storming of the road block and many had miraculous escapes, but none as incredible as Patteson's which combined heroism, tragedy and near-comedy.

As the tanks roared along at 35 miles an hour machine-gun bullets struck the armour like hammer blows. Patteson, standing up in the turret passing instructions to the driver through the intercom, rounded a bend and saw the whole of Shwedaung burning brightly in the distance and directly ahead the road block consisting of three over-turned vehicles. His immediate reaction was to get his tank off the road, and he shouted orders to the driver who yanked the right-hand lever, forcing the tank to spin off into a ditch. Machine-gun fire raked the rear of the Stuart and Patteson, anxious to get his tank into action, crawled off to find a way out. "I could see that in order to extricate the tank it would have to be reversed, but towards the enemy lines. The two Hussar tanks of the following troop had driven straight for the road block, and had somehow forced their way through on each side of the lorries; it was their machine-gun fire which had raked our tank from behind."

One tank left the road but managed to get back on it. Two went through at high speed and were hit several times and showered with petrol bombs which illuminated the way ahead where a massive tree trunk blocked the road. Another charged it like a steeplechaser taking a fence and it literally flew through the air and most of the crew sustained severe head injuries. The road block, however, remained intact.

Having found what he considered a possible way out, Patteson began to move back towards his tank when he suddenly found himself surrounded by enemy soldiers. He was kicked and pushed towards a bamboo hut where he was tied to the trunk of a tree and searched. He resigned himself to being shot; instead one of the soldiers started to scream something incomprehensible and proceeded to smash an earthenware pot over his head. As the others punched and kicked him an officer slashed his chin with a sword and then began to beat him with the flat of the blade. He thrust his face close to Patteson's and asked "How many tanks?" Despite the savage beating Patteson refused to talk until the officer asked him about artillery. Through his split and swollen lips the young tank commander replied that there was none. He felt that when the guns opened fire the enemy would be taken unawares, but the blatant untruth did not have the desired effect; the officer who possessed a sadistic sense of humour burst out laughing and ordered him to be untied and taken out onto the road and tethered to a wrecked ambulance.

As his captors took up their posts on either side of the road block Patteson wondered how long it would be before the guns of the 414th Battery Royal Horse Artillery began to pound the area. The answer came much quicker than he had thought.

"The first shell burst on the road itself, yards only from the over-turned ambulance, to which I was tied; the second burst high up in the palm tree branches, sending down a shower of splinters onto the road. Understandably the Japanese had gone to ground."

Sitting bolt upright with his hands secured behind his back and his ankles roped together, he reflected on the macabre sense of humour of the officer who had deliberately planned that he would be killed by his own comrades.

"Two further shells screamed overhead; instinctively, I hurled my full weight towards the ground. Whether it was the incompetence of the soldiers who had tied me to the running board, or by a miracle of a shell splinter, I shall never know, but in that brief second, the ropes behind me gave way, and I crashed headlong to the road. The ropes securing my hands behind my back were still intact, and I sensed that those around my ankles were still tightly fastened. I thought rapidly. The Hussar tanks would be advancing on the road block at any moment; frequently our tanks followed up so closely behind exploding shells that they were able to crush enemy infantry crouching in their weapon pits. I had to sever my connection with the ambulance as quickly as possible."

He kicked with his lashed-together legs until one shoe came off and with it a coil of rope. With agonising slowness he forced off the other shoe and with it the remaining rope.

He lay motionless as the shelling continued. Suddenly he heard a sound that had no connection with the noise of battle, the thundering of hooves from a herd of stampeding steers. He rolled over, scrambled to his feet and joined the panic-striken animals. Suddenly the shellfire stopped and the steers halted, turned and began making their way back towards the road block. Patteson hurled himself into the undergrowth. He heard two Japanese soldiers talking in low voices and decided to make a run for it. He darted between them shouting something unintel-ligible and raced through the jungle. At any moment he expected to receive a bullet in the back.

With his hands still tied and without the protection of shoes, progress was agonisingly slow. He had no compass but was able to take his bearings from the Great Bear and North Star. He had broken free at 2 pm, but it was well after dawn when he reported back to his squadron. On hearing his story his Commanding Officer said simply, "You need a drink."

"The memory of that night will never fade, which is hardly surprising. The rope marks on my wrist are still there to this day," said Patteson.

Lieutenant Palmer, commander of one of the tanks which had first broken through, reached the headquarters of the 17th Division and reported to Cowan. To his surprise Cowan made it obvious to Palmer that he thought he and his men were overdramatizing what they had been through. The Regimental War Diary commented caustically:

"March 29th, 1942. Lieutenant Palmer then got through to Prome, and reported to the 17th Indian Division H.Q. where he was very coldly and casually received, and they did not believe the seriousness of the situation."

Despite repeated assaults by tanks, artillery and infantry the road block remained intact; at times it was cleared but before it could be taken in force the enemy had re-established it. Brigadier Anstice sent an urgent message through to Prome saying that unless a heavy supporting attack was mounted all the untracked vehicles would be trapped.

Cowan's earlier cynicism had now been replaced by an acceptance that Lieutenant Palmer had assessed the situation correctly, and support was promised from the 63rd Infantry Brigade and a squadron from the 2nd Royal Tank Regiment, but for some unknown reason it was not mounted. At the road block it was decided that the entire force should attempt to break through, led by part of A Squadron followed by the regimental unit, then the infantry, guns and finally C Squadron.

Four of the leading tanks were immediately knocked out and a number of vehicles destroyed, and only two squadrons of tanks, the headquarters of the 7th Hussars and a small number of lorries managed to get through before the road block was replaced. Still ensnared were C Squadron, the infantry and the guns.

The tanks made a fresh assault but their progress was hampered by the tangle of wrecked and burning transport which littered the road making the block even more impenetrable. And to add to the confusion enemy aircraft began dive-bombing the bottled-up column of men and transport.

As evening approached it was decided that the infantry would have to abandon their transport and make their way out through the jungle, while the tanks and guns would make one final attempt to smash their way out. To continue to batter at the block was a senseless waste of life; the infantry had done their utmost, as the bodies littering the ground bore silent witness.

Among those killed was Major Victor Morton, the Gloucesters' second-in-command, who was riddled with bullets as he tried to drive away a jeep filled with wounded. His dying words were, "Get these lads to Prome as best you can. Goodbye, and good luck to the Gloucesters."

Major Morton's dying sentiments were wholeheartedly endorsed by Brigadier Anstice who had never had a great deal of faith in the value or merit of the operation. Getting the trapped men to safety was now his sole consideration.

Colonel Bagot, rallying his men in readiness for the march through the jungle, was hit by a tank and badly wounded in the leg. Someone in a passing armoured car hauled him aboard.

C Squadron hammered through houses and jungle on both sides of the road without losing a tank. The artillery, following hard behind, only lost two guns, a remarkable tribute to the skill of the drivers.

Alexander Morrison could see Prome ahead: "The whole place was an inferno. Even the massive trees on the roadside glowed red before crashing to the ground in the blaze of sparks. The tar on the road was bubbling and there was the smell of burning flesh."

As the battered force entered the town the cost was counted. The 7th Hussars had lost ten tanks, the artillery two guns, the infantry 350 men killed or wounded.

A brief entry in the War Diary of the 7th Hussars on 31 March stated starkly:

"The next morning we moved to where we had been before this useless venture had begun. The Regiment had only 38 tanks now and had lost a number of B vehicles. We had been forced to fritter ourselves away in a country entirely unsuitable to tanks."

The Chinese 200th Division fought to hold Toungoo with a fanaticism that was equal to that of the enemy, but, outnumbered by at least three to one, the outcome was inevitable. They put up a heroic resistance for ten days, anxiously waiting for relief and reinforcements that never arrived. When the town finally fell Slim considered it a disaster second only to the blowing of the Sittang Bridge.

He now had to consider whether it was worth trying to hold Prome. It was not an easy decision; although little remained of the town and cholera was rife among the refugees and spreading to the troops, a large quantity of stores, mainly rice, which was urgently needed by the army, was piled up on the quays by the riverside. Plans had already been set in motion to backload it, but as there was no railway out of Prome it had to be moved by boat. But the crews of the river steamers were reluctant to venture so far south where they were in danger of being straffed by enemy aircraft. The constant bombing had also resulted in the departure of nearly all the labour in the town.

As Slim weighed up the situation he doubted if he had the necessary forces to hold the town even if he wished to. With the enemy so close, he moved his headquarters to Allanmyo about thirty miles to the north. There he was visited by Wavell and Alexander. Little time was needed to reach a decision and Slim was ordered to begin the evacuation as soon as possible. At the same time he was told to speed up the backloading of stores. It was also impressed upon him how vital it was to defend the oilfields in the Yenangyaung area on which the army now depended.

Slim realized that the situation was indeed grim. The 17th Division, which had been fighting without pause since the start of the campaign, was in poor shape to repulse a strong and determined assault, and his problems were not made any easier by the fact that the division was spread out over a wide area. The 63rd Brigade was in the town itself and to the south; the Gurkhas of the 48th Brigade were at Hmawza some four miles to the east, and the 16th Brigade five miles to the north around Tamagauk.

General Bruce Scott's 1st Burma Division was moving in as fast as possible, but it was arriving in dribs and drabs. It was also poorly equipped and desperately short of carriers and artillery. Furthermore, it had been greatly depleted through desertions among the Burmese units. Its effectiveness was further diminished when Slim was forced to split it to meet Japanese threats on the west banks of the Irrawaddy.

But the withdrawal plans became somewhat academic; it was the enemy who decided the fate of Prome by attacking in great strength before the retreat started.

The first attack began at midnight on 1–2 April and was successfully repulsed by the Indian battalion holding the south end of the town. A second was immediately mounted and large numbers of the enemy infiltrated into the town and Brigade headquarters of the 63rd Brigade was almost overrun together with its gun positions. The ensuing battle was fierce and confusing and the brigade was forced to withdraw to the eastern exits. The Gurkhas of 48th Brigade were then attacked but held firm, repulsing the enemy with heavy losses. As the Japanese flooded through the burning town, Cowan ordered the 63rd and 48th Brigades to disengage and pull back under the protection of the Armoured Brigade.

The Gurkhas were loath to admit defeat and in one ambush the 1/4th slaughtered some two hundred of the enemy, holding their fire until they were only a few yards away and, when the ceasefire was ordered, moving in with kukris and bayonets. For much of the time, however, the enemy remained unseen, content to create chaos and confusion by a series of devastating mortar and artillery barrages. In some sections there was a grave danger of the withdrawal becoming a disorderly rout.

In the morning Cowan telephoned Slim to say that he had received reliable information that a big enemy force had cut through his flank and was approaching from the rear and endangering the entire division. His men were utterly fagged and short of food and water. Furthermore, the terrain was ideal for the enemy to introduce their favourite road-block tactics to which the British had yet to find an answer.

Once again the tanks roared to the rescue and two squadrons of the 2nd Royal Tank Regiment began ferrying the battleweary men back to Dayindabo. For eight hours the tanks ran a shuttle service and moved some 2500 men.

It was far from ideal country for the tanks covering the retreat, and on numerous occasions they had to tow each other out of dried-up river beds. A mere twenty minutes after the last of the infantry passed the tanks, the enemy was seen to emerge from the jungle a few hundred yards away and set up a road-block.

The men of the 17th Division now faced a new and terrifying ordeal. Instead of the lush, green vegetation, they had entered the 'Dry Belt,' a brown, arid area full of deep nullahs and stony, parched brown hills.

Most of the water courses were dry and the men were soon so tormented by thirst that when they found a pool of green-scummed water they crowded round it, presenting a tempting target for the dive bombers. But the enemy infantry, no doubt just as tired, made no attempt to pursue the dispirited and exhausted British, and they reached the Allanymyo area where they slumped to the ground, their last reserves of strength expended.

General Alexander knew that morale among the troops was not as high at it should be and unless more air support was provided would continue to slump. In a message to General Wavell he expressed the view that the 17th Division had not fought very well at Prome, but in mitigation pointed out that they had been fighting continuously for three months and units were getting weaker and weaker. Three questions occupied their thoughts; were they ever to be relieved; would they ever receive reinforcements; and how long were they to be bombed and machine-gunned without air support?

They were requests which Alexander must have suspected would not be met, as any reinforcements would have to be flown in and there were not enough aircraft available to do this on any great scale. As for fighters and bombers they were urgently needed for the defence of India. With remarkable insensitivity Wavell replied:

"Don't let them get too disheartened over the enemy's air superiority; it is nothing like so dangerous or destructive as artillery superiority such as we so frequently were up against in the last war."

What did not occur to Wavell was the harsh fact that morale had slumped as the men's confidence in their leader waned. Much as they prayed and hoped for air cover, many would have been immensely cheered by the appointment of a Commander-in-Chief who did not still think in 1914–18 terms. Seldom, if ever, can an army have been so consistently denigrated and quite naturally they resented it; but there was no outlet for their feelings; they could only voice their opinions to each other.

Nothing, however, could prevent the war correspondents from saying what they thought, and Leland Stowe was quick to come to the defence of the fighting soldier. He told his American readers that they had been faced with an impossible task from the outset.

"Bravery was not enough, but for all that, the British soldiers and the Indian troops in Burma fought with great courage whenever their leaders gave them the opportunity to fight. They did not fear to die and they were worthy of the finest and best in Britain's and India's military traditions. When they lost confidence in their commanders it was only after most soldiers would have lost all faith."

What angered the soldiers just as much was the failure to pass on praise when it was deserved. Later, during the withdrawal, the KOYLI fought a brilliant action at Myingun which saved the Burma Division from being cut off, and again at Magwe which saved the 1st Brigade. When the news reached London the Queen sent a personal message by wireless:

"Commander-in-Chief is requested to convey the following message from Her Majesty the Queen to the Officer Commanding 2nd Battalion K.O.Y.L.I. Begins. As your Colonel-in-Chief I have learned with pride of your splendid fight in recent days. You are all so much in my thoughts and I send my best wishes to all ranks. Ends. Please report when communicated."

Nothing could have done more to restore the flagging spirits of the Yorkshiremen. Unfortunately it was never delivered. It was not until five months later that the Commanding Officer heard about it. It was understandable that the troops in Burma should consider themselves the forgotten army.

Time after time incidents occurred which made the young officers wonder if anyone really knew what was going on, and, if they did, did they care? Ian Scott, who had proved his courage and that of his men on numerous occasions, was often reduced to hair-tearing frustration at the incompetence he encountered. After being cut off from his Division for several days during which he and his small group of men endured appalling hardships before regaining contact, he was surprised to be rebuked instead of congratulated on his initiative. A staff officer greeted him with the words, "You have no business to be here – you are posted as missing, believed prisoner-of-war."

It was not the only occasion when his confidence in his superiors was badly dented, and an ugly scene was only narrowly avoided by General Slim's tact and good humour. Scott, now a major commanding two companies, was totally bewildered by orders he had received from headquarters of Burcorps. "They were so vague and so ridiculous that I decided to go to Corps H.Q. to seek clarification. I was again feeling like death from malaria and dysentery and so was quite ready to have a fight with the first Staff Officer I met. On arrival I went in through a door into semi-darkness and started to feel my way up a narrow staircase. I sensed rather than saw someone coming down the stairs, we met, and a voice said, 'And who are you?' I was unable to distinguish the voice speaking, but saw that he was wearing a bush hat and he certainly did not look important. 'I am OC FF9,' I replied, 'and am looking for the halfwit who gave me these bloody stupid orders which I want to discuss.' There was a silence. The figure in the bush hat turned and started to go upstairs, saying 'Follow me.' I did and he entered a well-lit room where to my horror, I saw that he was wearing the insignia of General – he was General Slim, the Corps Commander. He said to his GI, 'This young man is looking for the halfwit who gave him some bloody stupid orders – must be you old boy.' He gave me a pat on the back and said, 'Give him hell,' and he resumed his descent down the stairs."

Scott succeeded in getting his orders modified. But many young officers lacked his boldness, preferring to carry out the most ludicrous orders rather than protest. Their docile acceptance of orders they totally disagreed with did nothing to bolster the morale of the men who felt they were simply being used as cannon fodder.

The Regimental History of the Duke of Wellington's Regiment stated, "There were few who fought in the Burma retreat who could not agree that a little more realism in the higher organization and direction of training in peace, and a little more foresight in planning, would have mitigated the worst consequences of the campaign and made our defeat less ignominious than it was."

The last reinforcements to reach Burma were the Royal Inniskilling Fusiliers who were flown into Magwe by aircraft which had been sent to evacuate civilian families. The "Skins" had been on internal security duties in Meerut. They were in the main tough, well-disciplined regulars who were anxious to have a crack at the enemy. They were Irishmen who had enlisted for long periods for various reasons; some wished to escape from appalling slums, unemployment, a murky past, or merely sought excitement. They had an infinite confidence in their senior N.C.O.s on whom they relied so much, for few ever had direct contact with their officers.

Company Sergeant-Major John "Tim" Finnerty was typical of that breed which had long been the unfair butt of the cartoonists and comedians. A Southern Irishman, he had enlisted in 1933 and epitomized the senior N.C.O: tough, thoroughly professional, dedicated to the welfare of his men, loyal to the Regiment, but more than a trifle cynical of the capabilities of some officers.

They did not have long to wait before they experienced their baptism of fire. Within a short time of landing at Magwe they lost their Commanding Officer, Lieutenant-Colonel Ralph Cox.

They met veterans from the Gloucesters, Cameronians, and the Yorkshire Regiment and it was not long before some of their bitterness rubbed off onto the relatively raw "Skins". At Shwedaung they heard a staff officer in a tight spot observe that it was "every man for himself", a sentiment which was contrary to all they had been taught.

Soon afterwards, when the "Skins" fought alongside tanks of the 7th Armoured Brigade, Finnerty found himself wondering why it needed a war for the infantry and armour to work together. Why had it not been done in peacetime?

But what rankled the troops most was the feeling that they were being deliberately kept in the dark; no one bothered to give them any information. "Unfortunately one got the impression that some of the staff of higher formations seemed to think that a well-starched suit of K.D. uniform would make the enemy feel he was fighting a lost war," commented Finnerty.

The poor system of communications often resulted in a lack of direct orders from Divisional Headquarters and units frequently remained in position waiting for instructions which never came.

Finnerty's own battalion was switched so many times from one brigade to another that there were times when the men did not know who their brigade commander was. It was not the ideal atmosphere in which to prepare for the most crucial part of the campaign.

CHAPTER 20

"What's the matter with us out here?"
an officer's wife

Maymyo, where the army had set up its headquarters, was to the Europeans in Burma what Simla was to their counterparts in India – a corner of a hot and humid land to which had been transplanted an English oasis. In peacetime it was the summer capital to which people escaped from the heat of the Irrawaddy valley and the stench of Rangoon. Now its population had almost quadrupled.

Earlier on it had been filled with refugees from Rangoon and this human flood had been swollen by the arrival of the wounded from Sittang and other battles. The situation worsened even more when Sir Reginald Dorman-Smith turned up and made it the seat of Government.

Now an air of decay and disintegration permeated the town, similar to that which had gripped Rangoon at the start of the campaign.

Leland Stowe wrote, "Like everything else in this land where empire is falling to pieces its days are numbered."

Maymyo was usually approached from Mandalay along a forty-mile stretch of road which consisted of more than two hundred tortuous bends and curves. But the journey was well worth the effort; when the visitor reached the top of the high plateau 3,500 feet above sea level, he was greeted by a scene of stunning beauty. The tarmac streets were shaded by towering elms and the spacious houses and bungalows were surrounded by lush green lawns and flower beds which presented a palette of dazzling colours. Gentle breezes fanned the air during the daytime, and at night one needed a log fire and a heavy blanket on the bed when you retired. It boasted a fine golf course, a polo ground, tennis courts and every other sporting facility that the English family on holiday could desire. The hub of social activity was naturally the European Club, a huge rambling bungalow-style building set in hundreds of acres of undulating countryside dotted with massive oaks and elms. When Stowe sat on the balcony for the first time he mused, "Everything is green and spacious and lazily restful, like a slumbersome village in Kent or Connecticut."

Food was plentiful and varied; there were strawberries in abundance and the Mandalay Brewery was still providing a very good beer, while the social round continued very much as before, even to the regular weekly dances. The hard core of regulars, accustomed to the leisurely tempo of an unalterable life, were determined to see that the sudden and unwelcome influx of refugees would do nothing to change it.

The Governor, his family and his staff were in the summer residence, where Army Headquarters had also been established. The peacetime barracks were grossly overcrowded with survivors from the Sittang, and the two hospitals were packed with sick and wounded soldiers, while more and more were arriving after each battle.

Mrs Finetta Bagot said, "Wives were rather unwanted and civil officials were not at all interested in them when they arrived."

The club facilities were made available to officers and those civilians whose status merited temporary membership. Officers wounded in battle and prematurely discharged from hospital to make room for more urgent cases discussed the progress of war with others who were recovering from dysentery and malaria. Their main topic of conversation was the manner in which it was being conducted and the lack of leadership among the army commanders. Tempers soared when the Sittang was mentioned, and whenever an officer from headquarters put in an appearance he was invariably subjected to a verbal assault. The oil men, timber men and businessmen from Rangoon protested volubly about the inactivity of the Governor, and when any of his officials dropped in for a drink they were left in no doubt as to how they felt.

The lounge was known as the 'snake pit,' for it was that part of the club most frequented by the women, most of whom were waiting to be evacuated to India. Understandably all were worried about their menfolk.

The uncertainty and the lack of information aroused deep resentment and an atmosphere of bitterness pervaded the 'snake pit' which often echoed to loudly voiced criticism of Sir Reginald, which, in normal times, good manners, etiquette, and a realism that to incur his displeasure could mean social ostracism, would have prevented them voicing. With few exceptions they felt they had been betrayed and misled by an incompetent administration which had not given a true picture of the military situation and had made no real effort to organize an efficient system of evacuation. Nearly everyone was convinced that priority was given to high-ranking officials.

But it was the Governor and his wife who were subjected to the most strident abuse. Everyone knew, or claimed to know, that a private plane was standing by to whisk them away to safety as soon as things got too hot. It was not true, but no one bothered to try to find out the truth. Sir Reginald was determined to remain in Burma and his wife wanted to be at his side, but the Governor considered it below his dignity to answer his critics and he remained aloof and silent. People continued in their belief that he did not care a damn for the refugees when in fact he had repeatedly urged the Viceroy of India to send more aircraft for the women, children and wounded. As for himself, he said he was determined that he would never occupy a seat that could be taken by a woman, child or sick person. He would, when the time came, walk to India.

But luckless Sir Reginald could do no right. There seemed no end to the stories chronicling his ineptitude and concern for his own comfort. If they could not confront the Governor face to face the women seldom missed an opportunity to vent their fury on any of his officials who were unwise enough to venture into the club. On one such occasion Lieutenant-Colonel Miller, an A.D.C., stormed out almost smashing the glass door behind him when a woman asked, "What's your stupid fool of a Governor going to do?"

"I resent that, madam. As an officer of His Excellency's staff I cannot tolerate such language."

Although bitter fighting was going on to hold Upper Burma, Maymyo had escaped the serious attention of Japanese bombers, which were more concerned with launching terror raids on the more densely crowded native cities, and this immunity did nothing to dispel the air of unreality. The town had suffered only one raid and that had not caused a great deal of damage. The anger that was engendered was not directed at the enemy but at the authorities' failure to give advance warning.

As time passed and the road to Mandalay became more and more choked with refugee cars, morale in Maymyo slumped even further. Conversation became increasingly more defeatist and the criticism more acrimonious. O. D. Gallagher commented, "They seem to be little interested in anything except getting out of the country, buying cigarettes, having parties and scoffing."

To some extent the mood of the civilians was understandable, even justified, for there was an acute shortage of reliable news.

News manipulation had created many enemies and when soldiers and civilians began pouring into Maymyo with different stories to those that had been broadcast it did nothing to enhance the credibility of the Government or Army Headquarters.

Surprisingly, or, as some said, typically, little was done to dispel the snowball of rumours which quickly developed into an avalanche. In fact some senior officers visiting the club went out of their way to highlight the rift that existed between the civil and military. One furious colonel announced at the top of his voice, "I wish someone would shoot the Governor. That would be one of the biggest improvements that could happen."

Such tactless outbursts did nothing to lift the pall of gloom and despondency which had settled over the town. The journalists, not usually prone to rumours, found it difficult to separate fact from fiction, for no sooner had they decided to ignore a particular story that was going the rounds than it was confirmed. Most of the stories emanated from the wives of officers who had no conception of what security meant; they simply wanted to score points. Gallagher was surprised to find himself the recipient of the contents of secret messages sent from the Army and the Government to India and London.

What was said in the 'snake pit' did not depict an entirely true picture of Burma at the time. There were still a great many men and women who displayed incredible fortitude and a grim determination to defeat the enemy. But they tended to shun the club and as a result their views were unheard. There were also many civilians working side by side with the army impeding the advancing enemy whenever they could by carrying out a policy of total denial.

That there was chaos and confusion is borne out by a secret message General Alexander sent to the Commander-in-Chief:

"I have had a long talk with H.E. about the civil side which had badly broken down – in my opinion his various officials have let him down badly – they have mostly packed up and seem quite incapable of even trying. H.E. has promised to get rid of his old and useless men and put in younger, more energetic fellows."

The rot, however, was too deep-rooted and no matter how hard and how earnestly the two men tried there was no stopping it. The smell of defeat was in the air.

Hutton, branded the pessimist, had with commendable foresight organized a system of backloading vital stores and equipment for the withdrawing army which meant that some things such as petrol were gradually becoming scarce in Maymyo. Unfortunately the need for priority being given to the army was not appreciated by the civilians who considered they were being given a raw deal.

It seemed inconceivable to the people in overcrowded Maymyo that there could be a shortage of petrol in a country that was one of the world's largest oil producers. The same applied to salt, for Burma had big mines in the south. As for food, how could there be a shortage in a place where there were strawberries every day of the year?

The atmosphere was not improved by the presence of so many soldiers who had recovered from their wounds and were anxious to rejoin their units, but who found that no arrangements had been made to post them. Blissfully ignorant of their plight, the civilians tended to dub them as line-dodgers.

As in Rangoon the evacuation scheme for Maymyo was a disorganized shambles. Mothers with children waited day after day for information, but nothing was announced. In the more outlying areas, men who had spent a lifetime working in the teak forests with elephants became so impatient with the inactivity of the authorities that they organized their own schemes and transported large numbers of refugees to the Indian border on the backs of the elephants.

Finetta Bagot was only one of many mothers who had endured agonies of suspense brought about by the vacillation and frequent changes of mind on the part of the authorities. The frustrations seemed endless. First she was told that the wives of her husband's soldiers would be leaving at any moment, then it was cancelled. When they did depart in a lorry she was told she would have to stay as it was not for officers' wives. Eventually she was told that those women without children or with children big enough would have to walk out. Her daughter Veronica fell into the latter class. Then when she was offered a flight out she felt forced to decline on the grounds that she could not possibly go when there were other more deserving cases, and her name was taken off the list.

When she and her daughter *did* leave they travelled in a grossly overcrowded carriage filled with Europeans and Indians with a hole in the floor for a latrine. They were given very little water or food for the journey to Shwebo, which took 24 hours. There they joined a waiting crowd of refugees until an American troop plane landed and the pilot said he would take off with as many as possible. Mrs Bagot, like the others, had nothing but what she wore and a few personal belongings tied up in a bundle. The aircraft was so overloaded there were women and children sitting on the floor.

When Anne Purton received orders to fly out, she and her baby were packed into an overladen car and driven to Shwebo where they slept on mounds of straw until an aircraft was available.

For scores of thousands there was no aircraft. For them the only way to safety was on foot to India. Years of complacency and a refusal to face up to reality had resulted in the almost certain loss of Burma, but India would be a rallying point from which it would be reconquered. Or so many thought.

Clare Luce, an American correspondent who had recently arrived in Maymyo from India, was not too optimistic. "There the slogan is, 'Come to India and forget the war,' " she told her colleagues. Events in Burma, she said, had done nothing to arouse a sense of urgency. People still dressed for dinner, while race meetings, bridge parties, dances and cocktail parties continued with undiminished zest.

Despite his wounds, Charles Bagot had insisted on remaining with his men, even though there were times when he had to be supported. It was only on the personal orders of Cowan that he reluctantly agreed to go to hospital in Maymyo. He travelled from Allanmyo to Mandalay with hundreds of other sick and wounded soldiers in a paddle steamer with barges lashed alongside. The trip took ten days and he was shocked at the conditions in which he had to live, and he appreciated the reason why so many of the less seriously wounded had refused to go to hospital, preferring to nurse themselves. They thought they had a better chance of survival.

The primitive launches had to secure alongside the bank every day while parties were sent ashore to gather timber for the boilers. Every barge contained at least 500 men and it was impossible to move across the deck without stepping on a recumbent body. The sanitary arrangements were impossibly primitive and inadequate. There was only one medical officer, one nursing sister and two Burmese V.A.D.s.

The medical officer who had until recently been a civilian brought the ominous flush to Bagot's neck. "He appeared to be callously disinterested in his charges and conditions on the ship. He spent most of his time closeted in his cabin."

The nurses on the other hand were magnificent, tending the men throughout the day and night, changing and washing bandages without a thought for their own weariness. Nothing, he found, was too much for them.

Later, he discovered, one of the barges had been abandoned with some of the wounded still aboard. One of the young nurses remained behind with those who could not walk, another set off for Assam with those who could. Many died on the way, some through lack of salt. On arrival at Mandalay the sick and wounded had to wait intolerably long periods as there was a shortage of trains to take them to Maymyo.

Bagot had remained remarkably cheerful until he reached Maymyo, where he realized he was witnessing the rapid deterioration of one of Burma's most important towns and he reflected that morale seemed to decrease the further one was from the front.

"Whenever the sirens sounded, and that was often, the offices and barracks emptied like rabbit warrens invaded by ferrets. Patients ran, hobbled or were carried out of the hospital wards. A few with a measure of self-respect left in them occupied slit trenches; for the majority salvation lay only in the jungle."

After two days in hospital he was told he was being evacuated to India, something which did not appeal to him in the least and he explained that as he could walk he should be allowed to live in a private house and attend hospital as an outpatient. Not only would that release a bed for a much needier case, but it would enable him to attend to regimental affairs. But when he went to army headquarters no one could tell him the present whereabouts of the Gloucesters, and he was told that it was doubtful if they still existed.

Knowing how every infantry unit at the front was desperately short of men he was appalled at the large number of soldiers aimlessly roaming the streets. Many of them, he discovered, wanted to rejoin their regiments, but no one was available to help them. There were others, however, who had no intention of going anywhere near the enemy and they simply kept well out of the way, knowing that when, or, if ever, their cases were dealt with in India there would be no witnesses or records available.

Sickened and dispirited by the slow paralysis which gripped Maymyo, Bagot, having at last discovered their whereabouts, wasted no time in rejoining his men. His batman summed up the feelings of the Gloucesters. "I had a feeling he would turn up all right. He's much too fly for those yellow bastards."

What none of the fighting soldiers knew was that General Wavell had virtually conceded defeat. He had informed Winston Churchill, "I do not think we can count on holding Upper Burma for long if the Japanese put in a determined attack." His own troops were still short of equipment, especially artillery and reinforcements in any strength were out of the question. Although he was anxious to accept as much Chinese support as possible, he was not banking on too much; "Chinese co-operation not easy and they are distrustful of our fighting ability and inclined to hang back."

CHAPTER 21

"Anyone who was in Yenangyaung on 18th and 19th April 1942, must have a clear idea of what the Hell of the Bible is really like"

History of the King's Own Yorkshire Light Infantry

The town and oil wells of Yenangyaung sprawled untidily over fifteen square miles on the banks of the Irrawaddy. It was not an attractive place to look at, the thousands of steel derricks resembled a man-made forest, but it was one of the richest areas in the world. It boasted 5,000 oil wells, three petrol refineries and the largest power station in the whole of Burma. The tremendous annual output had made the shareholders, many of whom had never seen the place, extremely rich. It was not an unpleasant place to work; the oil men and their families lived in beautiful bungalows with neatly laid-out gardens and were waited on by an abundance of servants. The clubs were among the best in the country.

The capture of Yenangyaung was vital to the Japanese. Having little of their own, oil was essential to their plans.

The oil was also of vital importance to the Imperial forces, for the entire motorized transport and armour of the army was now dependent on what was produced at Yenangyaung, and General Slim was determined to hold the oil fields until the last possible moment. He was equally determined that the enemy would not take possession of one workable well, and as with the refineries at Syriam a programme of total denial was prepared.

In a matter of hours Yenangyaung became a ghost town. The women and children and non-essential staff were given 12 hours to prepare for evacuation by river steamer.

The oil executive, Forster, and Captain Scott were again called in to supervise the work of demolition. General Slim personally inspected the oil fields and approved of what they had done. He was something of an expert himself having witnessed the oil fields in Syria and Iraq being prepared for demolition, only there the final step had not been necessary. Now he feared it was inevitable. It was simply a question of time, but the longer it could be delayed the better.

The Japanese, supported by large numbers of hostile Burmans, launched their advance towards the oilfields on 10 April, employing every possible ruse to confuse the British and Indian troops who at times were unable to tell friend from foe. The Japanese and their supporters mingled with genuine refugees trying to flee the battle area and only at the last moment did they reveal their true identity, often with devastating effect. Bullock carts piled high with hay would turn out to be concealed machine-gun nests, while the Japanese wore uniforms which had been taken off dead troops or prisoners.

Although a number of spirited actions were fought and strong enemy attacks repeatedly repulsed, it was becoming increasingly clear that nothing short of a miracle could save the oilfields. General Slim, who had set up his headquarters on a low, shrub-covered hillock on the bank of the Pin Chaung just north of Yenangyaung, had not, however, entirely given up hope. Alexander had promised to send him the 38th Chinese Division, but it seemed an agonisingly long time putting in an appearance.

Apart from the demolition squads and a small number of troops detailed to garrison the oil wells, Yenangyaung was deserted. For the seven officers and 170 other ranks of the Gloucesters who formed the main part of the force it was a welcome respite. After all they had endured during the retreat from Rangoon, Yenangyaung seemed like a holiday camp. The hastily abandoned bungalows provided every possible comfort. The speed with which the civilians had been asked to leave was brought home to the newly appointed Major Bruce Kinloch when he went into the kitchen of one house and found a half-eaten meal and a half-finished glass of wine on the table.

The unexpected oasis was doubly welcomed by the Gloucesters, for the last leg of their journey to Yenangyaung had been particularly arduous. Biggs recalled it: "I had about twenty or thirty men on my lorry and we were continuously harassed by Jap fighters; one in particular kept coming at us so I gave the order that whenever it approached, all the men were to jump off and take whatever cover there was nearby. Several times we did this but nothing happened, but on one occasion the lorry was sprayed with machine-gun fire; there were bullet holes everywhere but the engine wasn't affected and the tyres weren't hit. We felt we had had a lucky escape."

A little further on they were stopped by a strange apparition: "A man, all red and naked. I asked him who he was and he said he was a private in the KOYLI who had been captured, stripped and tied out in the sun. We took him along to Yenangyaung where he left us to find some clothes."

General Slim moved his inadequate forces with the skill of a chess master, strengthening a position here, meeting a fresh challenge there, and diverting tanks and infantry to where they were most needed, but he was never allowed to command the situation; it was the enemy who dictated his tactics. They seemed to call check mate at every move. His task was not made any easier by the fact that Army Headquarters held views with which he was not entirely in agreement. He would have preferred to have withdrawn the 17th Division from Taungdwingyi and recaptured Magwe, but Alexander insisted the town had to be held; he feared the Chinese would think they had been abandoned if the town was evacuated. Alexander could not risk offending his ally; he needed the promised troops, and knew it would not take much for the vacillating Chiang Kai-shek to change his mind; he made no secret of the fact that he thought the Chinese were doing the fighting while the British did nothing but retreat.

The support of the Chinese overrode all other considerations, for General Bruce Scott's 1st Burma Division was fighting for survival and retiring towards Yenangyaung. Without the Chinese they were more or less doomed.

On 15 April General Slim gave the order for the demolition of the oilfields and refinery. Only the power house was exempted; it was needed to provide electricity for a small oil field at Chauk which was still functioning and serving the army.

A series of earth-shattering explosions sent millions of gallons of crude oil up in flames. Columns of orange-black smoke soared hundreds of feet into the air and the ground shuddered under foot as machinery, workshops and buildings disintegrated. The drills were wrecked and cement poured down the shafts. Men with oxy-acetylene torches and sledge hammers destroyed intricate machinery and equipment.

The soldiers and 'last-ditchers' suffered terribly, for apart from the intense heat of the fires a pitiless sun burned down and there was hardly any water, as the tanks perched on the hills above the oilfield had been destroyed and the only water available was what remained in the pipes. Men, who a short time before had been splashing about in the swimming pools, would have given a month's pay for a mugful. The food plundered from the larders ran out and many of the men had to exist for an entire day on a wipe of tinned sardine on a hard biscuit.

The enemy launched a series of savage attacks employing their usual jitter attacks and setting up road blocks at vital points which resulted in some units being separated. Near Slim's old headquarters the Japanese captured some anti-aircraft guns which were covering the road along which some transport was withdrawing, but a stout action by infantry supported by some tanks resulted in their recapture.

South of the Pin Chaung a strong enemy force had penetrated Yenangyaung itself, too late to prevent the destruction of the oil wells, but in an ideal position to destroy the 1st Burma Division slowly making its way towards Yenangyaung. They presented a pitiful picture to Darrell Berrigan, the United Press of American correspondent. "Men, mules and horses were collecting, dog-tired, in the sand for a brief rest, then heaving themselves to their feet and again marching forward. Bearded, dust-caked men with their sweat dried white across their shirts, their water bottles clanking against the hips, fell into position as the sun sank behind the smoke from the burning city of Yenangyaung."

With his primitive system of communications it was almost impossible for General Slim to form an accurate assessment of the battle; no sooner did a trickle of news reach his headquarters than the situation altered entirely. The cynical use by the Japanese of uniforms taken from dead Burma Rifles, British and Indian troops, added to the number of misleading reports. But the most effective tactic was once again the road block, and it was a major blow for the beleaguered British and Indian troops when the Japanese captured the vital ford over the Pin Chaung, the only line of retreat and the only source of water. Fortunately for Slim he had just moved his headquarters back to Gwegyo otherwise he might have found himself in a situation similar to Alexander at Taukkyan.

Cut off in the area of the oilfields were the Inniskillings, the Cameronians, the West Yorks, the Gloucesters, Punjabis, Jats, Sikhs, Garhwalis, Gurkhas, Kachins and Chins from northern Burma.

When a party of Japanese infiltrated from a number of directions and reached the power house, it was the prelude to a battle which was one of the bloodiest and most ferocious of the campaign.

"I remember," said Biggs, "I had a fire going and was getting ready for breakfast when our H.Q. was attacked by the Japs with rifle, machine guns and mortars. I stayed until I knew we would be overrun, and as the only way out was down a deep incline towards the Irrawaddy I lost my lorry and everything in it. I only had what I stood in and a gin bottle for carrying water."

The party of about twenty men regrouped on the river bank and took stock; each man had a rifle or revolver and there was one Tommy-gun but only a few rounds of ammunition. They decided to split up and head for Magwe.

The power house was quickly recaptured by troops sent ahead of the main column of the 1st Burma Division, and at midnight on 16 April it was destroyed as there was no longer any question of production being continued at Chauk. The richest area in the country was now worthless, there was nothing to defend, but somehow or other the encircled British, Indian and Burmese troops had to be extricated. Tanks and infantry made a series of gallant attempts to smash the road blocks but no sooner were they cleared than the enemy rushed in reinforcements and re-established them. Although heavy losses were inflicted on the Japanese, very little transport was able to get across; they were sitting targets for the artillery and mortars carefully concealed on the higher ground around the ford.

Meanwhile General Slim displayed a coolness and confidence he did not feel, and prayed that the promised 38th Division of the Chinese Army would not be too long in arriving, for then he could launch an attack across the Pin Chaung to coincide with the breakout of the 1st Burma Division.

For the tanks fighting with the 17th Division and covering the withdrawal of the 1st Burma Division, there had been no respite. Like the infantry the tank commanders had great difficulty in distinguishing between friend and foe and they had to exercise the utmost caution as the Japanese had captured some Stuart tanks at Shwedaung and had rushed them into action. Apart from the danger of being fired on by a captured tank, commanders had to be extremely careful with their signals as the enemy could listen to their wireless. The danger of inadvertently passing vital information to the enemy was overcome by introducing a simple but fool-proof code. Anyone who came on the air had to answer a question the reply to which could only be given by a genuine tank man, such as being asked to give an officer or sergeant-major's nickname.

There was also a new and sinister weapon employed by the Japanese which the British tank crews had not encountered before – a glass grenade containing hydrogen cyanide, a knock-out gas, which could be thrown through the slits or into the open turret rendering the driver and crew unconscious. It was delivered by a soldier who accepted almost certain death as he had to rush the tank and almost drop the phial inside.

Above the din of battle British and Indian voices could be heard calling out for water through parched lips. The heat of the fires was made even more unendurable by a blazing sun which sent the temperature up to 114 degrees. As bullets cut through water pipes the thin trickle that was released sent men scurrying from cover to cup their hands below to catch a few precious drops of water. Many of them were cut down, but it was quicker and more merciful end than choking to death on a swollen tongue.

There was no shade and the ground was so hard it was impossible to bury the dead and soon the stench of rotting flesh fouled the air. When darkness came the experience gained on the North-West Frontier helped the trapped men to winkle out the snipers who were picked off when the flash of their rifles betrayed their position.

No one fought with greater courage than the 'Skins' who had barely had time to acclimatize, and none died more bravely. A long queue of wounded formed up in uncomplaining silence to be treated by the one medical officer, whilst another queue, resigned to the fact that death was not far off, lined up to see the chaplain to make confessions and receive the last sacrament before returning to their post.

As the mounds of dead grew higher, every man capable of pulling a trigger took up arms. Finnerty formed a company of 'odds and sods' which consisted of cooks, drivers, signallers and men who had become detached from their own units, but bravely as they fought, they were hopelessly outnumbered and they were forced to withdraw under a withering hail of machine-gun fire.

A great many wounded were packed into the Field Ambulance, but the enemy deliberately shelled it and set it on fire. Those who were able to scramble out were mown down.

As the hours passed and attemps to clear the road blocks and capture the vital village of Twingon, a mile to the south of the river, failed, Scott contacted Slim and informed him the enemy was now less than two miles from his own headquarters and his only hope lay in the Chinese counterattack.

General Slim's only contact with Scott was by radio from the headquarters of the 7th Armoured Brigade to the tank squadron attached to the 1st Burma Division. Slim was able to comfort his friend with the news that the Chinese had now arrived. Aware that the enemy was able to listen in, they adopted a personal code which they spoke in Gurkhali and often used intimate details obtained through their close personal friendship over many years. When they wanted to use numerals in order to co-ordinate the joint offensive in the morning they used the numbers of bungalows they had occupied in India, and the ages of their children and family birthdays.

A special cipher signal also informed Scott that the Chinese would identify themselves to the British, Indian and Gurkha soldiers by placing their caps over the muzzles of their rifles and raising them high above their heads. Somehow or other the Japanese heard about it with disastrous results.

The plan was for the 1st Burma Division to break out to the north, while the Chinese, supported by tanks from the 7th Armoured Brigade, would attack the road block at the Pin Chaung ford. It was the first time that British tanks had been commanded by a Chinese General, but Brigadier Anstice willingly agreed to it.

Slim waited on tenterhooks as the time passed and the Chinese gave no sign of beginning the assault. Slim realized that time meant little or nothing to his newfound ally. Major M. F. Rudkin, commanding C Squadron of the 2nd Royal Tank Regiment, reported to the Chinese and waited for the order to attack.

"It seemed most unlikely that the attack could start on time. I asked the British liaison officer with the Chinese what was happening and he informed me that as the Chinese realized that they would not be ready to attack at 0630 hours, they had put their watches back one hour, so that officially they were still attacking at 0630 though the time would in reality be 0730. They had, therefore, not 'lost face' by being late."

General Slim was fortunate in having Lieutenant-General Sun Li Jen commanding the Chinese Division for he had been educated at Virginia Military Academy, spoke excellent English, and was capable of making a decision without referring to Chiang Kai-shek.

After some hitches the attack was launched with a Chinese interpreter running alongside the tanks acting as liaison officer between the infantry and the armour. Within a short time the leading tank was hit by a 75mm gun concealed just north of Pin Chaung. The north bank was, however, cleared, but the vital road block remained in enemy hands. Some of the tanks were almost through when they got bogged down in the soft sand of the river bed and General Sun announced that he would need time to prepare for a fresh assault. The Chinese had fought with skill and bravery, but their casualties had been high, especially among the officers, as it was customary for them to lead.

The 1st Burma Division had attacked dead on time but the artillery support was far less intense than Bruce Scott would have wished; his guns had to be used sparingly as ammunition was so short. The enemy also counterattacked in considerable strength and one by one units of the Burma Rifles began to falter and break and Scott was forced to accept the unpalatable fact that the Burma Rifles Battalion no longer existed as an effective fighting force. The rest of his troops, however, were very far from finished.

Enemy aircraft bombed at will while Japanese artillery and mortars maintained an almost ceaseless barrage. Bruce Scott, as fatigued as his men, urged them on to repeated attacks against the enemy who held the nearby villages and the series of ridges that dotted the barren countryside. If a ridge was held by fifty of the enemy the British, Gurkhas and Indians had to kill forty-nine before they took it, though there were isolated exceptions. On one ridge the West Yorkshires attacked with bayonet and rifle butt, boots and fists with such ferocity that the enemy forgot about the nobility of death and fled in total disorder.

To the war correspondents caught up in the battle, it seemed beyond belief that the Imperial troops who had endured so much could still obey orders to make one more attempt to seize a seemingly impregnable position.

Scott employed his small force of tanks to try and flush the enemy out of Yenangyaung, but the narrow streets were not ideal for tank work. Although it was late at night when the first tanks entered the town, the fires from the burning oilfields were so bright that the crews could read a book inside the turrets. Every house and building seemed to conceal a sniper and they were able to pick off the men standing up in the open turrets. The slow-moving Stuarts were also ideal targets for men on the rooftops armed with Molotov cocktails. At one stage the Japanese pressed home their attacks with such indifference to their own fate that they often got within touching distance of the tanks, and commanders standing up in the turrets were forced to resort to using their pistols in self-protection. Again the anti-tank guns were so well hidden that one tank was hit six times at close range by a 75-mm gun before it had time to return fire.

As the casualties mounted Scott knew that, no matter how impossible the odds, it was imperative to attempt a breakout; to remain meant total annihilation. He gave orders for another attempt to be made to capture the village of Twingon, since all routes out of Yenangyaung converged on the village. But no sooner had the enemy been dislodged than they were back in strength.

Two companies of the Inniskilling Fusiliers did manage to fight their way through to the Pin Chaung where they saw hordes of smiling men with caps covering the muzzles of their guns. The Inniskillings heaved sighs of relief, thinking they had at last linked up with the Chinese army. The next minute the smiles froze on their faces, the raised rifles were lowered and the bewildered 'Skins' found themselves gazing down the barrels. They had been deliberately lured into an ambush by the Japanese.

Tanks made another desperate attack on the road block but once again it petered out when the tanks spun uselessly in the soft sand. Darrell Berrigan, the American reporter, watched as the utterly weary soldiers made attack after attack on the strongly held ridges. But no matter how many Japanese they killed there always seemed more to take their places.

An Inniskilling Major told him, "Our men were worn out, but they had guts. They crouched low with bayonets fixed and charged like the guards on a parade ground – or at least, they thought they did. The plain fact is that they were so worn out that they stumbled forward like drunken men hardly able to hold their rifles but they gave them hell. Irishmen and Indian they gave them hell and drove the bastards out of Twingon."

But sheer bravery and a selfless disregard for life were not enough. The men had passed the limits of endurance. They had given more than any commander could possibly have asked for and Scott knew it.

At half past four in the afternoon he contacted General Slim and reported that, although he could hold out that night, if he waited until the morning his men would be in no fit state to renew the attack. He, therefore, asked for permission to destroy his guns and transport and fight his way out that night. Slim thought of their long years of friendship, then issued a heartbreaking order "Hang on". He had ordered the Chinese with all available tanks to launch a fresh attack in the morning. If the 1st Burma Division broke out at the same time, instead of in dribs and drabs, losses would not be so heavy and the valuable guns and transport might be saved.

Scott promised to hold on and ended with a personal appeal to his friend, "For God's sake, Bill, make these Chinese attack."

Throughout the long night, Slim could only stand and listen as the enemy guns and mortars pounded away at Scott's encircled troops, his ears straining for the retaliatory boom of Scott's own artillery. But it never came and he realized that he was conserving his meagre supply of shells, down to about twenty rounds per gun, until the morning. As the bombardment continued, Japanese infantry launched attack after attack and the British and Indian troops, lacking the support of the now demoralized Burmese units, were stretched to breaking strain to repulse them.

The Chinese attack across the Pin Chaung towards Twingon was scheduled for first light, but once again it was delayed. Slim was informed that it could not be mounted until half past twelve at the earliest. No doubt with Scott's desperate plea still echoing in his ears, Slim launched a separate attack with a squadron of tanks and some West Yorkshires. They battled their way across the Chaung but were thwarted by another of those muddles that seemed to dog every battle; a report was received that the Japanese were advancing in force and the transport assembled around Gwegyo was in danger of being cut off and so the tanks and infantry were withdrawn to meet this unexpected threat. The Japanese were in fact Chinese and a valuable opportunity was lost through lack of efficient communications.

With the failure of the Chinese to launch their attack on time there was no point in Scott delaying his own break-out, for the toll of dead and wounded was mounting while more and more men were succumbing to thirst and exhaustion. At this crucial stage the Chinese announced that they would have to postpone their attack until 1400 and when that time passed they revised it to 1500. Slim had to accept it with resignation for he knew it was not cowardice that was causing the delay; General Sun's men were also desperately short of water and without bowsers every drop had to be carried. At 1500 the Chinese were at last ready to attack.

By now Scott had lost contact with Corps Headquarters and was therefore unable to co-ordinate his breakout with the Chinese assault. With the help of a friendly Burman the tanks had found a track that led to the Pin Chaung and Scott formed up the squadron as a vanguard and began the breakout. The guns took up positions behind the tanks and were followed by the crowded ambulances and what transport had survived the merciless barrages. It was imperative to get the wounded through, as many had been lying unattended for more than 48 hours. Suddenly the track turned into loose sand which brought the wheels of the transport to a complete halt. Reluctantly Bruce Scott ordered the destruction of all the ambulances, lorries and guns. As many of the wounded as possible were put aboard the tanks and what remained of the column struck out on foot towards the Pin Chaung. Many of the wounded were too sick to move and tears coursed down the cheeks of men as they looked over their shoulders at the comrades they were abandoning. The enemy did everything possible to halt the column: machine guns chattered incessantly while artillery and mortar fire devastated the area. The turrets and sides of the tanks were crowded with men who hardly had the strength to cling on, others just capable of remaining upright limped beside the tanks, while others were supported on the shoulders of more fortunate comrades who had so far escaped unscathed. The agony of the walking men was intensified by the fact that many had lost their boots. Darrell Berrigan watched the infantry, supported by tanks, race towards Twingon. "As the leading tank topped the rise ahead, a mortar bomb narrowly missed its tail. The second tank passed as a bomb from over the hills landed in the ravine. A third tank took a direct hit and remained on top of the hill undamaged except for a small fire on its front."

Enemy aircraft appeared overhead dropping bombs and directing the artillery and mortars. More men were killed and wounded and animals broke loose and careered away in a cloud of dust which obscured the fighting men. When it cleared the column moved off again. A tank, some anti-aircraft guns and numerous lorries were hit, but progress continued slowly but steadily.

A tank commander listening on his wireless shouted aloud, "Our Chinese allies have crossed the Chaung on our right." The long-delayed counterattack had at last been mounted.

The Chinese may have been slow to launch their attack but when they did they fought magnificently, spurred on by the unaccustomed support of tanks. As they stormed through Twingon they released a number of prisoners, including the Inniskillings who had been duped at Pin Chaung.

The mules of the released troops were the first to smell water. They pricked up their ears, pawed the ground, brayed loudly, then galloped pell mell for the Pin Chaung. Those soldiers still capable of walking unaided broke into a shambling gait and flung themselves face down in the muddy water.

One officer who had done so much to inspire the KOYLI was Captain 'Taffy' Phillips. When the breakout was ordered he had urged them to go straight for the enemy with the bayonet and 'bags of guts'. His words struck home and many a man owed his life to him as they reached the Pin Chaung. But 'Taffy' Phillips could go no further; having endured so much he sat down by the Chaung and slipped into a sleep from which he did not wake.

All that remained of the battalion which had gone into action three months before was 150 officers and men.

There were men who, having survived, were riddled with a sense of guilt that nagged like the nerve of an exposed tooth. The fate of the abandoned wounded was first and foremost in the minds of those who had got through and a young officer volunteered to go back and see if there was any hope of rescuing them. He found the ambulances where they had been abandoned but every man had had his throat cut or been killed by a bayonet.

Soon afterwards Slim visited the gaunt, red-eyed men who had survived the hell of Yenangyaung and felt a glow of pride; nearly everyone still held his personal weapon and some grenades. But the

Division had ceased to exist as a fighting force. When it had arrived at Yenangyaung its two brigades had been no more than the strength of one and in the ensuing battles 20 per cent had been killed or wounded. It had lost most of its transport, a considerable proportion of its howitzers and 25-pounders, and most of its Bofors and mortars, none of which could be replaced.

The Chinese, fighting with immense courage, penetrated into Yenangyaung and repulsed a determined enemy counterattack. But when there were signs that the Japanese were going to repeat it General Slim ordered a withdrawal to the Pin Chaung; there seemed little point in wasting more lives on the burned-out town and the useless oil wells. On their last day together Major Rudkin was asked by the Chinese second-in-command how many men there were in his squadron. When he replied that there were eighty-five the Chinese soldier had a whip-round and handed over 1 rupee for each tank man.

The Chinese attack had come too late, however, to save large numbers of men trapped in the area of the oilfields. Among these were Finnerty's party of Inskillings who were trapped with other soldiers in a saucer of earth below a wrecked derrick. He repeatedly blew morse signals on his whistle in an attempt to disclose their plight, but there was no reply. Many of the men were badly wounded. One man had twenty-seven shrapnel wounds while others were delirious through lack of water. The ground as far as the eye could see was littered with the dead and wounded of friend and foe; the air pungent with the sour smell of rotting and putrefying flesh. With so little ammunition remaining the 'Skins' were forced to withhold their fire until they were certain every round would count. For eleven hours they were subject to rifle, machine-gun and mortar fire, during which time all they had to eat was some Horlicks stirred into their precious hoard of water. A tank tried to rescue them but received a direct hit.

A voice in impeccable English called out, "Lay down your arms; resistance is useless; if you do not give up within five minutes we will mortar you out." Then, more insistent, the voice shouted, "Don't be foolish; the whole Division is surrounded; all are prisoners." The Japanese advanced through the wounded, confident the trapped men would not open fire for fear of hitting their own comrades. Sergeant

Finnerty received a violent blow on the head and one of his men said resignedly, "They're here."

Those capable of moving threw their rifles and other weapons down a shaft; at least they had denied them to the enemy. With quiet dignity the blood-soaked men in tattered khaki rose and helped their wounded comrades to their feet. Seven Japanese soldiers lined up a few feet away and at gunpoint ordered everyone to remove their equipment. One man refused to hand over his bible and was given a vicious clout with a rifle butt. When a soldier with a first aid bag began to attend the wounded, an officer strode up, kicked him in the face, and scattered the precious contents over the ground. The same officer then struck Finnerty on the chin for giving signals with his whistle.

On orders from the officer, Japanese soldiers dashed forward and pinioned everyone's hands behind their backs. An attempt was even made to tie up one soldier who had lost an arm; mercifully he bled to death. The captured men were then bundled into some stifling hot huts where one soldier, tormented by thirst, tried to drink his own urine.

The small group of Irishmen was swollen by scores of British and Indian troops until there was some 300 officers and men crammed into a cruelly confined area. Hour by hour the numbers dwindled. An officer broke loose and struck a Japanese officer and several men before he was shot. A young soldier started to sing Ave Maria, and it was some time before anyone realized he had gone mad.

No one was sure how long they were imprisoned before being bundled out into the sunlight, deprived of their boots and clothing, tied like a line of slaves and ordered to move off. Those who faltered were beaten with rifles and sticks, and those who collapsed were shot or bayoneted. A Yorkshireman who fell remained defiant to the end. As his bonds were cut he bellowed out, "You yellow bastards." Then he turned and thanked his comrades before being shot twice through the head. Another who was cut adrift from the line worked his hands round the front of his body in order to take one last look at a family snapshot before being stabbed with bayonets while Japanese newspapermen took photographs.

The last leg of their journey was in relative comfort, but there was not a man who would not have preferred to walk, for the lorries that they were herded into were British and American vehicles captured in Rangoon.

The convoy passed long rows of unmarked graves and more than one man would have readily exchanged places, fearing that what lay ahead was far worse than death. It was not an unfounded fear, for they were taken to the infamous prison in Rangoon, where those who survived remained until the end of the war.

The resilience and will to survive of men whose courage had been so frequently questioned was remarkable. Not only were they determined to invade the enemy, they were determined to carry on fighting. George Biggs and his party were a typical example.

Having narrowly escaped from the power house, Biggs, with a revolver and two grenades in the pockets of his shorts, decided to try and get his party to Mandalay, where he hoped to obtain information which would enable them to rejoin the battalion. They set off under continuous fire, seeking what little cover there was available on the steep ridges.

"Things were getting really tough. We had little ammunition, our clothes were torn and salt-encrusted with dry sweat, our boots had worn out and a lot of the men were wearing slippers."

Soon afterwards they came across a badly wounded captain who begged to be left behind but they refused to abandon him. For a hefty bribe they persuaded some Burmans to ferry them across a river. They then made their way to a village where they managed to get the owner of a bullock cart to help them. "From that day to this I cannot say where he took us. I do know it took all day before we reached a small river which must have entered the Irrawaddy some miles on. I paid him 60 rupees and he arranged for us to be carried on two small boats which took all night to reach the Irrawaddy proper."

Soon afterwards they were able to transfer to a hospital steamer. "I have never seen such a sight in my life," said Biggs. "Troops of all ranks and colour were lying around the decks, legs off, wounded, all covered in masses of flies and getting little attention owing to the lack of medical equipment."

The officer in charge pleaded with him to remain as discipline had collapsed completely, but Biggs felt his first duty was to return to the battalion; however, he agreed to take all the weapons and ammunition which he distributed among his own men.

Eventually they reached Mount Popa, an extinct volcano rising out of the surrounding plain, where they rejoined the battalion and for the first time in days were able to drink clean water in unlimited quantities. Biggs was awarded the Military Medal.

At Mount Popa the badly mauled but by no means defeated 1st Burma Division began to rest and regroup in readiness to meet the enemy again. But now an unseen and silent enemy attacked which no amount of courage could defeat – cholera.

CHAPTER 22

"The scene in Mandalay beggars description"
Lady Dorman-Smith

If Maymyo was Burma's Shangri La, then Mandalay was its Hades. Although only forty miles of bumpy road separated the two towns, they had little in common. Mandalay, hot, dusty and dirty, was almost universally loathed. It was the second city of Burma and once the capital of the kingdom of Ava. The sole remaining reminder of Thibaw, the last king, who surrendered to the British in 1885, was the walled and moated palace renamed Fort Dufferin. In the lofty rooms supported by pillars made from the entire trunks of towering teak trees, the old kings had once given audience to their subjects. Now it was a rambling hotch-potch of pagodas, barracks, military depots and the principal military hospital. Such a concentration of army depots in such a small area may have been convenient in peacetime; in war time it provided a tempting target for enemy bombers.

The civil lines to the south encompassed the offices of the local district authority, the police barracks, the houses of the railway and civil officers, and the European business community. It also contained the large railway station and marshalling yards which day and night emitted a deafening din of hooting whistles and shunting trains. On the river front were the wharves of the Irrawaddy Flotilla Company.

The rest of the town consisted of the native quarter – a warren of narrow, squalid streets lined with tin and wooden shanties.

Every day more and more refugees crowded into the already over-populated city. The station became a centre of refuge for many of the homeless, and the platforms were thronged with people whose eyes had the dead look of defeat. The stench was indescribable.

As the military situation worsened the road to Mandalay became an incredible sight. Day and night hundreds of cars, jeeps and heavy lorries thundered along at a reckless pace, churning up vast clouds of dust.

Horns hooted furiously at the plodding bullock carts laden with women, children and a few sticks of furniture. Indian women walked along the edge of the road with bundles on their heads and weeping children clinging to the hems of their saris. Many had walked all the way from Rangoon.

Some of the cars were driven by fleeing refugees, but most were driven by Chinese who were trying to get the last Lend-Lease equipment through to Lashio. Few were experienced drivers and they drove the left-hand vehicles on the crown of the road at a speed which seldom dropped below 60 miles an hour. Crashes were inevitable and deaths frequent.

The town itself was rapidly giving way to lawlessness, panic and disorder, and already there were signs of a breakdown in the essential services.

Mrs Gwenllyan Coward, living in a house near the station, had always had a loathing for Mandalay, and day by day it intensified. As the wife of a railway officer she was forced to remain, as no arrangements had been made for the evacuation of wives. Although, like many other women, she was prepared to remain with her husband she was appalled by the attitude of some officials who were solely concerned with getting out themselves. As supplies became scarce, prices in the bazaars soared and a flourishing black market in petrol developed, her home became a transit camp for refugees who were given a hot meal and a bath before moving on.

Frequently she witnessed examples of disgraceful cowardice – such as the time a senior railway official visited her home after fleeing from Rangoon. "He had shot his dog then commandeered the Governor's personal coach, a huge white palatial thing which His Excellency used when he went on tour. It had a day room with comfortable arm chairs, a dining salon with a bureau, carpets, bathroom, and a kitchen equipped with the finest glass, china and silver. It was a palace on wheels. He burst into the house while we were having lunch. He was unshaven and had a revolver on his belt and was only concerned with getting to India. He had walked out of his house leaving everything to be looted, taken the coach and ordered it to be attached to the mail train leaving for Mandalay. The train was packed with refugees who were clinging to the roof and sides of the carriages, and sitting on the buffers. Yet he travelled in solitary comfort and soon after arrival flew out from Maymyo."

Violet Kelly's journey to Mandalay had, by contrast, been full of discomfort and unpleasant incidents. It took her several days, during which she had passed long, straggling columns of refugees carrying their few possessions on their heads or pushing hand carts. Dotted among them were naked men released from the lunatic asylum. "I saw one train with people clinging to the sides, sitting on the roof and on the coal, and in front of the engine. I was told some had been decapitated when the train passed under a low bridge."

When her party eventually arrived in Mandalay, the true situation was not revealed to the hungry and exhausted party. "We were told we would stay in Mandalay for the monsoon and during the dry season we would return to Rangoon in a country that had been freed from the invaders," recalled Miss Kelly.

As time passed, food became limited and deliveries unreliable; even water became scarce and a crisis was only avoided by some of the staff who had remained behind volunteering to pump water up each morning which was then stored in huge jars. Sanitation was also a headache; there were only four latrines for the menservants and one for the women. "This we overcame by digging trenches which could be extended each day by putting wooden lattice-type covers over freshly dug pits, whilst the old ones were filled in. The row of new lavatories in the hospital were useless as they had not been connected to the water system," said Miss Kelly.

The difficulties at the hospital soon began to escalate as more and more trains arrived laden with sick and wounded soldiers. Fortunately not all remained in Mandalay, some moved on to Maymyo, but too often there were more agonizingly long delays for the wretched patients.

Mrs Coward and some friends eased their agony by setting up improvised canteens on the station. "The European women nursed the soldiers in the dark, stifling coaches of the improvised ambulance trains. They were as hot as ovens, and the men were wracked with pain as the journey often took three days or more. No arrangements had been made to feed them and often their wounds were gangrenous. There were few nurses or medical orderlies, and we had to cope as best we could. The stench was awful and often all they had to eat was biscuits and cheese which had been commandeered from refreshment rooms on the way," she recalled.

The plight of the wounded was improved slightly when a temporary hospital was set up in the sidings, and the overworked nurses were able to bathe the men and change their filthy dressings.

Dick Coward was busy organizing trains to move the Chinese Fifth Army to the aid of the withdrawing British, and when they arrived in Mandalay Mrs Coward had her first glimpse of the Chinese on whom so much depended. "They were a rabble in arms wearing poor cotton uniforms. Their colonel was dressed exactly the same as the men, but the discipline was extremely strict. When someone reported the theft of some tools from an engine shed, he paraded his men and had their kit examined. When the culprit was found, an officer cut off his ear with his sword and said, 'In future this man will be known for what he is.' Another refugee train arrived which had been sabotaged by dacoits and the occupants robbed. The Chinese hunted them down and crucified them against the walls of a pagoda as a warning to others."

For those with little to do to occupy their time, the British Upper Burma Club, an old teak building within the walls of Fort Dufferin, was an ideal place in which to blot out the harsh realities of life. As in Maymyo the bar was well stocked. People who for years had lived from season to season learned to live from day to day. Inevitably cholera broke out among the Indian refugees and corpses began to litter the primitive transit camp which had been set up about six miles outside the town.

With total air superiority, the Japanese indulged in a series of terror raids, and town after town was destroyed with high explosive bombs and incendiaries – Taunggyi, Lashio, Loiwing, Taungoo, Maymyo and Mandalay.

On 3 April, Good Friday, the sky was dark with formations of heavy bombers. Seconds later high explosives, fragmentation and anti-personnel bombs were raining down on the defenceless city. Not a siren sounded the alert, although a complicated system of air-raid warnings had been devised. It had been carefully planned but not rehearsed, and it broke down in utter confusion at the first real test. The familiarity of false alarms had lured everyone into a sense of false security.

Mrs Coward explained, "There were various colours to indicate the degree of danger. The sirens were to be sounded when the telephone exchange received the yellow and the Anglo-Indian girls manning the switchboard were to remain at their posts until they received the red, which meant enemy bombers were approaching. Then everyone should go to the shelters, but the girls downed their receivers and left on the receipt of the yellow.''

Without one anti-aircraft gun to keep them at bay, the bombers were able to fly in with the precision of a practice run. The club received one of the first hits and the old teak building was soon a blazing inferno.

Miss Kelly was busy in one of the wards when the first raid started. "As the sound of aircraft engines grew louder everyone rushed for the shelters. I looked up and saw the sky was dark with planes. The damage was tremendous and hundreds of people were killed and wounded, and the fires, helped by the Fifth Columnists, raged for several days. Most of the houses were timber and three-quarters of the city was destroyed as they went up like matchwood. One bomb, said to be the first, fell on the Matron's house and razed it to the ground, and part of the Mandalay General Hospital was hit and set on fire."

Her words give no real idea of the horror and devastation that was wreaked by the 36 bombers which came over in relays and released their bombs simultaneously at 6000 feet – a tactic the pilots had discovered was most effective in terrorizing civilian populations.

As in Rangoon, business was being carried on as usual in the native quarter and the people were entirely unprepared; the carnage was terrifying. Within minutes the tiny streets were littered with the shattered bodies of victims. Arms and legs were strewn over the road while people killed by blast bore no visible injuries and seemed to be sleeping. The raid lasted for three hours, and when it ended Mandalay lay in total ruin.

As the fires spread, hundreds of people were burned alive or buried under the debris of collapsing buildings. The crowded station was hit and scores killed and maimed. Blast hurled a great many into the moat where they drowned. Unofficial figures said that two or three thousand had died, with at least five thousand wounded.

The marshalling yards were choked with wagons containing equipment and material which had been back-loaded from Rangoon, but in the haste few of them had been labelled. This oversight added to the horror of the raid for one of the wagons contained R.A.F. bombs. A shunting engine was sent to move the wagonload of bombs to safety, but the fire reached it before it could be shifted and the bombs exploded. The engine crew were sucked out by the blast and hurled a considerable distance. The heavy footbridge across the station yard was thrown into the air like a piece of paper caught in a stiff breeze.

Ammunition trucks went up, setting fire to oil tankers, the electricity system was put out of action, plunging hospitals into darkness and cutting off the power supply to the operating theatres. Hours after the bombers had departed the blazing city was still being rocked by the explosions from delayed-action bombs. The streets were covered with glowing sheets of red-hot corrugated iron and burning telegraph and electricity poles, and a great many natives were electrocuted by falling wires. The charred skeletons of cars and lorries blocked the roads which were pitted with huge craters. The A.R.P. system fell apart and the fires burned and spread uncontrolled when the water supply for the hoses was cut off.

For some reason the ambulances were not filled with petrol when the bombers came over, and many lives were needlessly lost because the drivers had to go searching for fuel before they could move their vehicles.

From Maymyo Lady Dorman-Smith wasted little time in visiting Mandalay, and that evening wrote, "The scene in Mandalay beggars description. Acre after acre of streets are just completely flat . . . the fire station was knocked out and 30,000 feet of hose destroyed straight away, also the fire engines. The streets are littered with burnt trees – the telephone wires down everywhere – burnt-out gharries – some with the remains of the pony – just too appalling for words. . . . There was hardly a civilian to be seen. The hospital near the station was burnt out – luckily they managed to save the patients . . . the smell was awful – it looks absolutely hopeless to begin to clear the mess. There was no warning – the first thing were the bombs."

By the time the bombers had departed, Violet Kelly's hospital had admitted more than 300 casualties. "Though we had a room for an operating theatre, the authorities had not equipped it as we were intended to take only overspill and medical cases; the Mandalay General Hospital was meant to deal with air-raid victims. Our wards were filled to saturation and the floor of the empty theatre was littered with so many injured that a great many had to be placed on the floors of the corridors."

Thankfully an enterprising doctor turned up with an operating table and some instruments he managed to acquire from a hospital in a nearby town. Miss Kelly set up another emergency operating theatre in a basement kitchen. When fire threatened to engulf the Mission Hospital, the patients were transferred to her already overcrowded and overworked hospital.

The collection and disposal of corpses created an immense problem; bodies of men, women and children lay everywhere. As the water became polluted a new menace arose – cholera. People simply sat down by the roadside and died. In a short time six hundred people were dying each day, and the toll rose even higher when dysentery and smallpox broke out.

"There was only a small mortuary in the compound capable of containing two bodies, but soon it was crammed like an abattoir," said Miss Kelly. "No one came to claim the bodies, and it seemed the entire population had disappeared. I urgently requested for the bodies to be removed by the central authority, but there was no response, and several sweltering hot days passed before our insistent demands resulted in the arrival of some Burmans from the Mandalay Rescue Squad. They counted forty bodies."

A shallow hole was dug in the rock-hard ground in a field near the hospital; there was no time for anything more elaborate. "They took some wooden grids from a nearby ditch-crossing and placed them over the top of the hole. They then put on gas masks and began moving the bodies from the mortuary. As they prepared to pour kerosene over the bodies an Indian came forward to claim his wife's body which was the first to have been buried, and so was at the bottom. The situation was too gruesome to allow him to remain there protesting, and he was sent away before the rotting, foul-smelling bodies were removed and her body recovered."

As the nurses and medical staff continued to tend the sick and wounded, the mass exodus from the city continued until the roads were just a seething mass of bewildered leaderless humanity. Motor cars and lorries were bogged down by the plodding bullock carts and those who had to walk. Although there was a special cart track by the road few used it, and the air was filled with the blast of car horns. The Indians, never popular with the Burmese, were attacked and robbed of their few pitiful possessions.

Incidents regularly occurred which reminded those who had stayed of the kind of dangers they would be exposed to when the Japanese arrived. "One day a British sergeant, a big burly man, turned up. He showed me healing wounds in the middle of both hands and said he had been held captive by the Japanese and with some others nailed to a fence and used for bayonet practice. He had managed to tear himself free and made his way northwards," said Miss Kelly.

Amid so much human misery there were those who considered the destruction of the club the most serious loss. Within a day or two, a new building was found and it was back in business. "Every evening for an hour or so they forgot the war," said Mrs Coward.

Food became scarcer daily and in order to survive people had to resort to rustling. Violet Kelly, who would not take a thing for herself, had no qualms where her patients were concerned. On one occasion the sergeant who had been crucified stole a sheep from a flock being driven up-country away from the Japanese.

It was not until the end of April that the hospital staff received an order to move to Myitkyina where they were to set up a new hospital; their patients would be transferred to a local hospital at Katha. But when they arrived at Myitkyina they found that no hospital space had been allocated, and although they scoured the area they were unable to find a suitable site. The time had clearly come when they could no longer carry on nursing, and they were instructed to register with the officer in charge of evacuation.

All Violet Kelly possessed were a few essentials which she had packed into a canvas bag; her shoes hung in shreds, but she was determined to walk to India with a group of doctors. Her insistence was overruled and she was ordered to register for a flight out. She waited for more than a week and there was still no passage available.

When she finally arrived in Myitkyina the airstrip was covered with unattended wounded soldiers on stretchers who were waiting for a special military plane to evacuate them. "Their greatest need was shade from the relentless sun and so we got some empty drums and stretched some cover between them, and we also found some things they could use as primitive urinals."

Violet Kelly and her colleagues who had endured so much finally flew out on 2 May. Her description of that important day was typically laconic. "We had a comfortable journey to India. We learned later that ours was the last flight; the next day enemy planes came over and bombed the airstrip."

The time had also come for Mrs Coward to go. She was reluctant to leave her husband but she knew he had been ordered to slow the Japanese advance by demolishing essential parts of the railway system. Since the flight of the panic-striken railway official, the Governor's coach had been sitting undamaged in a siding. "As it had to be taken across the Irrawaddy and destroyed as far north as possible, it was agreed that my daughter Ann and I could travel in it to Shwebo. After the privations of Mandalay it was sheer joy to have a bath in His Excellency's superb bathroom.

"Shwebo airstrip was short and the Dakota so overloaded with people and stretcher cases I felt certain it could not take off, but it skimmed the tree tops at the very last minute, and we were on our way to freedom." The next day the airstrip was destroyed by bombs.

Day after day Chinese, American and British pilots risked their lives to fly out as many refugees as possible before the enemy arrived. As the weather worsened the flights intensified and the Dakotas flew over the Naga Hills which soared 17,000 feet between the Brahmaputra and the Irrawaddy in thick cloud and mist.

Many gave up all hope of flying out and tens of thousands of refugees began to walk to India. The trek which was to claim countless lives was one of the greatest human tragedies of the war. Badly mismanaged, it was doomed to failure from the outset, and few were in any doubt that the fault lay entirely with Sir Reginald Dorman-Smith; he had been too pre-occupied with saving his family and his own skin.

Contrary to the rumours that were rife, the Governor had stayed on and a series of urgent messages to the Viceroy showed that he was determined to remain until the bitter end and see what he could do about the refugee problem.

A message sent by the Agent to the Government of India in Burma to the Viceroy described the torments being suffered by Sir Reginald: "He realizes that he is not really doing any governing but he has to appear to do so. His staff spend most of their time doing nothing or nothing that matters."

The Governor, the message continued, was faced with an impossible task. "Things are very near collapse. The complete destruction of Mandalay, unopposed bombing of Maymyo and other nerve centres have now destroyed the morale of the public and subordinate services and the mechanical and physical means of communication. The postal service is practically non-existent. The telegrams are nearly as bad and only a few telephones work. Except for a few essential military trains, the railways are out of it and are terribly short of staff with daily desertions."

Meanwhile General Alexander was pressing him to leave, as his continued presence was only adding to his problems, but the Governor was reluctant and announced his intention to set up his headquarters in Myitkyina. "It looks as if I will have to continue my inglorious retreat. . . . I want to stay as long as possible in order to ensure that as many refugees as possible are backloaded."

The train he travelled in to Myitkyina was straffed by enemy aircraft, but he escaped unharmed. There he joined his wife, and again he appealed for more aircraft but once more refused to fly out himself, insisting that priority must be given to the wounded.

1st May to Viceroy: "I hope to get my wife off tomorrow. As for myself, I feel I must stay on and take my chances with the official people who may be left." If necessary he would walk out and he asked for air drops of food to be made at Shinbwiyang for the refugees. "I do not wish to take up a seat which could be used by a refugee. . . . We must do everything we can for the wretched people here even though it may mean taking risks."

When Lady Dorman-Smith flew out, Sir Reginald was too ill to walk. She left with 40 lbs of hand luggage – nothing like the vast amount she was accused of taking with her.

Lieutenant-Colonel "Wally" Richmond could see no point in the Governor remaining and he sent an urgent message to Air Vice-Marshal Stevenson: "Governor refusing to leave. Anxious he be got out quickly. Nothing more he can do here."

But it took Winston Churchill's personal intervention to make "Dormouse Smith" board a plane: "No point your remaining longer. Stop. You should leave at once; this is an order."

The much-maligned Governor replied, "Following for Prime Minister. With a heavy heart I will obey your orders. I can do no more here and will leave at dawn May 5."

A Blenheim bomber landed at Myitkyina and His Excellency boarded with some hand baggage.

When he arrived in India his wife recorded, "So that's the end of all our possessions."

The airstrip at Myitkyina on 6 May was crowded with hundreds of women and children along with large numbers of wounded soldiers, the victims of a train crash. Despite efforts to maintain some semblance of order and priority, it was sheer chaos, with refugees determined to board the aircraft on a "first come, first served" basis. Men remained deaf to strictures that only women and children and severely wounded would be flown out, the rest would have to devise their own means of escape. The wounded were suffering untold agonies with stoic resignation. They had been assured they would be flown out by the R.A.F., while the civilians would be ferried aboard civilian aircraft.

Hour after hour passed and still there was no sign of the promised aircraft; then a Japanese reconnaissance plane flew low across the strip with the pilot waving a red flag which everyone took to be a warning for an impending raid and promptly fled to the improvised shelters which provided some, but not much, protection. Then two R.A.F. aircraft appeared in the distance and there was an immediate rush onto the tarmac by the people who had taken shelter. In view of the unexpected appearance of the enemy aircraft, it was decided that some of the women and children should be taken as well as the wounded. When the aircraft was loaded well beyond its limit, preparations were made for take off. As the aircraft began taxying there was a loud bang and it lurched violently to one side hurling the occupants all over the place. At first it was thought the pilot had hit something, but when they tumbled out they realized that enemy aircraft were bombing the strip. Machine-gun bullets were stitching through the fuselage, and small high-explosive bombs were cratering the airstrip.

Mavis Gully, a young woman who worked with the Ministry of Information, saw the bullets ripping through the aircraft and heard the crump of exploding bombs and decided to remain inside the aircraft with several badly wounded men and provide a running commentary through the open door. It was a decision which saved her life, for seeing the aircraft had been immobilised the attacking aircraft concentrated on straffing the other plane and the refugees. When the Japs finally flew off, they had killed fourteen people and wounded thirty.

Eric Battersby, a member of the Governor's personal staff, was at the airfield although he had no intention of seeking a flight out; he had already agreed to "walk out" with the Deputy Commissioner of Myitkyina and his party, and had been at the airstrip to see what assistance he could render in the evacuation. After helping to bury the dead and carry the wounded to the ambulances which had raced to the scene, he assisted in the pointless task of filling in some of the craters, for everyone was sure the bombers would return to complete their devastation. Furthermore, with such an acute shortage of aircraft it was considered extremely unlikely that any further attempts would be made to land. As many refugees as possible were put on the last train with as much food as possible, and then taken to Mogaung. Shortly afterwards two more R.A.F. aircraft arrived and managed to land, due entirely to the skill and courage of the pilots. The remainder of the wounded were hastily taken aboard and room was found for Miss Gully, the last woman to fly out of Burma.

That night the Japanese returned and dive-bombed the airstrip, rendering it completely unusable.

The Japanese were now only nineteen miles from Myitkyina and the Military Governor made the decision to evacuate the town. The remaining women and children were placed in the care of nuns and Roman Catholic priests and those not one hundred per cent fit were advised against trying to walk out.

The next day the bombers returned and bombed the airfield and the town, and the last people began to move out. The day after the enemy occupied Myitkyina.

The devastation of the airstrip was to result in one of the greatest tragedies of the evacuation. It meant that the people left behind, many already weak and sick, had to walk through the almost unknown Hukawng Valley.

Most of them got no further than Shingbwiyang, a place which was to figure prominently in the weeks and months to come in the obituary columns of *The Statesman* and other English-language newspapers.

CHAPTER 23

"Their story is one story – of costly compromises and costlier blindness on the part of their Governments – of common sacrifice, a common courage, and a common glory"

Leland Stowe of the R.A.F. and A.V.G.

During the long retreat the majority of the troops roundly cursed the R.A.F. for failing to provide air protection against the constant bombing and straffing. In some respects their attitude resembled that of the men trapped at Dunkirk; because they did not see any aircraft, they assumed the "Brylcreem Boys" had let them down. At the same time, there were soldiers who fervently prayed that they would not see another R.A.F. or A.V.G. aircraft again, for, on the one occasion they had, they had been subjected to ruthless bombing and machine-gunning. But in Burma, as in France, the R.A.F., with the invaluable support of a handful of American mercenaries, had performed a near-impossible task that was unequalled in any other theatre of war. But for them the retreating army would never have reached India.

When war came to the Far East the R.A.F. in Burma was even less prepared and poorly equipped than the army. The fighter defence for the entire country consisted of sixteen near obsolete Buffalo fighters and one pursuit squadron of the A.V.G. equipped with Tomahawks originally intended to fight in China but which Generalissimo Chiang Kai-shek had agreed, in the best interest of his own country, should be stationed at Mingaladon in order to defend Rangoon.

The appropriately named Buffalo was an aeronautical disaster and the Americans were anxious and only too grateful to get rid of them on any European country which would take them in 1939 and 1940.

The British, having tried them out, decided they were quite useless against German fighters and they ended up in Malaya and Burma where their inferiority was not considered of great importance as the Japanese aircraft were even worse. The truth was quite the reverse. The

Zero was vastly superior to the Buffalo and the American P.40. The pilots also had an advantage which had nothing to do with modernity; they considered it a great honour to die for the Emperor.

The performance of the Buffalo prompted one American pilot, Captain Philip White, who flew one in combat, to comment, "It is my belief that any commander who orders pilots out for combat in a Buffalo should consider the pilot as lost before leaving the ground."

Burma was also deprived of an adequate warning system which would enable the fighters, already at a grave disadvantage, to become airborne quickly. Only one radar unit, already well worn and almost obsolete, could be spared for Rangoon. Apart from that, there was a chain of civilian observers who kept a visual watch and dashed for the telephone at the first sight of approaching aircraft.

The fact that it took so long for the Japanese to establish aerial supremacy was largely due to the existence of the American Volunteer Group and their Tomahawks, with the menacing teeth of a tiger shark on the nose. The pilots were all mercenaries who bore no rank, wore no uniform, and were invariably referred to as mister. They were the most unconventional combat fliers in the world. They were also the highest paid, though employed, ironically, by a country which paid its soldiers the lowest rates of any army. They started off in Burma as much despised young men who were only there for the money, but ended up as heroes.

Leland Stowe had first encountered them in the Silver Grill in Rangoon and found it a depressing experience. They were all extremely fit and experienced pilots who had relinquished their ranks in the American Air Force and Navy in order to pick up a salary of $600 a month with a $500 bonus for every aircraft they shot down. At home they would have been paid $175 a month. Ground crew, radio specialists and technicians had trebled their pay. They were all volunteers who, with the unofficial approval of the American Government, had been smuggled out of the services and surreptitiously transported to their destination. To some extent the secrecy was laughable for their passports described the boisterous young men who toted six guns as circus acrobats, artists, students and tourists – a ruse which fooled no one. But as they were considered vital to American war strategy the subterfuge had been considered necessary in order not to provide ammunition for the powerful anti-war lobby or contravene the Neutrality Act.

Stowe could not warm to, or feel proud of, the young men who made no secret of the fact that they were only there for the money. "They were attractive and lusty fellows alright, but somehow they threw you off a bit. They didn't seem to realize that Hitler and the Nazis were out to conquer the world and had been blowing people to bits and exterminating them like rats for years now. They didn't seem to realize the same thing about Japan."

Anxious to provide some good American copy he went to Toungoo to see how the A.V.G. were getting on with their training under Colonel Claire Chennault, a partly deaf, soft-spoken southerner, who had been retired from the American Air Force because of his unorthodox views. He knew more about Japanese pilots and their combat tactics than any man alive. He too was apprehensive about the attitude adopted by some of the young men who tended to complain about everything and everybody, and who considered downing enemy aircraft would be like "shooting fish in a barrel". He was quick to disillusion them, pointing out that the Zero had great advantages over the Tomahawk; it was more manoeuvrable, faster and could outclimb them.

During his visit, Stowe was present when the A.V.G. men were invited to buy raffle tickets to raise money to buy a British bomber; most declined. "They happened to be training on an R.A.F aerodrome, the best in Burma, and living in wonderful clean cement-floored barracks which had been built for the R.A.F. Even so, the vast majority of the A.V.G. boys felt not the slightest sense of gratitude to the British or any sense of ordinary social obligation. Later on, most of them were heroes but in little things many of them were also cads. During my stay in Toungoo I heard many things which made me ashamed of them as Americans; and they made it worse by assuming they were unquestionably better fliers than the R.A.F."

Colonel Chennault invited him to speak to his men, who seemed over-cocky and abysmally ignorant of what lay ahead.

"You fellows think you're good, and maybe you are," said Stowe. "But as far as any newspaperman is concerned, you're not good until you've shown it in combat. Whether you are an American or a Hottentot doesn't make any difference to a reporter. It's only how you perform."

Stowe continued his deflating lecture with accounts of what he had seen of the air war in other parts of the world, and concluded, "You fellows may be hot stuff. I hope you are. But you can't possibly be better than some of the R.A.F. pilots I've known. Nobody in the war can be better than they are. All I hope is that you will be as good – and if you are, every American will be proud of you."

When he left he jotted down in his notebook, "Most of them are one hundred per cent mercenaries . . . over-cocky and know-it-all . . . very critical and intolerant . . . a pretty lousy impression of America, if you judge by them . . . but a few are tops . . . and lots of good material, if they are given the works."

On Christmas Eve Stowe was only too glad to swallow his words. As the first bombs fell on Rangoon they left their drinks and raced out to the airfield. In an incredibly short time they were airborne and in action for the first time. They readily took orders from the R.A.F. and in the next two days twenty-two American and British fighters engaged vastly superior enemy forces of as many as 130 bombers and fighters. For the next three months the R.A.F. and A.V.G. were to fight against odds that were seldom less than 5 to 1, yet they came out on top.

Using the techniques instilled in them by Chennault, the Americans were far more successful than their British counterparts. He had told them, "Get in and get out fast. Hit them and run. Never stay in and fight with a Zero. He can turn in on you, outmanoeuvre you every time. But you've got more fire power than he has. The Zero can outclimb you, but you can dive faster than he can and stick with him on the level. Give him all the firepower you can, then get out and come back on your own terms."

The bragging quickly stopped and there was little talk about bonuses and lousy food. They could not wait to land and refuel quick enough to continue the battle high above the burning city. "I would rather fight those yellow bastards than eat," proclaimed one pilot renowned for his moaning.

On December 23 and 25 the 3rd Squadron, although unable to put more than half its aircraft into the air, shot down thirty-six enemy aircraft for the loss of five planes and two pilots. The R.A.F. lost three pilots. But between them the combined Anglo-American force destroyed twenty-eight aircraft. But it had not been entirely one-sided; the A.V.G. squadron had been whittled down to fourteen, many of which were badly damaged. The R.A.F. had only eight airworthy aircraft. The constant scrambling, in which they often took off blind because of the dust thrown up by the aircraft in front, at least took their minds off the hunger pains gnawing at their stomachs, for although it was Christmas, those responsible for providing food at the airfield had failed to deliver any to the aircrews since the first air raid. But it was not only food they were short of; the airfield still had no anti-aircraft guns, although there were large numbers lying in the docks. Exactly eighteen days had passed since Pearl Harbor, but the Chinese refused to relinquish any of the war materials America had so generously provided.

Stowe, Gallagher and Darrell Berrigan, of the United Press of America, decided to move out to the exclusive Mingaladon Golf Club close to the airfield in order to keep in touch with the aerial war. They drove past the bungalow of an Englishman whose life consisted of an unalterable routine: the office, the bungalow, and a round of golf. At first light he was hammering on the door of the crammed quarters which the three newsmen had been grudgingly rented.

"I say – excuse me, but you woke me up in the middle of the night. You came crashing past my bungalow, making a *terrible* noise. I thought it was enemy action. I jumped out of my bed into my trench. Would you please not do it again, or I shall have to inform the committee. This is a quiet country club. We know there is a war on, but we try to avoid as much of the unpleasantness of war as possible. Good morning."

It was not the only example of the apathy that gripped Rangoon or of the selfishness of the privileged minority who saw the war as an irritating interruption to a way of life that no one and nothing had a right to disturb, not even the tired and exhausted airmen who were fighing to preserve it.

The Buffalo pilots were not jealous of the success of the Americans or the publicity they got; they were only envious of their machines, and could not wait for the day when they would receive the long-promised Hurricanes.

In one day Flight-Leader Duke Readman, a farm boy from South Dakota, shot down five enemy aircraft, setting up a world record. One pilot set up another kind of record which resulted in merciless leg-pulling. He shot down two aircraft before being forced to crash-land himself. As he clambered out of his bullet-riddled Tomahawk, an English railworker living in a mobile carriage emerged and handed him an ice-cold beer. Soon afterwards he was back at the airfield, flying.

One of the A.V.G.'s most audacious exploits took place at the

Japanese airfield of Raheng in Siam where the Japanese had invited a number of influential Siamese to witness a large force of bombers take off for a raid against the British and American squadrons. A long and leisurely lunch had been laid on to occupy the time of the V.I.P.s until the aircraft returned in triumph from their mission. But a formation of Tomahawks, acting on information radioed from ground observers, sped off at full speed for Raheng, arriving at the precise moment that the Japanese were returning from their successful mission which had been carried out without loss. The P.40s went in with their guns blazing and the astonished spectators saw two Japanese aircraft burst into flames. Five more, lined up for inspection on the tarmac, were set on fire. Panic ensued and the Siamese made an undignified departure to the nearby jungle, but not before a Tomahawk, flying twenty feet above the ground, raked a truck racing across the airstrip and sent it cannoning into another parked aircraft. Seven planes were destroyed for certain, and several others badly damaged.

Overnight the Americans became the most popular white men in Burma. Girls swarmed around them, asking for dates, and men who a few days previously had cold-shouldered them insisted on buying drinks. The American reporters were inundated with requests from their offices for more and still more stories about the flamboyant, swashbuckling fliers.

There was something about the A.V.G. that fired the American imagination: the gay shirts and casual slacks which they wore as proudly as any uniform, the absence of rank and a dislike of spit and polish seemed to personify that individualism so admired by their countrymen. It was summed up by one young flier who said, "You don't need a uniform to fight the Japs. You need a plane, gasoline and ammunition," adding, "My idea of fighting is each for himself and no orders. Above all, no inspections. Inspections are the hellish part of military life. *They* must have been busy with an inspection on the day when we got our licking in Pearl Harbor."

Americans living in Rangoon, most of whom were engaged on Lend-Lease work, who had been embarrassed by the earlier conduct and attitude of the pilots, were now only too proud to claim the same nationality and could not do enough to demonstrate their pride. They organized a ferry service to the airfield which regularly provided sandwiches, iced beer, sweets, cakes and cigarettes.

By some unpardonable oversight, food was sent to the R.A.F. ground crews mess, but none to the pilots, who, when they found time, had to go into town and buy their own. Although they had the use of the club lounge the restaurant was closed to them and it angered the newsmen, who had been made honorary members, to be able to sit down to first class meals while the pilots were on what amounted to iron rations.

"The Americans got most of the planes and all the glory, and $500 per Jap plane shot down besides. The R.A.F's Brewster Squadron ran infinitely greater risks. Its pilots were mowed down, one after another, yet even a share of the glory was denied them. They, in all rectitude, were the greatest heroes of the air war in Burma," said Stowe. "They never faltered. They were badly fed and badly treated. Some of their own higher commanders sometimes forgot that they even existed. Yet their courage and patriotism were superlative. Finally, and in the greatness of their hearts, these British and New Zealand lads were above envy. 'Those A.V.G.'s are bloody wonderful,' they'd say to us countless times. Sometimes I wished that their American comrades in the air would say as much or more about them."

The R.A.F. pilots were not the only unsung heroes. Very little recognition was given to the ground crews who kept the Tomahawks and Buffaloes in the air. As undermanned as the aircraft were outnumbered in the sky, they performed miracles of improvisation and kept planes in the air by patching them up with tin cans and buying nuts and bolts from local shops, and cannibalizing aircraft that were no longer airworthy.

Despite the skill and dedication of the mechanics, several pilots were killed when their aircraft developed major defects in the air brought about by sheer fatigue.

After six weeks, only one of the twelve pilots in the Buffalo flight was able to fly. Four were in hospital and seven had been killed.

In January the first Blenheim bombers and Hurricane fighters arrived at Mingaladon. But there was no rejoicing at the golf club where about twenty boisterous Blenheim pilots, observers, gunners and navigators descended on the bar and drank vast quantities of beer, then settled down in the lounge for a quick nap, or stripped off their shirts and sun-bathed on the lawns.

The Club Secretary was immediately instructed not to serve them with any more beer and cigarettes. "After all," he was told, "the members' needs must be considered first. If we sell our stocks to these young fellows there'll be nothing left for the members."

That same night the Blenheims which had arrived from the Western Desert carried out the first bombing raid on Bangkok. Fortunately the ban on selling drinks was short-lived. The Secretary overruled his own members. "Damn the rules. Nobody's going to stop me selling beer to these lads who've just flown half way round the bloody world."

Among the pilots refused facilities of the bar was a young South African, "Hookey" Russell, from Port Elizabeth who sported the distinctive red shoulder flash of a Springbok who had volunteered to serve outside Africa. Soon afterwards Gallagher managed to wheedle his way aboard Russell's Blenheim for the second raid on Bangkok. The Blenheim crashed on landing at Mingaladon and was written off; it was not carelessness, the tyres were worn through.

The next time Gallagher heard of Russell he was in Toungoo where he was said to be dying in a military hospital. As he was landing at Toungoo one of his tyres burst and he was burned from the top of his head to his waist. He was so disfigured that he was kept behind screens and allowed no visitors. The night the town was set ablaze by Japanese bombers all the hospital patients were removed and put aboard a train for another hospital up country. All that is, except Russell. He was too ill to be moved unless the actual ward caught fire. Eventually he was flown to Calcutta in a Blenheim where doctors confidently predicted he would survive.

Back in Rangoon, the golf club still stubbornly refused to serve them food, although they were allowed to use the dining-room to eat the meals prepared by the R.A.F. cookhouse. It was, by common consensus, appalling. Breakfast never varied from week to week. It was always, tea, two meagre pieces of sausage on a minute piece of wood-hard fried bread, two slices of bread with no butter, and a spoonful of jam. Gallagher, who could eat what he wished, was so moved at the uncomplaining way the air crews put up with rotten food and the seeming indifference of headquarters that he wrote a scathing article for the *Rangoon Gazette* and soon afterwards there was a marked improvement.

The arrival of Hurricane fighters gave a much-needed boost to the exhausted Buffalo pilots, but an incredible blunder resulted in four out of seven of them being knocked out before they even saw action. Instead of being dispersed around the airfield at night as was the practice of the A.V.G., they were left in the open and four were destroyed in a night bombing attack. The Hurricanes were certainly an improvement on the Buffaloes but they were still hand-me-downs. There were several instances of pilots arriving from the U.K. who recognized aircraft they had flown in Britain or France and which had been discarded by combat squadrons.

When the Hurricanes appeared on the scene the Buffalo pilots were virtually ignored. One disgruntled young flier told newsmen, "Usually when there's a raid on they don't bother to inform us. We're just left there on the ground – waiting for the Japs if they come our way. Sometimes someone smells something's up and phones G.H.Q. to be told, 'Oh, hadn't you been informed?' So we're sent up half an hour late – just when we wouldn't have a chance if the Japs pounced on us. Headquarters doesn't really care whether we're in the fight or not." A few days later the young pilot was killed when his engine failed over Pegu. Unlike their American counterparts, the R.A.F. men who died remained anonymous heroes; British reporters were forbidden to give the rank or name of any personnel.

"For more than six weeks they had flown and fought in their suicide crates against hopeless odds, without chance of victory or glory. They were not so cocky and self-confident and dashing as the Americans. They were more tolerant and soft-spoken than most of the Americans. They were as brave and gallant as it is possible to be. After you knew them and had seen them go, they left you with a deeper feeling of humility and a new comprehension of greatness," Stowe wrote in a personal epitaph.

As the army continued to withdraw, the Japanese continued to bomb Rangoon by day and night, but the R.A.F. and A.V.G. prevented them from gaining the air supremacy so desperately sought. It was only through the handful of determined young pilots that the 7th Armoured Brigade and infantry reinforcements were able to disembark in safety.

On 2 February the Air Officer Commanding, Air Vice-Marshal D. F. Stevenson, DSO, MC, a veteran flier himself and a great advocate of offensive tactics, sent a message to Chennault – now welcomed back into the American Air Force with the rank of Brigadier-General – congratulating his group for having claimed its hundredth victim.

It was a conservative estimate, for no one knew exactly how many enemy aircraft had been shot down. Because such large sums of money were involved, the task of counting the "kills" was given to the R.A.F. and only those bombers and fighters which were found wrecked, or had been seen to crash into the sea by independent witnesses, were counted; many must have crashed into the jungle, but these were not taken into account.

The few Blenheims were so overworked they were literally wearing out. Pilots flew as many as five missions a day to bomb Japanese strongpoints. At one stage only two Blenheims remained serviceable, and pilots took turns in the cockpit to fly them on bombing trips in a desperate attempt to halt the advance on Rangoon. The pilots were almost asleep on their feet. The people in Rangoon, however, had no idea just how desperate the situation was for the *Rangoon Gazette* carried an effusive official statement from Major Cook which suggested that there was no shortage of bombers. "The widespread offensive activity of the R.A.F. bombers reported in Wednesday night's communique is a significant feature of recent operations which, as these increase, will render the Japanese communications more and more precarious."

Fortunately the next day six Blenheims flew in from India.

With the disaster at Sittang the loss of Rangoon was inevitable, but it was essential for the small Allied fighter force to delay it as long as possible in order that reinforcements could be landed. Realizing the situation the Japanese renewed their air attacks with increased ferocity, but the R.A.F. and A.V.G. continued to exact a punishing toll.

Although their fighting spirit remained undiminished the silence of grief brooded over the A.V.G. and R.A.F. messes. Few of the men that the newsmen had got to know so well at the golf club had survived. Stowe, so much older than any of them, viewed it with an almost fatherly concern. "You live with them. You drink and laugh with them. The planes take off once more – and one by one they do not come back."

The Japanese High Command became so infuriated at the inability of the Air Force to destroy the Allied force at Mingaladon that Tokyo radio broadcast in English that the airfield was to be subjected to mustard gas attacks. They did not carry out the threat, but the airfield suffered two devastating raids which almost, but not quite, brought it to a standstill. The runways were cratered, buildings wrecked and several Blenheims destroyed. But they did not ground the few remaining fighters and bombers. The 1st Pursuit Squadron shot down more than forty aircraft.

But there were no more victory rolls by the A.V.G.; they were scared that their Tomahawks would fall apart under the strain.

One of the last sorties from Mingaladon was flown by Battle of Britain ace Wing Commander Frank Carey, DFM, DFC and Bar, with eighteen German aircraft to his credit. He had already shot down a Japanese reconnaissance plane over Rangoon and destroyed three enemy fighters. When the fate of Rangoon was poised in the balance, information was received that a large number of enemy fighters and bombers were landing at the captured airfield at Moulmein. Carey scrambled his last remaining Hurricanes for a strike against the occupied airfield, but before the small force could rendezvous a force of enemy aircraft appeared overhead and Carey was forced to carry out the strike with just two other aircraft in support. One of these soon lost contact and Carey and the other Hurricane, flown by Pilot Officer Underwood, arrived over Moulmein to find the airfield packed with fighters, lined up in neat rows as ground crews fuelled and re-armed them.

Carey pounced on two fighters which were coming in to land with their wheels and flaps down. A well-aimed blast of machine-gun fire sent the rearmost fighter crashing onto the runway; the other tried to take violent evasive action, but its wing tip hit the ground and it cartwheeled into a line of parked fighters before blowing up among some hangars.

Glancing out of his cockpit he could see no sign of Underwood but the sky was full of enemy fighters. For several minutes he performed incredible feats of aerobatics in attempts to shake off the pursuing swarm of fighters. One flew across his bow and he caught it with a blistering burst. The Japanese aircraft, in their eagerness to claim the audacious Hurricane, managed to get in each others' way, and Carey opened the throttle and shot through a gap. Enemy fighers set off in pursuit but finally gave up, and Carey landed at Mingaladon with his Hurricane so riddled with bullets it resembled a colander. Underwood was unable to report his successes as he was hit by flak and forced to bale out. He was captured and spent the remainder of the war in a P.O.W. camp. Carey was awarded a second Bar to his D.F.C.

When the enemy launched their heavy attacks on Mingaladon, Stevenson dispersed the fighters to a number of makeshift airstrips which had been hewn out of the undergrowth and paddy fields by coolie labour. Although it reduced the risk of loss from air attacks, it was extremely difficult to get a sizeable force of fighters airborne at short notice. To deceive the enemy some extremely realistic dummy aircraft together with some damaged ones were left on the main airfield at Mingaladon.

As the evacuation was announced and orders issued for the demolition of all vital installations, the only warning system in Rangoon consisted of a solitary Hurricane flying above the city.

By then the remaining Hurricanes were based at a hastily constructed strip at Zigon to cover the withdrawal from Rangoon. Built at breakneck speed by inexperienced labour, it was so uneven that fighters were liable to break their backs on landing. One in five resulted in a crash of some sort, but due to the efforts of the ground crews the planes still managed to take off. One of the most common hazards was a broken rear wheel, and as there were no spares, mechanics fitted primitive bamboo skids.

For some unaccountable reason the one radar unit had remained under the control of the army, and one morning the R.A.F. and A.V.G. awoke to find that it had been moved without them being informed. Deprived of the early warning system, obsolete though it was, Claire Chennault issued orders for the last seven Tomahawks of the 1st Pursuit Squadron to prepare to leave and fly up-country to continue the war.

Before following the R.A.F. to Magwe, the A.V.G. destroyed everything that could not be moved and which might be of use to the enemy. When the Japanese arrived there was little left for them to seize.

Apart from a few Hurricanes at Akyab, the entire Allied Air Force consisting of one squadron of Hurricanes, one bomber squadron and the 1st Pursuit squadron, was now based at Magwe. It was an extremely slender force with which to protect the withdrawing army, but the pilots and ground crews were still full of fight and continued to carry the offensive to the enemy.

On 20 March a reconnaissance aircraft reported a huge concentration of enemy fighters and bombers at the abandoned airfield at

Mingaladon. A rough estimate indicated that the enemy now had at least 400 aircraft with which to attack the retreating army. The Blenheims were ordered to launch an attack and took off escorted by Hurricanes. The Blenheims were attacked by enemy fighters but shot two down and battled their way through to the airfield which they subjected to heavy bombing. At the same time the Hurricanes swept low over the airfield destroying sixteen aircraft on the ground and nine in combat. The surprise attack was so successful it was decided to repeat it in the afternoon. While air crews were in the briefing hut a report was received of a single unidentified aircraft approaching Magwe. Two Hurricanes immediately took off to investigate, but failed to locate it. Unknown to the people on the ground an even greater danger was threatening the airfield in the form of a massive force of fighters and bombers approaching from the north-east. Its presence was undetected, as the radar unit which had been brought up from Rangoon was facing south-east. As soon as the force was spotted, every available fighter took off, but they were pitifully few; after the morning's sortie there were only four Hurricanes and six Tomahawks.

The counterattack, in retaliation for the daring raid on Mingaladon, was carried out by 230 aircraft flying in waves at varying altitude. For twenty-four hours the airfield was bombed and machine-gunned, and when it ended there was only one Hurricane remaining that could fly and fire its guns. The tarmac was pitted with craters, ammunition dumps destroyed and administration buildings and living quarters reduced to piles of smoking rubble. Six Tomahawks and eight Hurricanes and three Blenheims were lost.

Orders were then issued for Magwe to be evacuated and those aircraft capable of flying, even if no longer operational, were sent to Akyab. When they arrived ground crews worked non-stop to get the few remaining aircraft back into fighting trim, and when the enemy next day repeated their tactics some managed to take off and shoot down four of them. But the losses on the ground and in the air were crippling and the small but valiant Allied air force virtually ceased to exist.

The R.A.F. withdrew to Calcutta and the A.V.G. to Kunming, leaving the withdrawing army completely devoid of air cover. It was not, however, the end of the air war in Burma. In order to keep in touch with the retreating army and provide some protection, a few battered and worn-out Lysanders were brought into active service. Mainly piloted by Indian officers, the reconnaissance aircraft were turned into maids of all work. They were used to pick up army messages with the gunner leaning out of the aircraft equipped with something that resembled a fishing rod; they dropped maps to lost units, food to starving refugees, flew out wounded and even performed as bombers. Some of the Lysanders had flown more than 600 hours above their normal life span, and one pilot recognized one as the same he had flown in at Old Sarum in England where it had been pensioned off as a trainer after seeing service in France and the Middle East.

A less glamorous role than that of the fighters, but nevertheless vital, was carried out by Dakotas, which became a legend during the campaign. They were so versatile that every sphere of war was clamouring for them and, as in so many things, Burma was last in the queue. At the beginning of 1942 there were only two serviceable Dakotas in the Burma-India theatre, and at the peak of the withdrawal the total had still only risen to eight. They were all rather ancient and some had already flown more than 10,000 hours when the R.A.F. took them over from the Americans. They were so urgently needed there was no time for proper examination, not that it mattered for there were no spares. In some miraculous way they were kept flying, and it was not uncommon for an aircraft to have a 550 h.p. engine on one wing and a 700 h.p. on the other.

They flew unarmed in the most appalling weather and thousands of wounded soldiers, sick refugees, women and children, owed their lives to the pilots who, although flying far more missions than would normally be expected, asked for their work load to be increased after witnessing the plight of the helpless hordes stranded in Upper Burma.

With the withdrawal of the R.A.F. and A.V.G. from Akyab, the Japanese had at last achieved the air supremacy so essential for the successful completion of their plans, but the cost had been astronomical. Between them the R.A.F. and A.V.G. had performed superhuman feats on a scale that no one could have hoped for. And with the monsoon not far off they had provided the necessary breathing space for the army to stand a reasonable chance of reaching India still intact as a fighting organization.

CHAPTER 24

"If somebody brings me a bit of good news, I shall burst into
tears"

General Slim

As April neared its end it was obvious that Burma could not be held; the
Chinese army was slowly disintegrating and Lashio was in imminent
danger, which meant the Burma Road would be cut. General Stilwell
had rallied the faltering Chinese with a huge cash bribe and retaken the
important town of Taunggyi, but it was a victory that could not
drastically alter the situation.

On 25 April Alexander, Slim and Stilwell met at Kyaukse 25 miles
south of Mandalay to discuss the next move. Alexander decided
reluctantly that the top priority was to get his army back to India with
as few losses as possible, and he gave orders for the withdrawal over the
Irrawaddy to commence and the supplies backloaded to Mandalay to
be moved and dumps set up along the route to India. General Wavell,
meanwhile, would do the same thing from the Indian end.

Stilwell, who rarely made the slightest attempt to disguise his dislike
of Alexander, was convinced that the British were deserting him and the
Chinese, and he did not hesitate to say so. As events developed and he
realised the Chinese could not be depended upon, he modified his views,
but only slightly. He thought Alexander had got the wind up and there
was no fight left in the British who had lost faith in their leader. No one
disputed Stilwell's courage, but he was often guilty of letting his
inherent mistrust and dislike of the 'limeys' blur his judgement about
the fighting qualities of the British and Indian troops. Alexander's
leadership was open to criticism, but his personal courage was beyond
question. The reason for what Stilwell saw as unseemly haste was the
fact that Alexander knew the withdrawal had developed into a race
against time; he had to get across the Irrawaddy and then the Chindwin
before the monsoon set in: once the rains started the army would be

bogged down as the rough track from Kalewa to Tamu would become impassable.

The Ava Bridge, on the Irrawaddy, near Mandalay, was the only one over the river and Alexander, haunted by the spectre of a repeat of the Sittang disaster, had ordered rafts and ferries to be laid on south of the bridge and north of Mandalay.

By no stretch of the imagination could it be described as an orderly withdrawal, but, considering the overwhelming problems, it was carried out with commendable efficiency. It was not the disorganized, disorderly rout Stilwell claimed it was.

As the army withdrew there was numerous savage encounters involving tanks and infantry in which heavy casualties were inflicted on the enemy. The brunt of the fighting fell on the 17th Division and the 7th Armoured Brigade which formed the rearguard for the Chinese V Army which General Slim had asked to be allowed to accompany him to India.

To ensure that the crossing of the Irrawaddy was successful, it was vital for the town of Kyaukse to be held, and it was there that Cameron's Gurkhas fought one of the most brilliant and defiant battles of the campaign. It was a hellish backcloth against which to stage a major action on which the survival of an army depended. The predominantly wooden town was ablaze and the streets were littered with the dead of its inhabitants and their animals. There 1700 men, supported by tanks, faced and repelled repeated assaults by an enemy force of 4000 men, despite being dive-bombed, shelled and mortared without respite. At one position the Gurkhas erected barricades of sharpened bamboo stakes which disembowelled so many that even the most fanatical Japanese were deterred from repeating their suicidal attacks. They held the position for 48 hours, and when the time came to withdraw to the Ava Bridge the ground was littered with the bodies of hundreds of Japanese.

The Japanese were not the only enemy; armed Burmans and dacoits indulged in a frenzy of blood-letting by attacking the columns of refugees which hampered the progress of the army. The Burmans were guilty of committing their most appalling atrocities on the Indians towards whom they bore a particular hatred.

At Pakkoku another spirited action was fought and a number of prisoners taken. "I have never seen such a grim looking lot, men sitting crosslegged in a line along the roadside, heads bowed, with their dead piled up in heaps everywhere. After two days the smell was awful though squadrons of massive vultures were doing their best to counteract the situation," said Corporal Morrison.

During the race for the Ava Bridge, Morrison was caught in an ambush. "The Old Man told me to stop the car and he got out and looked around. I suddenly realized what was going through his mind: it was a place which could mean disaster to our brigade, a natural bottleneck. The only sign of life was a bullock cart on the other side of the clearing, loaded with hay and heading in our direction. It seemed a peaceful scene until a shot rang out and a bullet passed through the rear window and out through the windscreen. I hit the road as a second shot tore through the roof. At the same time I sighted the sniper, high up in a tree overlooking the road. I fired instantly and a Jap came crashing down. The Old Man ran back to the car and got behind the wheel, and as he did so another Jap ran into the road. But I was expecting this and dropped him too. I got in and the Old Man exclaimed, 'The bullock cart'. It was Japanese, for I saw flashes of machine-gun fire from under the hay. As we sped away I had a quick shot at it."

As the car raced back to warn the approaching brigade, the Colonel turned to Morrison and said, "How does it feel to shoot a couple of Japs?" and Morrison replied, "Good. I wish I could shoot a few more."

"It looks as if you'll get your chance on the way back," said the Colonel.

They were prophetic words for when the brigade reached the scene of the skirmish a road block had been established, and the area was being pounded by mortars and guns. Lorries and ambulances were hit and set on fire and tanks had to bulldoze them off the road for the vehicles behind to pass through.

"With their few 25-pounders the R.H.A. fired over open sights from the roadside amongst the trees while two Bofors with only two shells remaining, fired them off and blew a gun to pieces in true artillery style. Guns were no use without ammunition and every available man had to grab a rifle and fight, knowing we were trapped."

Morrison waited for his turn to break through. "I could see the shells exploding in the road in front of me and the wreckage of vehicles scattered all around. Bodies were spread out on either side of the road and Jap snipers were hanging by their feet from the trees. There was a body in the road directly in my path. I must have hesitated for a second as the Colonel said in my ear, 'Keep going, keep going'. I felt the bumps as we almost jumped over the body and the Old Man banged his head against the roof. A couple of shells exploded nearby and we felt the impact of a lump of shrapnel hitting the radiator and tearing a great gash across it, almost cutting the bottom tank of the radiator in two. But I kept going and we ran the car until it seized up. We poured petrol over it and set it on fire."

At one minute to midnight on 30 April when it was considered that the last man and the last vehicle of Burcorps were over, there was a deafening explosion as two spans of the bridge toppled into the Irrawaddy.

Slim watched the destruction with mixed feelings; it was "a sad sight, and a signal that we had lost Burma".

Corporal Morrison, who was with a party which had lost contact with the bulk of the brigade, arrived at the river only to see a tangle of girders protruding above the yellow water. They decided to make some rafts and ferry their vehicles across and make their own way to India. But the rafts were only partly completed when the Japanese attacked. Although they repulsed the attack they knew they could not hold out against another and they destroyed some guns and all the vehicles except a three-tonner which they loaded with essential supplies.

A raft was hastily completed and it was decided to try and cross under cover of darkness. Morrison camouflaged the lorry with branches and crawled underneath with another soldier while six Gurkhas kept watch on the raft. They had three hours to wait and each minute seemed an eternity. The bulk of the party formed up into infantry units and set off on foot to find a suitable crossing place.

As he lay under the lorry a Gurkha sidled up and whispered, "No chance, now, sahib. Japs all round. Other side of river too. Better burn motor and go quick."

After setting fire to the lorry they sped off into the jungle, Morrison doing his utmost to keep up with the fleet-footed Gurkhas.

"I was lucky to be with them; the finest soldiers in the world. The jungle got thicker and thicker but it didn't stop the Japs pursuing us. Then a Gurkha whispered, 'Japs sahib', and motioned me to keep down. Then he and another Gurkha drew their kukris and slipped off into the undergrowth.

"At this moment I saw two Japs, rifles and bayonets in their hands at the ready, walk past, obviously without seeing us. The two Gurkhas sprang out and only the cracking of the necks of the two Japs sounded in the eerie silence. Then we moved off again. As we passed the two bodies I noticed that the head of one was completely severed from the body, a spurt of blood was shooting from the neck and the body was still trembling."

Eventually they caught up with the remainder of the brigade in the Irrawaddy valley where they were told it was intended to make a stand before crossing the Chindwin. Morrison clambered into a ditch with twenty-five soldiers and waited for the enemy. "I remembered one man I had seen after the Japs had finished with him. He had been tied upside down to two bamboo trees which had been roped together. He had been torn in two when the ropes were cut. I admitted to myself, 'I'm scared stiff, but I'll take a few Japs with me if I can.'"

Suddenly the jungle was filled with the clamour of birds and monkeys and a line of Japanese appeared about 100 yards away. The order "Fire" shattered the silence and several Japanese fell to the ground. Some were killed, but the wounded continued to fire. Most of the enemy were hiding behind trees and a voice shouted, "Pick your targets. Don't waste ammunition." Soon afterwards the same voice bellowed, "Cease fire," and then, "Advance and make bloody sure they're all dead." Later, as they sat down to rest, someone produced a small wireless set.

"We listened to a broadcast from Radio India and the news sounded real grim. We heard that the Burma Army was doomed and trapped in the Irrawaddy Valley, completely cut off and with no hope of escape, and that they were holding a national day of prayer in Britain. I said, 'Hell, they're talking about us,' and a soldier smashed it with his rifle and said, 'Remember the old saying, Nilo Ilijitimo Carborundum [sic]', and I said, 'I know, don't let the bastards grind you down'."

Not long afterwards they came across a river bed where a party of soldiers had been ambushed trying to get across. Bodies lay half in and half out of the water. Then mortars opened up from both banks.

Morrison and his friend Shorty were pinned down by heavy fire for a considerable time; when it ceased they realized they were on their own. They moved downstream through the darkness as stealthily as possible, but after covering twenty-five miles they had still not made contact with the brigade. They hid under the bank and decided to try and swim over in the dark and make for India some 200 miles away. They agreed that one would keep watch while the other slept, but they were so exhausted both fell asleep and at four o'clock woke up to find themselves encircled by grinning Japanese. They were jabbed to their feet and dragged into the open where they were thoroughly searched. They were marched off at bayonet point to where an officer stood waiting. His first action was to strike Shorty in the face for smiling.

In the clearing were sixteen other prisoners sitting on the ground covered by a machine gun. Morrison was relieved to recognize four of his Gurkha friends. Then their captors formed them up in single file and loaded them like pack mules. A rope was passed over their heads to prevent the ammunition boxes, each weighing 55 pounds, from slipping. Several of the men were badly wounded and just did not have the strength to carry such enormous loads.

"Within a couple of hundred yards one lad dropped to the ground. He was stuck with a bayonet about four times. The rest of us carried on through the night. Before the night was over two more of the boys died by the bayonet when they fell."

They marched for five days with hardly any food. "My feet were covering in blisters, the skin had gone from my back and I had passed the hunger stage a long time ago. Numbed with pain my legs just plodded on automatically. Six men died en route, leaving just twelve of us. Whenever a man dropped the Jap who bayoneted him was careful not to kill him outright, but invariably left him squirming to die in agony. One or two put up a fight but they were too weak to win. We had no idea where we were and we couldn't have cared less."

Having successfully crossed the Irrawaddy, Burcorps now headed for Shwegyin where it was proposed to cross the Chindwin, the last river in Burma. For more than 100 miles the road was little more than a cart track which wound like a snake through jungle; the rough ground was veined with dried-up streams with soft sandy bottoms which presented serious obstacles for the transport. But at least they were fordable; when the monsoon started they would be impassable. The greatest problem, however, confronting the troops was the acute shortage of water. There were stretches, sometimes forty miles long, which were completely dry, and men had to manage on a few swallows in conditions when they needed several pints a day. At Shwegyin the track petered out into a horseshoe-shaped basin from where it was proposed to ferry the army six miles upstream to Kalewa.

Army headquarters was doing everything possible to establish water and food points along the route and similar steps were being taken from India. Although all non-fighting vehicles had been allocated to the task there was no hope of providing all that the army – already on half-rations – needed to meet the requirements of the tens of thousands of refugees.

Meanwhile the Japanese were heading by road and river in considerable strength to cut off the retreat. Six hundred amphibious troops captured Monywa and the race intensified. If the enemy reached Shwegyin, Kalewa or Kalemyo first, the route to India would be cut.

Outwardly Slim remained calm and unruffled, inwardly he was full of apprehension. He told himself, "If somebody brings me a bit of good news, I shall burst into tears." He remained dry-eyed.

As the enormous convoy of vehicles ground on, more and more broke down and had to be abandoned. The roads were littered with the decomposing bodies of refugees. Although they were seriously impeding the progress of the army, on humanitarian grounds alone they were provided with as much food as possible, and as much precious transport as could be spared without affecting fighting efficiency. But nothing could stop the death toll from increasing.

Inevitably disease soon spread among the troops, enfeebled by hunger, thirst and lack of sleep. Concern was also growing for the wounded who were undergoing insufferable torments. As more and more ambulances broke down, men with appalling wounds had to be shifted into lorries and the few civilian buses which had been acquired, and every inch of the uneven road in the poorly sprung vehicles was sheer agony.

The Japanese continuously harassed the strung-out column of troops and refugees, and every town and village was bombed. At Shwebo so many were killed that huge funeral pyres were lit to avoid further pestilence.

Despite the unfavourable odds the retreat went surprisingly well, and by the end of the first week in May the bulk of the 1st Burma Division had been ferried over the Chindwin.

As more and more troops arrived, Shwegyin became one vast

bottleneck of soldiers, animals, lorries, tanks, guns and refugees. The road petered out at what was called the 'Basin', a relatively flat area about a thousand yards wide and dotted with small clumps of dense undergrowth. It was surrounded on three sides by a 200-foot-high jungle-covered escarpment which was almost vertical. From the top the whole of the basin was visible. If the Japanese occupied it the basin would become a death trap. A heavy air raid would end any hopes of a withdrawal to India.

Six river steamers had been laid on to ferry men and equipment upstream to Kalewa and engineers had erected a rickety pier to facilitate loading. Each of the steamers was capable of carrying five or six hundred men if packed like sardines, but only one lorry, two or three guns, and about the same number of jeeps. Loading was extremely slow and every gun had to be manhandled on to the deck where they frequently became jammed against the stanchions.

Although loading went on throughout the day and night, it became apparent to Slim that it would take the steamers several days to clear everything, and he decided that a considerable amount of transport would have to be abandoned and priority given to those with four-wheel drive.

Then what every man had feared occurred – Japanese aircraft began to bomb the almost imprisoned troops. Fortunately casualties were not high, for by now the troops had perfected the art of digging in, but a considerable amount of exposed transport was destroyed and damaged. None of the ferries was hit, but the raids had a demoralizing effect on the native crews who deserted in large numbers, while those who did remain refused to make the return trip from Kalewa. Armed guards were put aboard to force them to return to Shwegyin, but whenever the opportunity arose the sailors slipped overboard and disappeared.

Slim, who had set up his headquarters in the jungle near Kalewa, was so concerned at the delays caused by the continuous bombing that he visited the basin to see if he could speed things up. As he stepped onto the deck of one steamer a stream of tracer bullets passed over his head, followed by intense rifle, machine-gun, mortar and artillery fire. Shwegyin was under attack from a large enemy force which had been landed by naval craft. In a short time they occupied the knoll overlooking the basin which was soon being heavily mortared. Several attempts were made to dislodge them but all failed.

Enemy aircraft continued to fly overhead but their bomb bays remained closed; in the confusion it was impossible to distinguish their own troops from the British.

Three skippers, assisted by some civilians, brought their steamers close inshore below a cliff which provided some shelter from the mortars and took aboard the remaining wounded and some administrative staff. They were almost the last trips; nothing could induce the crews to return.

There was only one way out of Shwegyin for those remaining and that was by foot over the rough riverside tracks. There was no question of taking any of the tanks or remaining transport and Cowan reluctantly gave the order for them to be destroyed. It was with heavy hearts that the tank crews set about wrecking the Stuarts which had brought them so far and performed so well.

The last task of one tank before it was destroyed was to batter the Governor's Rolls Royce to pieces. It was an ignoble end for a vehicle which had graced so many ceremonial occasions, but it died nobly and proved a testimony to British workmanship; it survived several head-on charges before disintegrating.

Tony Mains saw the same tank smash the American Ford which had carried him all the way from Rangoon. He and his sergeant packed a few personal belongings and some food which they attached to a bamboo pole and carried coolie-fashion over their shoulders. Their only luxury was a bottle of whisky and before setting off they drank a toast, "Farewell to Burma".

The soldiers spread out their possessions on a blanket, selected the most precious, then set fire to the rest.

As evening approached Cowan ordered every remaining gun to open fire on the escarpment and for the first time the gunners did not have to stint on ammunition, and they laid down the heaviest barrage of the campaign as a cover for the withdrawing soldiers. When the last round was expended, they were destroyed. Shortly afterwards the Basin became one big funeral pyre.

Colonel Thornton who had taken over command of the 1/3rd Gurkhas described the scene. "As the march started, all the abandoned vehicles were set alight, and by the time darkness fell the whole jungle to the east, where the cliffs ended, was a blazing inferno. The roar of bursting shells, bombs and small arms ammunition of every calibre was

249

intense, and everyone had a rather uncomfortable time with the inferno only a hundred yards away and hot metal flying in every direction. The whole nullah was floodlit by the blaze and packed with slow-moving troops, and we thanked God the Japs were keeping quiet."

Ahead lay a long and arduous march along narrow precipitous tracks to Kalemyo opposite Kalewa. The infantry, accustomed to such ordeals, faced it with typical stoicism, but the tank men viewed it with obvious distaste. They were ragged unmercifully over their initiation to footslogging, especially the Hussars. But the Hussars showed their true metal. The officers donned their distinctive cross belts to show they were still tankmen and marched. The Reverend Metcalfe, an incorrigible optimist, burdened himself with a load of prayer books in order to hold a full service of thanksgiving when they arrived in India.

As the weary men and the mule transport moved along the track it was so dark it was difficult to see the man ahead. "The delays can be imagined, advance 20 yards, then halt for half an hour. As we were to be rearguard we took a very poor view of the pace the column was making. Things got worse and it became obvious that we would be lucky to be on the move before daylight. The Japs had packed up for the night apparently; but that obviously meant they were feeding and resting preparatory to being very unpleasant next day. For us to be found where we were at dawn could have had but one result, weak as we were," said Colonel Thornton.

Fortunately the Japanese did not pursue them; they had suffered heavy losses and for the moment had had enough.

"The track proved to be something that Dante could hardly have imagined. Up and down the houses was not in it, and the heat was awful," said Thornton. "We passed lots of stragglers, some obviously suffering from heatstroke, but nothing could be done and they had to be left. We had thrown away our reserve small arms ammunition so that the mules could carry heatstroke cases."

When the bedraggled men reached Kalewa they were ferried upstream to Sittaung to continue the final phase of the withdrawal to India. Next morning they were awakened by torrential rain, an ominous warning that the monsoon was about to break. At Sittaung the ferries were sunk and the long march to Tamu began.

George Biggs buried his two grenades. "I had carried them long enough. The ferry crossing did not take long and after that it was march,

march, march for everyone. Men died on the way as it was a long climb to Tamu, about 6000 feet up."

It was a typical understatement by the old soldier. Ahead lay the 90-mile slog through the Kabaw Valley to the relative safety of Tamu. With every justification it was known as Death Valley because of the particularly virulent form of malaria which struck those foolhardy enough to try and walk it. It was to live up to its evil reputation with a vengeance.

CHAPTER 25

"They might look like scarecrows, but they looked like soldiers to me"

Field Marshal Slim – *Defeat Into Victory*

The long columns of troops that writhed along the dusty track like a snake with a broken spine had lost all sense of time. Days and nights merged into one nightmarish blur; one foot followed another, propelled by a burning determination to survive. Bearded, emaciated, wide-eyed with fever and covered with festering sores, they were totally oblivious of the terrain. Many were only kept upright by improvised crutches or bamboo poles and those fortunate enough to have clothes were infested with lice. Occasionally an officer or N.C.O. croaked out an obscenity followed by an order to keep going whenever anyone showed the slightest inclination to sit or lie down for a short rest; there was a grave danger they would not rise again. A considerable number were suffering from beri-beri, while others silently endured the agonising cramps of dengue fever. All were ravenously hungry and dehydrated. There were also men suffering the agonies of dystentry who did not have the strength or enough control over their bowels to walk to the roadside. But for the fact that so many carried weapons they were barely distinguishable from the thousands of refugees who walked with them.

The wounded were in an even worse state, for with transport so limited little could be done to ease their suffering. They were crowded into lorries and jeeps and strapped to the side of mules and the few available elephants. All were sorely in need of expert medical treatment.

Despite the appalling state of the troops, General Alexander assumed responsibility for the hordes of refugees – estimated at 150,000 – who clung to the army as their only hope of survival. Whenever possible room was found aboard the already overcrowded lorries and bullock carts, for the more sick and feeble. Tremendous efforts had been made to provide food and water at points along the route but there was still a desperate shortage.

There had already been one or two heavy showers which had begun to turn the dust into a syrupy quagmire, and on 12 May the monsoon broke in its full fury. For the leading groups a long journey remained, while the rearguard was still in the vicinity of Kalewa. The torrential rain had, however, one immeasurable blessing: it halted the Japanese pursuit.

At night the troops huddled under the odd blanket or a cover of palm leaves in an attempt to keep off the rain which chilled to the bone limbs that a short time before had been protesting against the heat. The particularly virulent malaria of the infamous Death Valley had already claimed many lives, and as the heavens opened more and more succumbed.

There were several routes out of Burma, some minimally less difficult than others, but whichever one was taken there was no escaping the voracious leeches. With few exceptions those who survived the trek to India agreed that they created the worst horror. No part of the body escaped their attention; they crept up nostrils, into ears, and even entered the penis. Men who were dreaming of a meal in a Calcutta restaurant awoke screaming to find that the imagined meat they were eating was a leech clinging to the roof of their mouth. They squeezed through the lace holes of boots, and their presence only became known when blood squelched out. They battened onto their victims until they were four or five inches long. As many as one hundred had to be removed each day, a process demanding meticulous care for they had to be extracted without leaving the head behind. The end of a cigarette or a pinch of salt was the most effective, but not everyone had them and were reduced to scraping them off with a bayonet. The leeches also injected a liquid into the wound which prevented clotting and the diamond-shaped marks quickly turned into maggot-infested sores.

From Tamu onwards the going should have been relatively easy for heroic efforts had been made to build a road from India to provide transport on the last leg, but the Indian drivers of the convoys sent out to meet the approaching army were reluctant to go too far down the road as they were petrified by stories they had heard from recently arrived refugees about the atrocities committed on them. Instead they drove off the road and hid their vehicles in the jungle. The convoys were only kept going when a soldier was placed alongside each driver to make sure he obeyed orders. In this way many of the sick and wounded were carried to safety.

The majority, however, still had to make it on foot, but with safety so close there was a discernible stiffening of shoulders and an attempt to form into orderly columns. They were determined to arrive looking like soldiers.

With a stupidity that defies belief, there were officers at Tamu who had not heard a shot fired in anger but felt the need to impress their authority on men who had been fighting and withdrawing for the best part of a thousand miles. After a five-hour march the KOYLI arrived there only to be told by an officious officer in newly starched khaki drill that they had arrived too early and could not possibly have covered the distance they claimed in such a short time, and they were sent back five miles to rejoin the rest of the column.

The Gloucesters, forming part of the rearguard, marched into Tamu with Lieutenant-Colonel Bagot in his customary place at the head of his men.

"Tamu was a most unhealthy place," said George Biggs. "It was malaria-ridden and I witnessed the most awful sights. Men and women, thin and starving, were dying by the roadside."

After a brief rest the march continued towards Palel where Biggs noticed that the trees were covered with sheets of paper containing long lists of names written by those who had made it.

As the Gloucesters plodded on they had occasion to wonder if anything had been learned from the débâcle of Burma. An Indian Army staff officer drew up alongside the totally exhausted men, jumped out of his jeep, took up position at the head of the line and set off at a brisk marching pace. When he found that he was well ahead and alone, he turned back and berated them from their slowness, and commented to Bagot on the lack of physical prowess of his men.

The stench and pollution caused by the dead and dying on the road from Tamu to Palel was so overpowering that soldiers at the Indian end, detailed to assist with clearing the corpses, had to be issued with respirators before they could stomach the task of piling them into huge mounds and cremating them.

The incidents involving the KOYLI and the Gloucesters were not isolated ones. The remnants of the Burma army were to encounter many more examples of hostility and insensitivity before the trek was over. They were criticized for just about everything. Yet they had achieved the near impossible through those qualities which so many said they lacked.

Captain Tony Firth, despite the agony of his wounds, had never faltered in his determination to reach India and return to Burma with a new and re-equipped army. "If anybody says we did not bring out our weapons it is a lie. I personally helped to carry out a Boys anti-tank rifle, a more completely useless symbol of discipline you could hardly imagine."

There were many others with the same feelings: 2nd-Lieutenant John Randle, still short of his twentieth birthday; Major Bruce Kinloch who had seen in such a relatively short time more action than most senior officers had experienced in a lifetime of soldiering. There was Brigadier Ronnie Cameron, badly wounded in both legs, who had remained at the side of his Gurkhas, who would, if they had been ordered to, have turned round and done it all again in reverse. There was Major Calvert and his commandos.

As the defeated army marched, walked and staggered into India, Slim was there to watch, from a bank beside the roadside. "They might look like scarecrows, but they looked like soldiers to me," he wrote with pride.

CHAPTER 26

"They did not expect to be treated as heroes, but they did expect
to be met as soldiers, who even if defeated, were by no means
disgraced"

Field-Marshal Slim

Not everyone reached India through the two most recognised routes.
There were many who, without maps or compass, had to find their own
way out through tracts of land that were mainly unexplored. They
included "last-ditchers", both military and civilian, who had remained
behind the main army carrying out vital demolition work to impede the
Japanese advance and prevent any encirclement from enemy forces
moving through little-known tracks from the east. To survive they had
to live off the land. Boiled monkey, roast parrot and snake soup were
delicacies indeed.

There were others, like Corporal Morrison, who had been captured
and were being led like yoked slaves towards an unknown future or
mercifully brought to an abrupt end by a bayonet if they stumbled,
or a ceremonial beheading if an officer felt that way inclined. Morrison
and his party, who had resigned themselves to certain death, were
unexpectedly reprieved. Without any warning the Japanese were
ambushed by a large force of Chinese guerrillas.

"They butchered the hundred or so Japs as they stood with their
hands in the air. While this was going on one of our men dropped his
load, ran forward and leapt at one particular Jap, savagely tearing at his
throat with his bare hands."

Although unable to converse, the Chinese were friendly and gave
them some wild pig and rice to eat, along with some concrete-hard
biscuits which lasted all day. They also gave them large lumps of salt
which through hand signals they indicated should be rubbed over backs
and feet. After a thirty-six-hour rest they moved on to Lashio and over
the border into China. After a month with the guerrillas, only five of

the party were still alive: Morrison, "Shorty", two Gurkhas, and "Sparkie", a young soldier from the Signal Corps who had been badly wounded.

When they reached China the officer invited Morrison and the two other Englishmen to remain with them as captains, but they declined, saying they would rather take their chances and head for India. They were handed what equipment could be spared and they set off in a north-westerly direction. For food they were given some salted pork and a bag of rice. "Sparkie" was no longer able to walk and they made a stretcher and took turns to carry it. Morrison teamed up with "Shorty", and the Gurkhas comprised the other team. "We had lost all sense of time, but it must have been about the end of June," Morrison estimated. It was a peaceful journey for the first two weeks, then they ran into a party of Japanese and after a brief engagement withdrew as fast as they could with the enemy in hot pursuit. " 'Sparkie' was in great pain, his legs black and evil smelling," said Morrison. "Then he decided he could go no further and rolled off the stretcher. He had plenty of guts, that lad. Knowing we stood a chance without him, and knowing he was dying, he had decided to make a stand against the enemy on his own. It was useless trying to talk him out of the idea. The Japs were close behind us as we propped him up against a tree, a loaded Jap Tommy-gun by his side. Anyway, it would be a quicker death than the gangrene would give him. After a last handshake, our last Chinese cigar alight in his mouth, we moved off quickly, still heading north. Ten minutes later we heard a Tommy-gun firing in short bursts. We stopped and listened in silence. Then we heard rifle fire, and 'Shorty' broke the silence, 'Sparkie's saying goodbye'. Then it was silent again. The Gurkha sergeant major said to me, 'Sparkie was a very brave soldier, Sahib.' "

Week followed week during which they waded rivers, clambered up and down precipitous hills and hacked their way through dense jungle with no idea where they were.

"There were days when we never saw the sky. It was the worst country I have ever seen," said Morrison. "We drank from coconuts and bound our cut and bleeding feet with palm leaves and urinated on them to try and harden them."

After two days of crossing an arid, scorching plain they ran out of water and food and were convinced death was near as there seemed no end to it. Suddenly in the distance they saw what looked like a big black snake sidling along. As it got closer they realized it was a line of black chanting men, with fuzzy hair and no clothes apart from bracelets of teeth around their arms and ankles, and with rings and bones through their noses. They were armed with bows and arrows and spears and they never ceased their chanting. The two British soldiers were about to shoot when the Gurkhas assured them they were friendly. The wild-looking men relieved them of their equipment and in sign language indicated that they should follow them.

"We walked for several hours during which the tribesmen kept up a trotting dance around us, chanting all the time. Shorty turned to me and said, 'After all we've been through, we're going to end up in a flipping pot'. They took us to a village of round straw huts built on bamboo stilts, about five feet off the ground, and surrounded by a bamboo fence on which were human skulls."

The Gurkhas told them they were in Assam and the tribesmen were head-hunting Nagas. The entire village turned out to greet them and they were ushered before the chief who was extremely fat and naked except for a black top hat. To their surprise he shook hands and addressed them in perfect English. They were given food and water, and that night they slept on tiger skins in a hut festooned with skulls and teeth. The next day the chief told them that the men and women of the tribe were employed by the British who were building the Burma-Assam road.

In the village the Gurkhas and the two British soldiers parted company. The Gurkhas set off for Nepal while Morrison and Shorty decided to try and link up with the army. After a two-day rest, Morrison and his companion were escorted by the tribesmen to a stony track and told to keep going. They walked through an entire day and an evening. "Then we saw a cloud of dust ahead and heard the sound of engines. Then around a bend came two lorries filled with Sikh soldiers. Shorty and I stood with our hands above our heads and walked slowly towards them. We were bedraggled figures with long hair, long beards and in tattered shirts and shorts."

They travelled a whole day in the lorries and were taken to a refugee camp filled with women and children and about 300 troops, among them some comrades from the 7th Armoured Brigade who were flying the Desert Rats emblem over their primitive quarters. The camp was appropriately named Dysentery Hill. But they had made it.

The Burma Army had marched and fought non-stop over one thousand miles in three and a half months – the longest retreat ever carried out by a British army – in order to delay the Japanese advance and to give India an opportunity to prepare her defences. The tenacity of the troops aided by the monsoon had halted the enemy in his tracks, but the cost had been tragically high. The total mechanical transport at Imphal amounted to 50 lorries and 30 jeeps. More than 13,000 men had been killed, wounded or were missing, and that figure did not include those who had been evacuated sick. The army had also lost the bulk of its guns and tanks.

Earlier in the war the British Army had evacuated from Dunkirk and when the weary men reached England they were greeted like returning heroes and given every available comfort by a grateful people. The Burma Army looked forward to a similar reception; instead they were treated as something of a nuisance and subjected to a great deal of sarcasm and bullying from some commanders and their staff. Brigadier 'Taffy' Davies, Slim's Brigadier General Staff, commented at the time, "The slogan in India seems to be, 'Isn't that Burma Army annihilated yet?'" General Slim commented later, "They did not expect to be treated as heroes, but they did expect to be met as soldiers, who, even if defeated, were by no means disgraced. Yet the attitude adopted towards them by certain commanders and their staffs was that they were only to be dragooned into some show of soldierly spirit by hectoring and sarcasm."

The troops were understandably bitter and it was a tribute to their discipline that they did not mutiny when they were put into camps which were every bit as filthy as some they had encountered during the long retreat. Their sense of grievance intensified when, instead of being sent on leave in India, they were told they were expected to hold off any Japanese attack on Imphal as there were insufficient troops available in India to relieve them.

As more and more men fell ill and died, it seemed to the survivors that there was a determined effort by the authorities in India to complete what the enemy had failed to do.

General Slim deeply resented the reception his men had received and when Burcorps ceased to exist he felt that he was deserting them.

Too many officers, although deeply concerned for the welfare of their men, preferred to keep a tight-lipped silence when outspoken criticism would have been more beneficial. Charles Bagot was not one of them. Already he detected "Burma Blight", which had resulted in the loss of the country, and unless someone spoke their mind the same thing would happen in India. The monsoon had set in with a vengeance and the camp the Gloucesters were sent to was not only under water, it had been frequented by refugees who had turned it into one huge latrine. Bagot sent off some officers and the more seriously sick in the one available administrative lorry and told them to set up camp in better conditions some twelve miles away. But conditions there were just as bad. The few tents he was able to borrow were given to the sick, many of whom were suffering from malaria and exposure. The Field Ambulance was overflowing and little could be done to ease the plight of the patients as there was no transport to move them.

When a staff officer visited the camp, Bagot protested that his battalion was threatened with destruction by exposure and neglect. Totally unruffled, the officer reminded him somewhat icily that there was only one railway and one road from India to Assam which was inadequate to meet the needs of the marooned army. Before leaving he told Bagot "not to let the men grouse".

Soon afterwards Charles Bagot, three officers and twenty other ranks were invited to Calcutta to meet their Colonel-in-Chief, the Duke of Gloucester, and it was only then that the plight of the battalion was ended. Royal intervention resulted in the men being moved to comfortable barracks at Kohima. The chosen few who had met the Duke were extremely lucky in another sense. It was considered to be quite out of the question to meet him in the clothes they had worn since Rangoon, and they were kitted out with new uniforms at Fort William before being ushered into the Royal presence.

Other units who encountered His Royal Highness failed to arouse such compassionate interest.

Captain Ian Scott and a considerable number of men from the Frontier Force were put in Milestone 105 Camp. "With the rain came sickness, mainly malaria and dysentery, and soon we were evacuating men at the rate of 200 a day to Dimapur. After the rain had done its damage tents were allocated and some tarpaulins, but not sufficient to house all the men. However, the rain stopped the day before General Wavell dropped in to see us. He saw about 2000 men of the B.F.F. all lined up and trying to look like soldiers. He did not of course see the 1000 who were lying sick, or the 200 or more wives and children of the men of the B.F.F. who were camped in terrible squalor in the area. I heard him say to the Camp Commandant: 'There's a lot of weeding out necessary here'. No doubt he was right."

Scott, like many others commanding native troops, invariably put their welfare above his own, and he was incensed at the indifference displayed by the evacuation authorities. "The treatment given to the families of the soldiers of the B.F.F. was disgraceful. No arrangements were made for their evacuation to India although every day hundreds of civilian evacuees were sent out by truck. Eventually, I decided to take the law into my own hands. Early one morning I told the families to pack up their kit and come down to the road where the convoys of evacuess were gathered daily for evacuation. I got hold of the officer in charge of the convoy and told him that General Goddard* had ordered that space was to be made on the convoy for them, even if it meant removing some of the civilians. I knew very well that General Goddard would not be around at that time of the morning (4 a.m.), and nobody was likely to query my orders; and I was right, as space was made and all the families left. I wish I had done it earlier, as they left behind three women and six children who had died from exposure."

Major Tony Mains was among officers and men who arrived at Kanglatongbi desperately in need of new clothing and equipment, but the officers were unable to get anything from the Ordnance Depot on the grounds that they were not entitled to free clothing, but should purchase them from the Officers' Shop, despite the fact that such shops did not exist in the area.

Hearing that there was a bulk canteen at Dimapur station the officers had a whip-round and Mains and a fellow officer borrowed a 3-ton truck and made the tedious drive over the mountains to Dimapur. On arrival they were told that no traffic would be allowed to return after 1 p.m., which meant that there was not time to load up and get back to their own camp in the agreed time. After a lot of pleading they were given thirty minutes' grace only to find that the Burmese money they had was not acceptable in India, although the notes had been issued from the Reserve Bank of India's Rangoon Branch. They differed only from

* Lieutenant-General Sir Eric Goddard, Alexander's Chief Administrative Officer.

Indian currency in that the numbers were printed in red instead of black.

"I was determined to get those stores which included toothbrushes, toothpaste, razor blades and such-like articles – vital necessities to those of us who had not seen a shop or canteen for at least two months. In fact my determination was such that I was on the point of drawing my pistol and taking the stores by force, (an act which would have had the direst consequences for me), when the canteen's British Warrant Officer said, 'Don't worry, Sir, pay me and I will see the money is changed.'"

The only thing that did not seem to be in short supply was inspections.

At Imphal General Wavell inspected the remnants of the Gurkha battalions.

"He hardly looked at, let alone spoke to, a single officer or man as he walked down the ranks, and his short address was a series of apologies and excuses. Before or since I have never heard such angry mutinous muttering from the officers, some very senior, whom he was addressing," said Major Kinloch.

At Ranchi, east of Calcutta, Ian Scott was told to prepare for an inspection by the Duke of Gloucester. "We had already been inspected by many generals including Wavell, Alexander and Slim, and it was difficult to persuade the men that this inspection was any different. I told them that it was no less than the brother of His Majesty the King who was coming, and they made a great effort and looked good when the time came. We fell in along the road on either side by companies. We were kept waiting for ages during which time it rained, and the men did their utmost to remain dry under groundsheets to retain the creases in their clothes. Eventually the great moment arrived and we saw a car approaching. The company first in the line was called to attention and presented arms. The car did not stop but continued right down the line, and the Duke sat like a stuffed pudding in the back, never looking right or left or returning the salute. He spoke to nobody, and it was all over in seconds. Bahadur Khan said to me, 'If that is the King's brother you can keep him'."

Ranchi was designed to cater for a small peacetime garrison, and the understaffed hospitals were soon overcrowded, and many died without the doctors or nurses becoming aware of it. For the local staff officers stationed there before the sudden influx of survivors life went on as before. While the tattered remains of Slim's army had no clothes to wear the garrison officers had plenty of dhobi wallahs to wash and iron their immaculate uniforms, for slovenliness was not tolerated in the local club where they drank ice-cold drinks, or by the ladies who would not be seen in the company of an officer who neglected his appearance. And so while the Burma veterans shivered and shook with fever under their primitive shelters, the local staff officers enjoyed regular dances, got drunk and ordered gargantuan meals of eggs and bacon at midnight from yawning servants.

Corporal Alexander Morrison was living in a tent, the floor of which was covered with bamboo and branches, in a camp that was continually waterlogged, when General Wavell paid a visit. "He walked along the lines of troops, pausing occasionally to shake a man's hand, mine included. The men were silent, many looking down as he came by, avoiding his eyes, for Wavell's popularity had taken a hard knock: the men felt he had let them down by sending them into the hell of Burma merely to act as cannon fodder for the Japs."

On arriving in India he was issued with new clothing and sent on leave. In his pocket he carried a message from the Commander-in-Chief which contained the passage:

"Your main task during these months has been to occupy and delay large Japanese forces so as to give time for the defence of India to be reinforced and organised, and this you have most successfully and gallantly accomplished in spite of the difficulties."

Unfortunately, as the survivors of the long withdrawal gazed around them, they could see little sign that India had taken advantage of the respite their gallantry had provided.

CHAPTER 27

"In the horrible Hukawng Valley the bodies of the sick were dragged down into the stinking mud and the souls drawn out as if by suction"

Diary of Eric Battersby

While there were countless thousands who could not get out of Burma fast enough, there was a band of resolute missionaries who were reluctant to abandon the work of a lifetime. They knew from observation that the land clawed from the jungle quickly reverted to its original state once abandoned, and that, they feared, was what might happen to their congregations. But they were motivated by considerations other than spiritual; there was also the physical well-being of their communities to be taken into account. And nowhere was this more evident than at the headquarters of the mission station in Mohnyin which administered a vast area of Upper Burma.

Stanley Farrant Russell exemplified all that was best and noblest in the small religious community. When he was a young medical student he had showed such outstanding abilities that everyone who knew him predicted an illustrious and distinguished career as a surgeon. Instead, however, of aiming his sights at Harley Street, in 1930, at the age of 27, he went to Burma to run the Bible Churchmen's Missionary Society Hospital at Mohnyin.

The small town of 7000 people was 600 miles north of Rangoon in a rich rice-producing valley 80 miles from Myitkinya.

The modest little hospital was being built when he arrived and when it was completed it had twenty-four beds and an out-patients' department to meet the needs of the people in an area of 60,000 square miles. His first amputation was carried out with the crudest instruments which included a specially adapted screwdriver. Slowly but steadily his equipment and facilities were modernized. His first wife died eighteen months after going to Burma, and in 1934 he married Muriel, a missionary recruit. By the outbreak of war she had borne him three children and a fourth was on the way.

With the passing of time his reputation spread throughout Upper Burma and countless people of all races spoke of owing their lives to the man whose motto was "Tender care and prayer".

There were six other missionaries in the area who carried on working when war broke out, having been assured that Burma would be held.

The Reverend Wilfred Crittle, the mission's field secretary, was told by a senior Government officer, "It will probably be over in six months."

The trickle of refugees which began to pass through soon after the first bombing of Rangoon developed into a steady stream, but there was still no cause for alarm, let alone panic. And so they put their trust in The Lord and carried on through January and February into March and April.

But as the military situation deteriorated, Wilfred Crittle began to consider evacuating the women and setting up a permanent camp at Kamaing, which was his own base.

The District Commissioner, however, still held the view that there was no need for any hurry as everyone would be able to leave when he did.

Once again the lack of cohesion and organization in the evacuation scheme manifested itself; within a short time the order was given that all the women had to leave before it was too late.

On Sunday 12 April, three weeks after most of the women and children had flown out of Shwebo, an urgent message was delivered to Russell's bungalow:

"From Deputy Commissioner Myitkyina – cannot agree to family remaining longer Mohnyin stop proceed Myitkyina for evacuation India Sixteenth without fail stop Depcom."

Three days after they were due to depart, Mrs Russell and her family finally took off for India. Crittle continued setting up refugee camps at various points on the road from Kamaing. He was virtually isolated as he had no radio and had to rely on what others passed on to him. "No one who did not experience it could have any idea of the complete chaos of communications during the last few weeks," he said.

By the end of April Russell accepted that it would not be long before he and his fellow missionaries joined the long trek north. "Day by day the long trains, crowded with refugees, rumbled their slow way up the valley towards a possible means of escape from Myitkyina. Day by day our hopes of remaining in our station until the tide turned grew fainter."

His anger mounted at the abysmal ignorance of officials who were advising people to walk out. "The authorities had no idea what conditions were like in the north. They had told the refugees that there were tea shops all along the route. Some Indian typists arrived with light shoes and attaché cases and asked where the buses for Calcutta left from. They did not realize they had three hundred miles of death confronting them."

In addition to civilians, trains arrived crammed with wounded, medical personnel, and much of the equipment from the two military hospitals which had been evacuated from Maymyo. They had been travelling for six days and nights with hardly any food or water.

"A long line of bullock carts brought wounded and sick to our little hospital, from which our own patients had been hastily cleared, and filled it to overflowing. It was a very busy afternoon, dressing wounds, many of which were desperately bad ones and heavily maggot infested, putting plasters to fractured legs, preparing gangrenous limbs for amputation, and settling in the less seriously injured."

Twenty-four hours later they were all placed back aboard the trains for Myitkyina. That same day, 2 May, the members of the mission held a meeting with some army officers and officials to discuss plans for going overland to India. Store cupboards were opened and tinned food distributed to each man with Russell advising on the most nutritious food to take. His own load consisted entirely of medical supplies.

Farrant Russell went to bed planning to get a good night's rest before boarding the train which would take him and the rest of the party to Mogaung, the last station before the long hike through the little known Hukawng Valley, but at 2 a.m. he was awakened by two army officers who burst into his room to tell him to leave as soon as possible. "They had left their own train to warn me that it was quite possible that within a few more hours no more trains would arrive. Earlier in the day there had been a terrible smash at the junction fifty miles to the south when half a train had rolled back down a steep hill and crashed into a parked ambulance train. "This nocturnal visit settled our few remaining doubts, and showed us clearly that the time had come for us to go."

No matter how urgent the question of departure had become, Russell could not abandon the injured to their fate and he hung on until they began to arrive at Mohnyin. When he had done all he could, he handed over his bungalow to a Kachin family and returned to his hospital for the last time to remove vital parts from the lighting plant and carry out a miniature "scorched earth" policy so as to deprive the Japanese of anything that would assist them. Then the party of twenty-five men, which included a number of officers and other ranks, set off to catch the last train only to find there was no room on it. Fortunately, they found an abandoned coach in a siding which they manhandled into the station and linked on to the waiting train. It was 4 p.m. on 4 May and the enemy had already taken Bhamo and were sweeping towards Myitkyina.

Wilfred Crittle prepared to leave Kamaing, to which he had devoted so much of his life, to see what could be done to alleviate the plight of the thousands now streaming towards the Hukawng Valley. It was not long before he accepted that the evacuation had degenerated into a disorganized race for survival. Lorries originally intended to transport rice careered along the dirt road perilously overloaded with civilians, British, Indian, and Chinese troops. The drivers had strict instructions that they were to provide a shuttle service, and as soon as they had unloaded their human cargoes as far up the road as possible, were to return and collect more refugees. But they were more concerned with their own safety and simply abandoned their vehicles at the end of the run.

Russell's party which Crittle joined presented a strange picture as it joined the exodus. They had eight cycles which were not intended to be ridden but were utilized as wheeled mules. Bundles of food hung from the crossbars, handlebars and saddles. "It was slow work pushing them, but far better than abandoning the foodstuffs which might make all the difference between starvation and safety in the days to come," said the surgeon. As the long river of humanity flowed northwards, the worsening conditions brought out the best in some and the worst in others. Heavy rain reduced the track to a glutinous mess that bogged down the vehicles and the air was filled with the whine of wheels spinning uselessly in the churned-up mud. Passing elephants sometimes halted to haul out stranded vehicles, but many had to be abandoned. Those on foot found themselves trying to wade through a porridgy morass that was often thigh-deep. The effort was too much for some and they simply sat down by the roadside and gave up. Survival of the fittest took on a menacing meaning; many of the more able-bodied were prepared to attack, rob and even kill the less strong if it guaranteed their own safety.

As the mass migration moved northwards a problem no one had envisaged presented itself; the thousands of Indians fouled every halt. The stench was indescribable and inevitably cholera and dysentery broke out, and the road became littered with corpses.

It was not just human corpses that fouled the water and spread disease. Bullocks and ponies were abandoned when they dropped through sheer exhaustion or hunger or drinking polluted water. "City people had no knowledge of animals," said Crittle. "The thought that an animal's strength was not inexhaustible never occurred to them. So day after day we saw worn-out animals flogged along long after they should have been unloaded. In many cases they collapsed in the mud leaving their owners stranded."

Well-organized as they were, and well equipped in comparison to many of the refugees, there were nevertheless moments when they came perilously close to despair. Even the redoubtable Crittle, after one particularly arduous day, confessed, "I really felt that if the Japs did overtake us that night they were welcome to do so, and I did not care whether I lived or died." But such moments of despondency were rare; something always seemed to occur to convince them they had not been forsaken and their prayers were answered. By an act of almost divine providence they were given Maggie, an elephant belonging to the Reverend C. E. Darlington who was leaving the remote station at Maingkwan, the last missionary post in Burma, as his wife and new-born baby could not cope with the enormous beast.

There were other occasions which fortified their belief in the power of prayer. A most frequent prayer was for news of loved ones with whom contact had been lost. One night as they were sitting in an abandoned hut a tall, fair-haired woman dripping wet and caked with mud, walked in and said quite calmly, "Someone told me you were here." Victor Green, one of the party blurted out, "My God, it's my wife." Throughout the journey he had agonized about the whereabouts of his wife and small son. She had been working for the Civil Defence Department and had been assured that she and the boy would be flown to India, but at the last minute the senior officials had flown out and told her she must find her own way. A few minutes later the ten-year-old boy arrived in a similar condition to his mother. "He did not seem particularly surprised to see his father," said Crittle, "and in a very short time he was eating away and talking as if being a refugee was the most natural thing in the world."

As food became scarcer looting became more widespread. Armed Sikhs and deserters from the Frontier Force and Military Police acted atrociously towards the unfortunate families who could not retaliate. They stole their money at gun-point, commandeered their animals and jumped the queue at swollen rivers where thousands had been waiting for several days for their turn to cross on the rafts. Such activities were not confined to renegade soldiers; there were dacoits and Chinese troops who preyed on the refugees, and it was not uncommon to see Indian women with blood streaming from mutilated ears and noses from which jewels and rings had been torn.

When weather conditions premitted, aircraft from India dropped supplies by parachute which immediately became the target for looters. In their haste to grab the supplies they often put aside their rifles which enabled the mission party, assisted by the soldiers with them, to demonstrate the church militant in action. They frequently retrieved the food at gun-point and made everyone form into an orderly queue in which women and children were given priority.

Meanwhile, the outside world remained blissfully ignorant of the plight of the refugees. In fact there was deliberate deception. During one halt Crittle found a jettisoned radio and by chance tuned in to a broadcast from Delhi by Sir Reginald Dorman-Smith. "He was telling the world how well everything had been organized and how magnificently everyone had stuck to their task. We, who were in the middle of the chaos, were not amused and his speech was greeted with loud jeers."

The spectacle of more and more people dying was agony to Russell who had devoted his life to medicine. "Again and again one had to tell the sick that there were no drugs available for their particular complaint." Even so, many owed their life to his ministrations. In the midst of so much death there was also new life. Along a corpse-strewn stretch of road he came across an Indian father supporting a groaning woman and two small screaming children. "They had come from far-away Lashio and the third member of the family had decided to enter this unfriendly world at a most inopportune time. In place of sterile scissors I used my rusty penknife whilst a piece of parachute cord had to do for ligatures. A drink of stale rainwater as a restorative and the population was increased by the arrival of a fine baby girl. The next day I saw the mother, apparently none the worse for her experience, down by the river and I was able to give her a lift across on the elephant."

For the thousands who had endured so much the road seemed never-ending. They climbed mountains, struggled through dense jungle, crawled on hands and knees through thick mud, and waded rain-swollen streams. Their miseries were indescribable. "One would need a fire-proof typewriter and asbestos paper," said Russell.

Towards the end of May the mission party reached the banks of the Namyaung River which presented the most formidable obstacle they had so far encountered. Hundreds of people had gathered on the steep bank overlooking the gorge, waiting for the swirling water to subside before attempting to cross. They had seen too many home-made rafts smashed to matchwood and the occupants swept away. As the vast crowds waited for the level to drop, food became scarcer and many who had waited so patiently died on the banks of the river which was the last real hurdle.

Overhead they could hear the drone of aircraft engines and markers were spread out and fires lit, but visibility was so bad their plight went unnoticed. The mission party ransacked nearly every house in the vicinity for pieces of rope to provide a lifeline across the river to help those who had no animal transport to carry them across. Then when everyone feared the water would never drop, it stopped raining and people prepared to take the risk. Maggie managed to ferry many across, while a considerable number made it on their own before the rope snapped and crossing was halted until an aircraft dropped a steel hawser. Hour after hour Maggie carried men, women and children across on her enormous back and frequently went to the rescue of small groups stranded in midstream.

"Wealthy Indians were offering Rs 1000 for a lift across, but the only qualification was helplessness; all others had to wade, or wait until the river sank further," said Russell.

While the mission elephant worked until she was too exhausted to carry another load, parties of wealthy refugees passed over on their own elephants, totally deaf to agonizing pleas for a lift.

Eventually they reached the Pangsau Pass which marked the

boundary between Burma and India. Once over that they were assured there would be a chain of ration camps, with waterproof shelters, set up by the India Tea Planters Association.

At Nampong, the first of the rest camps which also had a hospital tent, an orderly attended to lacerated feet while a Canadian doctor treated the more serious cases. There were shelters too, roofed with thatch and tarpaulins and nearby a kitchen which served rice, dhal and onions, biscuits and cheese and mugs of scalding tea.

All animals had to be handed over to prevent the track ahead being too churned up, and jeopardizing the efforts of the coolies delivering food supplies. Maggie was passed on to assist in bringing in refugees, but the elephant which had served so nobly had different thoughts.

"That night she disappeared," said Crittle. "She snapped her leg chain and though we followed her traces through the jungle we soon lost them, and were quite unable to find any trace of her. She was heading for Burma, by the direction of her tracks."

On Tuesday 2 June, the party set off on what was to be the last leg of their heroic journey. Ahead lay more mud and a steep climb which proved to be among the worst few miles of the entire trek. A string of stretcher-bearing coolies had been laid on to carry the sick down to the camp below, but the coolies, reluctant to make the perilous descent, often dumped their patients by the roadside. Others even more callously simply pitch-forked people over the edge of a precipice.

It was here that they saw the last roadside corpse. "It was that of a sweeper who had worked for me at Kamaing for a long time," said Crittle. "He was sitting by the road huddled up as if asleep, and I did not think he was dead until I went across to him and a cloud of flies arose from his face."

After a brief halt at the camp they set off again.

"Then, without warning, it happened," said Farrant Russell. "At 2 p.m. coming down a long slope, we all heard the hoot of a train. The last time we had heard that musical sound had been a month before, and three hundred miles away. As we went down our weariness forgotten, we burst into the strains of 'Glory, glory, Alleluia'."

No one who passed through the Hukawng Valley and reached safety would ever forget Shingbwiyang. The tiny Jinghpaw village was at the end of the valley and it was estimated that some forty thousand troops and civilians had descended on it during the evacuation. Many were never to leave. Desperate efforts were made to feed them and provide medical attention, but fresh faces arrived at the rate of eight hundred a day. The R.A.F. dropped leaflets urging them to press on to India, but many took one look at the Naga Hills looming in the distance and simply lay down and died.

The death rate soared to twenty a day, until a situation arose when there were almost as many living as dying. When the monsoon broke they were stranded. The diary of a young private in the Duke of Wellington's Regiment epitomizes the incredible courage of thousands doomed to die.

Private Donald Warner did not begin his diary until 20 May when he was approaching the village camp. "Passed six bodies, they stunk rotten."

Two days later after wading through knee deep mud he wrote: "I had a terrible experience. I was about to pinch a truck, everything was ready for starting, so I went round to get in. I opened the door and found myself face to face with a skeleton. Gosh! I didn't know whether to shout, run or what to do. Anyway the stink decided me."

The next day he rested as his wounds were causing a great deal of pain and at the end of the next day wrote, "We passed sixteen bodies, three were women. Frank gave a Wog a good hiding and burst his knuckle for the troubles." It was the first of many attempts to deal with the gangs of looters who terrorized the refugees.

Tormented by thirst, he remarked how indifferent they were to the risks they ran. "The water looked like urine, but we drank it."

His description of the natives revealed how the young soldiers had been encouraged to view them, but the harsh words could not conceal the compassion. "The Wogs are dying in dozens, it's cruel to see them. I shot one this morning to put him out of his misery, he was unconscious in the mud and every time he breathed he swallowed more and more mud. I hated to do it, but it was the only thing that could be done. Today we passed twenty-eight bodies." The next day he and his small party reached Shingbwiyang after a particularly gruelling march which never exceeded half a mile an hour.

They decided to rest there a couple of days before pushing on but the rains delayed them. "Even as I write this it is simply pouring down and the hilltops are covered with clouds. I saw supply planes come over, but they didn't drop anything. One of them was making signals as to what was most needed. The M.O. here has asked me to help with the looters as the last time food was sent a load of Wogs helped themselves. He told me to shoot. I said nothing would give me greater pleasure. Anyway, the plane didn't drop anything, so I had nothing to shoot at. Ken gave me his watch today as he thought he was dying. The M.O. came and gave him a good chewing up and told him not to be a b . . . fool and act like a man. Gosh! but Ken soon changed his mind about dying; he's quite lively now."

As the rain continued to hammer down he asked how far he still had to go, and he was told it was 115 miles to Ledo. "Oh, well, seventeen days walk, and two days train will see us in India, I hope." But as the monsoon showed no sign of easing he realized that if he did not move within the next few days he would be trapped, but he remained remarkably cheerful. "I have a nice job for the next two or three days. I'm looking after two sick men in the hospital, cooking and everything . . . Gosh! but it's hot. I've almost forgotten what a fag looks like. I've been smoking country baccy in newspaper, and all sorts. I shall be a non-smoker soon."

The days passed and his diary entries repeatedly stated, "Nothing happened," until he wrote, "Poor old Ken died at 3.45 p.m. of heart failure following dysentery. We held a burial service and buried the body at about 7 p.m." Then Warner went down with fever which delayed his departure even longer. Sick as he was, with a temperature of 105 degrees he still tried to enforce discipline. "I have just thrown a Wog out for being indecent, he would not put his clothes on and there were both women and youngsters." But the rains continued and he confided, "Now thanks to this lousy weather, we are stuck here till after the rains (six months at least). Anyway my fever is a bit better. My temperature came down to 100 degrees. The worst part is that I feel so dithery and weak." Soon afterwards he noted, "Well – the second member of my party died at 2.30. That's Ken gone, Frank gone. There's only me left."

His frustration mounted as he was unable to walk far. "Still hanging around with nothing to do. Rained like hell again. The only things that seem to like this place are the flies. Gosh! but there are millions of them." The Chinese continued to loot whenever there was a supply drop and Warner wrote, "One cockeyed swine was going to shoot me until I planted my fist on him."

Two days later he recorded, "MY BIRTHDAY. And what a birthday. It rained all day. We are getting used to it by now. I got Frank's pencil yesterday, I've also asked for his pen." Then, "I had a rather busy day today. First of all I buried a little girl of six and made a wooden cross for her grave. I think she died of dysentery. This afternoon I decided to clean my revolver. It badly needed it as it was getting rusty."

The weather improved slightly and the supply drops continued but a message from one of the aircraft warned the refugees they would have to remain as the rivers were still impassable. Warner's wounds were "paining like hell", and he watched helplessly as more died. "An old lady of seventy died in our hut of heart trouble. She died quite suddenly. I have just seen a Chink and a Gurkha shooting it out with each other. Don't know who won. I didn't stop to see."

Another bout of fever laid him low and he recovered to record, "There is a young woman here in terrific pain. I doubt if she'll live much longer, her pulse is down to 40. She has just this minute died (10.42 p.m.)."

Death was now so commonplace that under an entry beginning "Nothing happened", he wrote, "Chinks stole all the supplies. Another young girl died this morning. That's three in a week. Managed to get some bacco." Then, "Buried the young girl today, and what a day, nothing else but rain. I have got another dose of fever, that makes three doses in three weeks." As his condition worsened the entries became briefer and a note of despair began to creep into his jottings:

"Old Mrs Halpin died this morning from dysentery. Apart from that nothing happened out of the ordinary . . . I got fever and it's slowly getting worse . . . Mrs Halpin's cousin died this morning. Rained all day . . . Old Taffy died very early this morning. I have been made hut haircutter . . . Nothing happened except a Chink got killed for looting." Another was shot next day, but he was able to record, "Had a pretty good day."

His diary for the first two weeks in July recorded:

"One youngster died. I've had nothing else but pain from my wounds. Ron down with fever . . . McQueen died today. Rained a lot . . . Mac still not buried, beginning to smell . . . Mac buried today . . . rained all day . . . nothing happened. Rained all day . . . nothing happened . . . plane sent supplies. The day was nice and warm . . . nothing happened . . . Got some chocolate, had to pay Rs 50 for it . . . Two Gurkhas shot for looting . . . Had a nice day . . . I got a bad fever . . . About ten planes dropped supplies. I got bad fever . . . Nothing happened . . . nothing happened. I have got some kind of disease (sic) and honestly there is nothing left but bone. Oh, well! We'll have to trust in God and faith."

The entries became shorter as the month drew to a close, and for two days there were none at all as he lapsed into unconsciousness. When he recovered he began to say his rosary twice a day "as every Sunday". His steadfast faith gave him fresh hope and his spirits rose, "At long last. It's getting near the time to leave. Hope to start on the 1st of next month." As more and more of the people he had befriended died, he still clung to the belief that he would be leaving soon. But September came and he was still in Shingbwiyang.

On 3 September he made his last entry. "Had an injection for dysentery today. Gosh! but I am weak. I've got two operations waiting for me in Ledo. The reliefe (sic) party should be here soon."

It was not until 18 September that Private Donald Warner's body was buried alongside his friends. Even his indominatable courage and unquenchable faith were not enough to survive the hell of Shingbwiyang.

CHAPTER 28

"The people seemed blissfully unaware that there was a war
on"

Mrs Gwenllyan Coward

Calcutta, one of the world's busiest ports, was the commercial heart of
India. Almost overnight it became the reluctant host for many who had
survived the trek from Burma. But not many of its residents cared, for
the city was sweltering in a heatwave which was hotter than any since
1860. Indians were dying in the streets in unprecedented numbers and
their bodies went uncollected.

Among the early arrivals was Leland Stowe who felt he had stepped
from one nightmare into another. The same ostrich-like attitude he had
witnessed in Rangoon existed in the city. "It offered the same pageant of
folly and stupidity, simply staged on a grander scale and at a far greater
risk. You looked and scarcely could believe your eyes. The province of
Bengal – and some insisted most of India – was merely Burma all over
again."

The lobbies and dining rooms of the hotels and clubs were packed
with men and women in dinner jackets and evening dresses and officers
in smart uniforms, who seemed solely concerned with enjoying
themselves. There were dances and cocktail parties every night at which
many drank to excess. Nothing, it seemed, could be allowed to affect the
endless social round or impart a sense of urgency. Stowe was honoured
to be invited to the exclusive Saturday Club which actually saw a virtue
in its snobbishness. "It had never accepted a member without first
examining his family tree and social status most minutely." Instead of
being impressed he was appalled.

"More then 500,000 natives had fled the city for fear of the Japanese
air raids and 57 Allied ships were tied up in the river, and the port itself
was almost paralysed," he said.

Some of the ships had been held up in Rangoon before managing to escape; now they had been waiting for more than a month as no berths alongside were available, and there was a shortage of dock labour. There were also ships laden with Lend-Lease materials – including one which carried forty-nine much needed aircraft. But the port was not the only scene of inertia; the railways had almost ground to a halt. Only enough coal had been stored to keep them running for three months, and General Wavell reported to London that the chaos was so bad that it took seven weeks to move a brigade to the Assam frontier, a journey which normally took 36 hours. Sunday remained a day of rest, eagerly observed by the goods section, which meant that if a wagon reached its destination on a Saturday it often remained in a siding until Tuesday. The loss of the Burmese oilfields – India's main supplier – had also led to a desperate shortage of petrol.

A practice air raid was enough to denude the streets of thousands of people and, as in Rangoon, many of the staff of the larger stores deserted, never to return. If there had been a real raid it would have had devastating effects on the entire country, for three-fifths of India's production of war materials was located within bombing range of Calcutta. The rest of the country's industrial potential had been deliberately neglected for fear it would adversely affect Britain's own industries. With an appalling lack of foresight there was only one rail line out of the city and only one bridge.

Although the nation was being urged to fight the threatened invasion, nothing could induce the white population to lower the rigid class barriers which would convince the Indians they had something worth fighting for. Wilfred Burchett, the *Daily Express* reporter who had arrived via the Hukawng Valley, was rudely reminded of this when he took an Anglo-Burmese girl of a good family and education whom he had known in Rangoon to a dinner-dance at the Grand Hotel. Sitting at a nearby table was an R.A.F. officer and an English girl he had dined with the previous evening. "She looked at me as if she had never seen me before, and without replying to me, stood up with assumed dignity and asked her escort to take her away."

In Simla Sir Reginald Dorman-Smith was leaning over backwards to grant interviews to reporters in order to expound his views on the kind of Burma he wanted to see after the war. They were surprisingly enlightened; he believed the country should be granted independence. With commendable candour he admitted the British had made a hash of things and it was essential after the war to bring in younger and more energetic men to put the country on a sounder and fairer basis, economically, administratively and socially. There were few Europeans in India who would have endorsed his views if he had been speaking of the sub-continent. India, they argued, would collapse if the British handed over the reins of government.

Not all voices were mute in acceptance of the status quo. The *Calcutta Statesman* felt it was time India was allowed to develop beyond the toddler stage politically and industrially. "The future is indeed all-important. But what is of ill omen is the determination of the men who have failed to burke all responsibility for their failure and to retain power in their incompetent hands." Industries, urged the editor, should be developed and power transferred from London and a national government set up which would be a working model for the future. "We need indeed a political settlement. But above everything else we need a governmental machine more suited to waging the war – a clean sweep of the present bureaucratic methods."

Letters also began to appear in other British-edited newspapers from people who were beginning to read the writing on the wall and realize that unless a more enlightened attitude was adopted and control removed from those who believed they had a divine right to run the civil service and the forces, the future of British rule in India was bleak indeed.

"An old woman" wrote in the *Bombay Standard*:

"It would be interesting to know the age and physical condition of all officers above the rank of acting lieutenant-colonel . . . to know how many years they have moved from office to office and job to job in Delhi and Simla; to know just how long it is since they had active experience of the matters they are supposed to control . . . and how much longer the physically unfit and the failures will be nursed."

An editorial in the *Standard* endorsed her views:

"Is it not a fact that so many in the higher ranks of the army stick with the tenacity of leeches to their positions in spite of their obvious inability to live up to modern conditions? Social pull, indirect influence, family connections, nepotism, the old school tie – these place unsuitable men in responsible positions. These keep them in there in spite of the ludicrous bunglings, these keep them there with exorbitant emoluments until at last they are gracious enough to retire on a pension."

It was an echo of what had been said of Burma.

Such strictures, however, were small pebbles which barely rippled the surface of the great sea of complacency.

Violet Kelly recalled, "Miss Maxfield and I arrived in Calcutta in pretty good spirits and we went to book in at the Great Eastern Hotel, but the reception desk took one look at our bedraggled appearance and announced there were no rooms to let."

She also encountered the impregnable race barrier. "I had applied to join the Q.A. but changed my mind after hearing some thoughtless sisters mimicking the voices of young Anglo-Indian nurses. I decided instead to join the Indian Military Nursing Service, remembering the nursing staff at the Rangoon General Hospital had been Anglo-Indian and Anglo-Burmese and no praise was sufficiently worthy of the great work they did."

Major Bruce Kinloch, wearing the ribbon of the Military Cross, said, "We hoped we would receive a great welcome and we had made a book with drawings showing plenty of nudes and lots of whisky, but all we encountered were blimps and brass hats."

Mrs Gwenllyan Coward went to Poona. "It was quite an incredible place. The people seemed blissfully unaware that there was a war on and the garrison troops were still going round in white trousers and smart uniforms."

Anxious to play a more active role in the war she volunteered for the Women's Army Corps and was made a staff captain. "Although I did not know a thing about the army, I reported to a colonel who asked me what I wanted to do. I said I would like to be a driver, but he said, 'No, I'm afraid only Indians do that.'"

Most of the soldiers – officers and men – who had made it safely to India accepted the snobbishness and muddle with the resignation of men who had lived close to death and learned there were more important things in life than background and social status. They had seen comrades who had both die fighting back to back with men who had neither. But what did grieve them was the disbelief and irritation they frequently encountered when they talked about Burma. When they mentioned the privations and the bestiality of the enemy, eyebrows were raised, and the general attitude was that they were simply stories made up to explain the defeat.

"I heard many people say that they considered the stories of Jap atrocities to have been largely exaggerated. Many found it hard to believe that, for instance, the Japs used live prisoners for bayonet practice," said Ian Scott.

In Delhi the top-heavy Army Headquarters staff bemoaned the petty irritations the war brought on their well-ordered lives. Overtime, they complained, was having a disastrous effect on their social life and they were expected to work in the oppressive heat of the city without the customary well-earned visit to a hill station.

On 25 May, the sixty-year-old General Joseph Stilwell arrived in Delhi having walked out of Burma like an ordinary infantryman. He told the assembled reporters, "I claim we got a hell of a beating. We got run out of Burma and it is humiliating as hell. I think we ought to find out what caused it, go back and take it."

His blunt words upset Army Headquarters; they were contrary to the official line that the withdrawal had been a brilliantly planned delaying action in order to give India time to prepare for invasion. Every attempt was made to dissuade British reporters from cabling it, and when that failed every effort was made to delay transmission of their copy.

The newspapermen who had covered the campaign and those who had survived it felt that one had only to look around to find the answer to Stilwell's question.

SOURCES

Rangoon to Kohima – Terence Dillon – Regimental Headquarters Gloucester-shire Regiment.

A personal memoir on the campaign by Lieutenant-Colonel Charles Bagot, M.C. – Headquarters Gloucestershire Regiment.

The Seventh and the Three Enemies – Brigadier G. M. O. Davy, C.B., C.B.E., D.S.O – W. Heffer & Sons Ltd, Cambridge.

War Diaries of the 7th Queen's Own Hussars.

Regimental History of the Malerkotla Sappers and Miners.

History of the 5th Royal Gurkha Rifles (F.F.).

Regimental History of the 3rd Queen Alexandra's Own Gurkha Rifles, and War Diaries of the 1/3rd Q.A.O.G.R.

The History of the Duke of Wellington's Regiment.

History of the King's Own Yorkshire Light Infantry (Vol V) – Lieutenant-Colonel Walter Hingston.

Official History of the Indian Armed Forces in the Second World War – the retreat from Burma – Combined Inter Services Historical Section, India and Pakistan.

The Burma Campaign, by T. L. Hughes, C.B.E. – based on a lecture given to the Royal Asian Society, London 1943.

Seconds Out – Sergeant Ken Chadwick – a History of the 2nd Royal Tank Regiment.

Despatches of General Sir Archibald Wavell – Supplement to the *London Gazette*, 5 March, 1948.

Report of Sir Reginald Dorman-Smith on the campaign in Burma.

Times Literary Supplement – 4 and 11 September, 1969, 2 October, 1969.

India Office Library and Records: Linlithgow Collection EUR 125; Dorman-Smith Collection 215E; Eric Battersby, an account of the retreat into Assam EUR 2155.

Diaries of Lady Dorman-Smith EUR 215E 41.

Imperial War Museum: Alexander Morrison, an account of his service with the 7th Armoured Brigade. Major John Finnerty, memoirs. Captain H. B. Toothill, diary. J. R. Gardiner, a diary of his trek through the Chaukkan Pass.

By permission of the Trustees of the Liddell Hart Centre for Military Archives: The papers of Lieutenant-General Sir Thomas Hutton, which includes his report to General Wavell on operations in Burma, December 1941–March 1942. A personal memoir and numerous official and private letters; signals and correspondence relating to the campaign.

BIBLIOGRAPHY

Defeat Into Victory, Field-Marshal Viscount Slim, G.C.B., G.C.M.G., G.C.V.O., G.B.E., D.S.O., M.C., Cassell, London.

The War Against Japan (Vol II), History of the Second World War, Major-General S. Woodburn Kirby, C.B., C.M.G., C.I.E., O.B.E., M.C., H.M.S.O.

The Second World War (Vol IV), Winston S. Churchill, Cassell, London.

Wings Of The Phoenix, Official History of the Air War in Burma, H.M.S.O.

The Campaign In Burma, Lieutenant-Colonel Frank Owen, O.B.E., H.M.S.O.

The Stilwell Papers, Macdonald, London.

Wrath In Burma, Fred Eldridge, Doubleday & Co., New York.

Milestones, a memoir, Sir John Smyth, V.C., M.C., Sidgwick and Jackson, London.

Trek Back From Burma, W. G. Burchett, Kitabistan, Allahabad.

Retreat In The East, O. D. Gallagher, George G. Harrap & Co., London.

The Longest Retreat, Tim Carew, Hamish Hamilton, London.

They Shall Not Sleep, Leland Stowe, Alfred A. Knopf, New York.

Walking With Warriors, Eve Curie, Doubleday, Doran & Co., New York.

Sinister Twilight, Noel Barber, Collins, London.

A Million Died, Alfred Wagg, Nicholson & Watson, London.

The Chief, Ronald Lewin, Hutchinson, London.

Wavell Supreme Commander, John Connell, Collins, London.

All Quiet On The Irrawaddy, Major John Finnerty, B.E.M., New Horizon.

Alexander Of Tunis, Ronald Lewin, Hutchinson, London.

Slim As Military Commander, Geoffrey Evans, B. T. Batsford Ltd.

Leadership In War, Sir John Smyth, V.C., M.C., David and Charles.
The Retreat From Burma, An Intelligence Officer's Personal Story, Lieutenant-Colonel A. Mains, W. Foulsham & Co.
Tank Tracks To Rangoon, Bryan Perrett, Robert Hale Ltd.

INDEX

A Selection of Arrow Bestsellers

☐ The Lilac Bus	Maeve Binchy	£2.50
☐ 500 Mile Walkies	Mark Wallington	£2.50
☐ Staying Off the Beaten Track	Elizabeth Gundrey	£5.95
☐ A Better World Than This	Marie Joseph	£2.95
☐ No Enemy But Time	Evelyn Anthony	£2.95
☐ Rates of Exchange	Malcolm Bradbury	£3.50
☐ Colours Aloft	Alexander Kent	£2.95
☐ Speaker for the Dead	Orson Scott Card	£2.95
☐ Eon	Greg Bear	£4.95
☐ Talking to Strange Men	Ruth Rendell	£5.95
☐ Heartstones	Ruth Rendell	£2.50
☐ Rosemary Conley's Hip and Thigh Diet	Rosemary Conley	£2.50
☐ Communion	Whitley Strieber	£3.50
☐ The Ladies of Missalonghi	Colleen McCullough	£2.50
☐ Erin's Child	Sheelagh Kelly	£3.99
☐ Sarum	Edward Rutherfurd	£4.50

Prices and other details are liable to change

ARROW BOOKS, BOOKSERVICE BY POST, PO BOX 29, DOUGLAS, ISLE
OF MAN, BRITISH ISLES

NAME . . . .

ADDRESS . . . .

. . . .

. . . .

Please enclose a cheque or postal order made out to Arrow Books Ltd. for the amount
due and allow the following for postage and packing.

U.K. CUSTOMERS: Please allow 22p per book to a maximum of £3.00.

B.F.P.O. & EIRE: Please allow 22p per book to a maximum of £3.00

OVERSEAS CUSTOMERS: Please allow 22p per book.

Whilst every effort is made to keep prices low it is sometimes necessary to increase cover
prices at short notice. Arrow Books reserve the right to show new retail prices on covers
which may differ from those previously advertised in the text or elsewhere.

Bestselling War Fiction and Non-Fiction

☐ Passage to Mutiny	Alexander Kent	£2.95
☐ Colours Aloft	Alexander Kent	£2.95
☐ Winged Escort	Douglas Reeman	£2.95
☐ Army of Shadows	John Harris	£2.50
☐ Decoy	Dudley Pope	£2.95
☐ Gestapo	Rupert Butler	£4.50
☐ Johnny Gurkha	E.D. Smith	£2.95
☐ Typhoon Pilot	Desmond Scott	£2.95
☐ The Rommel Papers	B.H. Liddel Hart	£5.95
☐ Hour of the Lily	John Kruse	£3.50
☐ Duel in the Dark	Peter Townsend	£3.95
☐ The Spoils of War	Douglas Scott	£2.99
☐ The Wild Blue	Walter J. Boyne & Steven L. Thompson	£3.95
☐ The Bombers	Norman Longmate	£4.99

Prices and other details are liable to change

ARROW BOOKS, BOOKSERVICE BY POST, PO BOX 29, DOUGLAS, ISLE OF MAN, BRITISH ISLES

NAME...

ADDRESS...

....

....

Please enclose a cheque or postal order made out to Arrow Books Ltd. for the amount due and allow the following for postage and packing.

U.K. CUSTOMERS: Please allow 22p per book to a maximum of £3.00.

B.F.P.O. & EIRE: Please allow 22p per book to a maximum of £3.00

OVERSEAS CUSTOMERS: Please allow 22p per book.

Whilst every effort is made to keep prices low it is sometimes necessary to increase cover prices at short notice. Arrow Books reserve the right to show new retail prices on covers which may differ from those previously advertised in the text or elsewhere.

Bestselling Non-Fiction

☐ Everything Is Negotiable	Gavin Kennedy	£3.50
☐ The Cheiro Book of Fate and Fortune	Cheiro	£2.95
☐ The Handbook of Chinese Horoscopes	Theodora Lau	£3.50
☐ Hollywood Babylon	Kenneth Anger	£7.95
☐ Staying Off the Beaten Track	Elizabeth Gundrey	£5.95
☐ Elvis and Me	Priscilla Presley	£2.95
☐ Maria Callas	Arianna Stassinopoulos	£4.95
☐ The Ulysses Voyage	Tim Severin	£3.50
☐ Something Understood	Gerald Priestland	£3.99
☐ Fat is a Feminist Issue	Susie Orbach	£2.50
☐ Women Who Love Too Much	Robin Norwood	£2.95
☐ Rosemary Conley's Hip and Thigh Diet	Rosemary Conley	£2.50
☐ Intercourse	Andrea Dworkin	£2.99
☐ Communion	Whitley Strieber	£3.50

Prices and other details are liable to change
